X

A MEMOIR

IMPACT PLAYER

LEAVING A LASTING LEGACY
ON & OFF THE FIELD

Bobby Richardson

WITH DAVID THOMAS

TYNDALE HOUSE PUBLISHERS, INC.
CAROL STREAM, ILLINOIS

Visit Tyndale online at www.tyndale.com.

TYNDALE and Tyndale's quill logo are registered trademarks of Tyndale House Publishers, Inc.

Impact Player: Leaving a Lasting Legacy On and Off the Field

Designed by Daniel Farrell

Edited by Anne Christian Buchanan

Unless otherwise indicated, all Scripture quotations are taken from the *Holy Bible*, King James Version.

Scripture verses marked *Phillips* are taken from *The New Testament in Modern English* by J. B. Phillips, copyright © J. B. Phillips, 1958, 1959, 1960, 1972. All rights reserved.

Scripture quotations marked NIV are taken from the Holy Bible, *New International Version,*® *NIV.*® Copyright © 1973, 1978, 1984, 2011 by Biblica, Inc.™ Used by permission of Zondervan. All rights reserved worldwide. www.zondervan.com.

Library of Congress Cataloging-in-Publication Data

Richardson, Bobby.
    Impact player : leaving a lasting legacy on and off the field / Bobby Richardson with David Thomas.
       p. cm.
    ISBN 978-1-4143-7273-0 (hc)
    1. Richardson, Bobby.   2. Baseball players—United States—Biography.   3. New York Yankees (Baseball team)   I. Thomas, David, 1968 June 21-   II. Title.
    GV865.R4279166 2012
    796.357092—dc23
    [B]   2012018899

Printed in the United States of America

18   17   16   15   14   13   12
 7   6   5   4   3   2   1

To my wife, Betsy.

I can't find the words to express my love and appreciation for you and your faithful companionship and support. I'm so thankful for your love for our Savior and for His mercy and grace, which have kept us going these fifty-six-plus years.

CONTENTS

FOREWORD

I REMEMBER THE FIRST TIME I walked out of the clubhouse at the old Yankee Stadium. All I could think was, *Wow—this is the same tunnel that guys like Yogi Berra, Mickey Mantle, Roger Maris, Bobby Richardson, and Whitey Ford walked through. I've really made it. I'm playing in New York for the New York Yankees.* It was a really special feeling—and one I'll never forget.

That great dynasty of '55–'64 is one every Yankee player looks up to. I had the privilege of winning three championships with the Yankees in '96, '98, and '99, but these guys were doing it almost every single year. They taught us that you should never be satisfied with winning one, two, or even three championships, but that you need to go out there and play your very best every day, every game, every series, and try to earn another one. They set the bar the rest of us strive to meet. There's a tremendous sense of pride that comes from being a New York Yankee, and those guys played a huge role in creating that.

There have been a lot of great Yankee players over the years and a lot of guys who have won championships. But I think the greatest players are the ones who strive to make the people around them great. That's what Bobby Richardson did. He was a real impact player—and I don't just mean on the field.

On the field, an impact player is someone who can change the game at any time. One play—be it on offense or defense—can change the course of an entire game. An impact player is a guy who makes that play on a consistent basis. But in my mind, a real impact player is one who also makes a huge contribution to the clubhouse.

You go through so much as a team during the course of a season. When I think back to the four years I played with the Yankees, I remember how many of the guys I played with lost their fathers during the season, how many of them went through cancer battles, how many of them were dealing with rough patches in their marriages. As a manager, I can tell you that it's not just about keeping a team together *on* the field; it's also about dealing with everything that's going on *off* the field.

Every club has to have that guy players feel they can turn to when things are not going well—someone they can talk to, someone who can provide comfort during difficult times. Bobby Richardson was one of those guys—the kind who got along with everybody, who helped bring everyone in the clubhouse together, and who genuinely cared about the people around him. A true leader.

With Bobby, it all came down to his values and his Christian faith. I'm sure he had his struggles like everyone else, but you can just tell when you look at his face and see his smile that there's a peace there—peace, humility, and a lot of love. And I think other people feed off of being around a guy like that.

As a Christian athlete, you want people to look at you and think, *What's different about that guy? I want what he's got.* Of course, then you've got to be able to walk the walk. I think that's one of the biggest challenges of being a Christian athlete. You have to live up to a lot more, and that can be extremely difficult at times. But it also takes the pressure off, because you know that God's always going to put you exactly where He wants you— not where *you* want to go, but where *He* wants you to be. That's God's plan.

Bobby knew that God had a plan for his life, both during and after baseball. And I believe that's what gave him that sense of inner peace, contentment, and humility that drew others to him and made them want to be better players, teammates, and human beings.

As a fellow Christian, I admire Bobby for never shying away from the opportunity to share his faith in Jesus with those around him. He understood that he was given a great gift and a great platform, and throughout his life he has used both to make a positive impact on those around him.

When I look at Bobby Richardson, I see someone I strive to be more like—not because of his stats, the records he holds, his World Series rings, or his place in baseball history, but because of his character, his values, his humility, and his beliefs.

There's no question: Bobby Richardson is a true impact player in every sense of the word.

Joe Girardi

PROLOGUE

THE MAJESTIC MELODY from the organ resounded throughout the packed sanctuary. The accompanying voices of the mourners were thick with emotion as they sang:

Just a closer walk with thee.
Grant it, Jesus, is my plea.

On the platform, I sang along in my head, though not mouthing the words. I alternated between looking down at my one page of notes and looking out over the crowd. I could see former New York Yankees players . . . Yogi Berra, Whitey Ford, Moose Skowron, Johnny Blanchard, Bobby Murcer, and Tony Kubek. Texas governor George W. Bush and his wife, Laura, were near the front, close to my own wife, Betsy, and Randy Maris, son of Roger. Comedian Billy Crystal stood to the right. I spotted Bobby Cox, the manager of the Atlanta Braves and a former Yankee, and took note of Yankees owner George Steinbrenner and broadcaster Pat Summerall.

My heart was moved when I looked to the family. Some dabbed tears. Others stood arm-in-arm with the loved one next to them as they lifted their voices along with the rest.

When my feeble life is o'er,
Time for me will be no more. . . .

I had been privileged to speak many times at the funerals of friends and teammates, and often to crowds much larger than this one that had gathered to bid farewell to a husband, father, grandfather, brother, friend, teammate, and baseball hero. Yet I was more nervous than usual that day. I was very nervous, actually.

Mickey Mantle's home-going had set off a dizzying two days. There had been so much to do, so much to plan, a message to prepare. But, as had happened many times during the previous week, I sensed a peace coming over me from the prayers of hundreds.

In just moments, I would be recounting the life of my friend of four decades, not only to a church crammed full with more than two thousand people, but also to a live, nationwide television audience that had to number in the tens of thousands.

I looked back to the keywords jotted on my notes and once again asked the Lord to give me the strength and ability to say the words He would have me say. I would be sharing old stories about Mickey that I had told many times before: about his fake mongoose in the locker room, about the rubber snake he hid in a teammate's pants, about his high-interest loans from Yogi, about our basketball game at West Point. But there at the bottom of my notes was a story from my final days with Mickey.

It had already become my favorite, and I couldn't wait to share it.

Chapter 1
SHARING A DREAM

"**SOMEDAY HE'LL BE** in the major leagues," my dad declared the day I was born. The date was August 19, 1935—not just during baseball season, but at the point in a season when pennant races begin to heat up.

I don't know whether Dad was predicting or hoping, but his words came true. I was privileged to play twelve seasons in the major leagues. And because I spent my entire career with outstanding teammates in the pinstripes of the New York Yankees, I was able to take part in more pennant races than most ballplayers could hope to experience.

Blessed with good health, I played 1,412 games in the majors, but only one with my dad in the stands. At least that one was a World Series game. Health issues and other circumstances prevented Dad from seeing me play more. He didn't even get to see all of my career. My family suffered a great loss when he passed away in 1963, three years before I retired.

My dad loved coming to my games when I was growing up. Unless it was one of our out-of-town games too far to travel to, or one scheduled during the day, before he could slip out of work, Dad was in the bleachers. He wasn't my loudest fan, but he was my biggest.

I was Robert Clinton Richardson's only son. He gave me his name—he went by Clint; I was Robert—and he passed on to me his passion for baseball. In return, I lived out his dream of playing in the majors.

I wish Dad could have been at Yankee Stadium for Bobby Richardson Day in the final weeks of the 1966 season, my last year in the majors. I know he would have been proud when my career accomplishments were listed that day: playing in seven World Series, winning three, and being chosen Most Valuable Player of one; earning five Gold Glove awards; being selected to seven All-Star teams. But what I think would have made Dad most proud was when and why I was walking away from baseball.

Age wasn't an issue, because I was only thirty-one at the time. Skills weren't a concern either, because I had just made my fifth consecutive All-Star team. Injuries, thank goodness, had never been a problem during my career. The only reason I had missed thirteen games in my final season—the most I had missed since 1959—was a request by manager Ralph Houk. He had asked if I would mind sitting out games late in the season so the Yankees could give playing time to my expected replacement at second base.

I hung up my spikes in 1966 feeling I was still in my peak years as a baseball player. But at that time I was also in what I felt should be my peak years as a father. Betsy and I had four children. Our fifth, Rich, would join us two years later. My oldest son, Robby, was nine years old, and Ron was eight. Both were playing baseball, and I was missing too many of their games. Our daughter Christie was almost six and missing her daddy, and two-year-old Jeannie often would cry when I was away.

As much as my dad valued my time in the major leagues, and as much as he enjoyed keeping up with my games on television, radio, and in the newspapers, I know he would have approved of my early retirement. His constant presence in my life was the best gift he had ever given me, and now it was time for me to give the same gift to my children. I felt confident he would have agreed with that.

Dad had been a tombstone maker, spending his lifetime inscribing the names and dates and words of hundreds of people to be remembered. Every time I visit Dad's grave, I read the words my sister Ann suggested be placed on his tombstone:

ONLY ONE LIFE,

IT WILL SOON BE PAST;

ONLY WHAT'S DONE FOR CHRIST

WILL LAST.

Those are the same words Betsy and I made "ours" at the beginning of our relationship. My dad had helped me inscribe those words on a small stone for us to share.

I was the second of three children born to Clint and Willie Richardson, the only boy, born between Inez and Ann. We were raised in Sumter, South Carolina, a small town about forty-five miles east of the state capital of Columbia. I still call Sumter home, and the folks who live here still call me Robert instead of Bobby. It was in Sumter that the foundation was laid for my baseball career and my spiritual journey.

In addition to my parents, three people stand out in my decision to accept Christ as Savior: Bill Ward, Pop Owens, and J. H. Simpson. The first two were my Sunday school teachers at Grace Baptist Church.

Mr. Ward was a farmer who loved to say, "Praise the Lord!" and made each of us boys in the class take turns teaching a lesson.

I have had the honor of speaking to tens of thousands of people at Billy Graham Crusades, but I'll tell you that it is an entirely different type of nervousness when you have to stand in front of a small Sunday school class of your peers and deliver a message.

Mr. Owens worked for the Carolina Power & Light Company, and I remember there would be Sunday mornings after a big storm had blown through when he would have to miss class to help restore power in the area. But when Mr. Owens wasn't called away by work, he was faithful in bringing God's Word to us every Sunday.

What those two teachers instilled in me as a young boy was that I needed to live my life for God and that the first step in doing so was to receive Jesus Christ as Lord and Savior. Their lessons prepared the soil of my heart to the point that I knew I needed a Savior. J. H. Simpson, the pastor of our church, was the one who then came in and brought the salvation message home, so to speak.

When I was almost twelve, at the request of my mother—and, I believe, also at the urging of Mr. Ward and Mr. Owens—Rev. Simpson came by our house for a visit. To my surprise, instead of visiting with my parents, he started talking with Inez, Ann, and me. I didn't know much about Rev. Simpson, other than what I had observed of him at church. But I was impressed that he knew my name and my sisters' names and also seemed to know a little about each of us. As he talked to us, it was obvious that he wasn't just making small talk. He was sincerely interested in hearing about our lives and our activities.

At some point in that visit, Rev. Simpson shifted our conversation to God's plan of salvation. I was quite familiar with it, having heard it many times from the pulpit and also from hearing it described by Mr. Ward and Mr. Owens in Sunday school. I'm sure that I had not completely understood all that was explained to me as a young boy, but I believed I needed a Savior and that Jesus loved me enough to suffer and die in my place. That day in our living room, though, I felt different than in times past as Rev. Simpson explained the plan once again.

Rev. Simpson recited a verse we knew well—John 3:16: "For God so loved the world, that he gave his only begotten Son, that whosoever believeth in him should not perish, but have everlasting life." Rev. Simpson told us that all of mankind had sinned and needed God's gift of salvation; then he asked the three of us whether we each knew that we, too, had sinned.

I don't recall being asked that question before. I know it had been posed by Rev. Simpson during his sermons and by Mr. Ward and Mr. Owens in Sunday school. But it definitely was the first time I remember someone looking directly at me and asking if I knew *I* had sinned. Because God was working in my heart, it caused me to confront the question personally in my life.

Of course, I knew my answer had to be yes. I knew I had done things wrong in my life. I was aware of thought patterns and actions the Lord was not pleased with. And I knew there was a consequence involved in sin and that it was separation from a holy and just God forever in a place Scripture calls hell.

I wasn't what others would call a bad boy. The most trouble I got into was for talking back to my mother or sneaking out of the house to play baseball when I was supposed to be cleaning my bedroom. Of course, there were those "shady excuses" to avoid punishment, and my habit of annoying my sisters. That's not bad considering what a young boy could have gotten into, but there are no degrees of sin. Sin is sin. I was disrespecting and disobeying my mother, and I knew that did not reflect the heart God wanted for me. He gave His commandments to reveal His righteous requirements. Lying and not honoring my mother were sins. I needed forgiveness and a new heart.

After Rev. Simpson read Romans 3:23—"For all have sinned, and come short of the glory of God"—I admitted aloud that I knew *I* had sinned. The pastor then aptly explained to us how the mere fact that we had been born made us sinners, because human beings have been sinners by nature since Adam and Eve disobeyed God in the Garden of Eden. Yet as John 3:16 points out, God provided a means of escape from our sinful nature through the life, death, and resurrection of His Son, Jesus Christ. Jesus came to become the sacrifice for the sins of all of us. He was the Lamb of God, sent to take away the sin of the world.

I had heard all that in church services and Sunday school, but it didn't become personal to me until Rev. Simpson sat in our living room and detailed it directly to my sisters and me. For the first time, I understood that Jesus had died for *my* sins. His death on the cross and His resurrection became personal to me. It's interesting how we can hear the gospel message, as I had for years to that point, and still not really *hear* it. We can know that Jesus' death paid for all the sins of everyone in the world, yet the moment of true salvation does not come until we grasp that Jesus shed His precious blood to redeem one person in particular: me.

That is what I meant earlier when I said that Rev. Simpson was the person who took the plan of salvation and brought it all home for me.

"Do you believe that Jesus died for *your* sins?" Rev. Simpson asked.

"Yes," I answered, "Jesus died for me."

My sisters answered the same way, and Rev. Simpson prayed then and there with the three of us as we asked Jesus Christ into our hearts. Inez and I were baptized in church the following weekend, and a few weeks later Ann was too.

Starting at Home

My mother maintained a strong spiritual presence in our home. In fact, Mom's was the strongest presence in our home, period. Her personality was powerful, and to a young boy it was at times a little overwhelming. But I knew she loved me, and boy, could she cook!

Mom attended church every Sunday. She took part in a number of activities, including her beloved women's group, and she made sure we attended too. Dad, on the other hand, wasn't much of a churchgoer, though he never objected when Mom and the three of us kids went. Sometimes he would even drive us to church and drop us off, though the church was within walking distance of our house. I felt confident that Dad knew the Lord because every night at home I saw him on his knees, praying. As I look back now with an adult's perspective, though, I wonder how much he grew spiritually.

The truth was, Dad faced some limitations. He had made it only through the third or fourth grade. I don't know whether he could read, but I do recall that he made all his purchases with cash—no writing checks—and that Mom handled the business affairs around the home.

Dad also struggled with emphysema. He was owner and manager of Richardson Marble and Granite Works, and the dust from the sandblasting associated with his work contributed to his health issues. I know that the need to rest after a long week of work was one of the reasons Dad did not attend church with us more often.

Dad didn't make a lot of money from his company, but business was good enough for him to support us. We may not have been able to buy everything we wanted growing up—and there's nothing wrong with that—but we did always have everything we needed. At Christmastime there were presents for all of us.

My sisters claimed I was spoiled because I was the only boy, and there may have been some truth to that. I remember one year receiving a Cushman motor scooter before I was old enough to drive it legally on the streets. But I took it out on the streets anyway—until the police stopped me and told me to push it back home and keep it there until I was old enough for a license.

Being the only boy did give me an advantage sportswise with Dad. Inez, my older sister, was more into baby dolls and pretty dresses than sports. My younger sister, Ann, was interested in sports, but because I came along before her, I had a head start.

Growing up, I didn't really have a favorite sport. I was most interested in whatever ball was closest to me at the moment. If I could throw it, catch it, kick it, bounce it, or shoot it, I did. Over time, though, baseball and basketball emerged as my favorite sports.

Baseball was the sport I could best play by myself during my free time. We had a two-story house with a big chimney, and I would bounce tennis balls off that chimney to practice fielding ground balls, getting down to the nitty-gritty details like working on my backhand pickups and scooping up tricky short hops.

For variety I would throw the balls up on the roof and practice catching fly balls as they rolled off. There was a gutter around the roof, though, that liked to catch the balls before they could fall to me. That would mean a trip to the upstairs bathroom, where I could stretch my arm out the window to retrieve the ball from the gutter. After a few of those trips upstairs, I'd decide that fielding grounders off the chimney was more efficient for getting in as much practice time as possible. Who knows? Perhaps that gutter is why I became an infielder instead of an outfielder.

The back of our house was nice for practicing by myself, but it wasn't perfect. If I missed the chimney with a tennis ball, the impact of my throw would knock small pieces of plaster off the inside walls. The sound of falling plaster would get Mom's attention, and she'd come to the back door to express her disapproval. I would apologize and explain that I couldn't hit the chimney every time. I was never banned from throwing balls against the chimney, but the fear of that happening could be a major reason I was an accurate thrower in my later years.

I also spent a lot of time practicing baseball in front of our house, where we had a concrete walkway leading to stone steps. I could have bounced balls off those steps and fielded grounders on that walkway all day long. Some days, I think I did. But there was also a danger to playing in the front yard. Balls could hit the edge of the steps and ricochet into the screened front door or up against the siding. The clunk of a ball hitting the house or knocking plaster off the walls would bring Mom to the front door, too. I think my practice sessions caused my mom to wear paths to our front and back doors.

The highlight of the day came when Dad arrived home from work, because then he would go to the backyard with me to throw a ball around for a few minutes or to hit some pop-ups to me. My dad had been a pretty good ballplayer himself growing up. He never told me that—he wasn't the type to talk about himself—but his friends made sure I knew of Dad's abilities. He might even have been good enough to have his own dreams about playing pro ball. But since Dad had to work a lot to help his family, he was never able to position himself for a chance to play professionally.

I still hold wonderful memories from those times my dad and I played catch in the backyard. Even though he knew a lot about baseball, he never overcoached me. He was a man of few words to begin with, so the most he might offer would be a simple tip here or there. For the most part, he limited his speech to encouragement—"nice catch" or "good throw."

A Chip off the Old Block

Dad allowed me to spend time with him at his marble and granite company. Although he stayed busy, I was able to further hone my baseball skills at the work site. Dad's company would take quarried slabs of rock and shape, polish, and engrave them to make tombstones. The process generated lots of granite chips, and in the hands of a young boy with big league dreams, those chips became baseballs.

Unfortunately, stop signs became first basemen's mitts. I'm embarrassed to admit that I plunked a few stop signs in my day.

Dad let me earn money from his company. Sometimes I would hop into the back of the truck when one of Dad's employees, who went by the nickname of Crawfish, delivered tombstones to cemeteries. Small metal plates from the funeral home served as temporary grave markers until the tombstones arrived. I would dig up those markers and turn them in to Dad for five dollars per plate. That was good pay—no, great pay—for the work.

I think letting me help around the company was Dad's way of slipping me a little extra spending money, because the funeral homes paid him five dollars per plate as well. It also provided a chance for us to spend extra time together. Even when he was busy working and I was off nailing stop signs with granite chips, my hours at Dad's company still counted as father-son time for both of us.

Another job I had around Sumter was delivering the local newspaper, *The Item*, right after school. I had a delivery route of 128 papers, but 7 of those went to one stop—the YMCA—and a good number of them could be quickly delivered in a set of apartments. I could finish my route in less than twenty minutes, so that part of the job was easy. The part I hated was collecting. I think I had to collect a quarter per week from each customer. I would go around my route with a little pouch that I'd slip the payments into. But I didn't like having to remind people they hadn't paid. Even worse, sometimes customers wouldn't be home, and I'd have to go back later to collect. Those extra trips cut into my sports time. Still, I stuck with that job for a couple of years and made good spending money. I even tried to add an early-morning route for the morning edition, but that meant picking up my papers for delivery at 4:30 a.m. I lasted only a week or so on that route.

One job I really enjoyed was coordinating sports activities at a community center in a poorer part of town. The work was right up my alley, and I liked knowing that the sports we offered were help-ing some people who probably couldn't afford to take part in some of the larger organized-sports leagues around town. The people were great too. My friends from the center and I would take a quick break to walk over to a little country store for a MoonPie and an RC Cola. I still have friendships in Sumter that I made working at the Jenkins Community Center.

This doesn't technically qualify as a job, but I did make a little money playing table tennis against Oliver Stubbs. The YMCA was one block from my house, and Oliver liked to practice table tennis there. The problem was, Oliver was very, very good. In fact, he would eventually win the national championship. Not many people at the Sumter Y wanted to play against him, so his dad would pay me one dollar a night to meet Oliver at the Y and practice with him. I spent many nights playing game after game after game against Oliver. I noticed that on nights when I used part of my dollar to buy Oliver a MoonPie and an RC, I had a slightly better chance of win-ning a game every now and then—but only slightly. I did, however, get something out of all those poundings I suffered at the nimble paddle of Oliver Stubbs. When I was fifteen, I was runner-up in my age group at the South Carolina state table tennis tournament.

Table tennis, of course, was never a serious threat to my two favorite sports. For me, nothing could compare with baseball and basketball—although I did have a not-so-glorious, one-day career as a football player. My sophomore year in high school, Coach "Hutch" Hutchinson, who also was my American Legion baseball coach, talked me into coming out for the football team. He said that with the good hands I had displayed on the infield, he could envision me as his quarterback.

It took a while for him to convince me to give football a try, but I finally relented. I joined the team late, during two-a-day practices. I knew nothing about football, really, but Coach Hutchinson put me in right away at quarterback. On the first play, I was supposed to take the snap from center, turn around, and hand the ball to the halfback. Well, I took the snap and made one step. I must not have stepped where I was supposed to, because the halfback hit me from one side and our linemen hit me from the other side.

This would be a good point to inform you that I have never been a big guy. When I played for the Yankees, I was listed at five feet nine and 170 pounds, and that was a generous listing. As a sophomore in high school, of course, I wasn't close to that. Between the halfback and the linemen, I was pressed about as flat as the marshmallow filling in one of those country-store MoonPies.

I could never seem to find my way in the backfield, and after two workouts that day, I called it a career. My dad never said so, but he probably considered my early retirement from football one of the best decisions I ever made. He'd been concerned that I might get hurt.

Football, then, was never a serious threat to my future in baseball. Basketball was a different matter. During high school, in fact, I'd say it was my best sport. I was an all-state guard my junior and senior seasons and even received two scholarship offers to play basketball in college. Norm Sloan, a college coach who would win more than six hundred games at schools such as the University of Florida and North Carolina State, offered me a scholarship with the Presbyterian College Blue Hose. Georgia Tech also offered a basketball scholarship.

I loved basketball, and though I don't want to bill myself as a better player than I was, I handled the ball well. I was able to break the first line of a defense, and then, when another defender would step up to block me, I could pass the ball to the open player for him to score. I was a good free-throw shooter, too.

Ultimately, however, I was smart enough to recognize that,

largely because of my height, basketball was not the best sport for me beyond high school.

Clearly, baseball was my sport.

Musial's Lasting Influence

Dad was a St. Louis Cardinals fan because in Sumter, as in many locations in the South, the only station we could pick up that broadcast major league games was KMOX out of St. Louis. When KMOX carried Cardinals games, Dad would invite me to listen along with him. Then when I was a little older, about twelve as best as I can recall, Dad took me and a group of my friends to Columbia to watch an exhibition game between his revered Cardinals and the Cincinnati Reds. On the car ride over to Columbia, we all talked about getting to see the great "Stan the Man" Musial play for the Cardinals. Musial was one of my dad's favorite players.

I had never gotten anyone's autograph before, but after the game I went up to Musial as he walked toward the team bus, and asked for his autograph. He gladly signed for me. I don't remember how long I kept that autograph or what eventually happened to it, but I do recall that for a time I walked around Sumter saying, "Hey, I've got Stan Musial's autograph." I also remember how excited Dad was for me to have it.

Enos "Country" Slaughter was another well-known player on that St. Louis team. Although Slaughter is most remembered as a Cardinal, we were teammates on the Yankees near the end of his long career. During the 1958 season, my second son, Ron, and one of Enos's daughters were born on the same day at The Valley Hospital in Ridgewood, New Jersey.

When Enos passed away in 2002, his family asked me to be a part of his memorial service in Roxboro, North Carolina. Musial was among the teammates who came in for Enos's funeral. I had never had the opportunity to play against Stan in a World Series, but I had gotten to know him after retirement through Old Timers' Games we participated in. At the dinner following Enos's funeral, I told Stan, "I know you don't remember this, but when I was about twelve years old, I got your autograph at an exhibition game in Columbia, South Carolina."

I have to tell you, that made Stan cringe a little bit, because I was just shy of my sixty-seventh birthday when I told him that. Stan was already in the majors when I was twelve, so you can do the math.

"Honestly," I told Stan, "yours is the only autograph I ever asked for as a kid."

"Rich," Stan said, using the name most major leaguers called me, "I can't believe that. But I sure am glad I signed and didn't turn you away."

Throughout my career, I remembered how much that one signature meant to me at that age. That is why I always made my best effort to sign as many autographs as possible. Plus, as many players from my era did, I always used my best penmanship when I signed. Nowadays, professional athletes tend to save time by making only the first letters of their names readable, followed by something that looks more like a squiggly line than part of a name.

If you see my autographs, you'll note that my complete name is readable. And let me tell you, "Bobby Richardson" isn't the shortest of names. Sometimes it would be nice to have been named something short like "Bob Lee." But I take the time to make the signature nice because Stan Musial did that for me. I have never forgotten how much something as simple as a signature could mean to a young boy with major league dreams—or even to his father.

Chapter 2
BECOMING A YANKEE

ALONG WITH MY DAD, there was a second person who played a key role in developing my baseball skills: Harry Stokes.

Harry was seven years older than me, and I must have been about seven or eight when I met him.

We lived in downtown Sumter near an elementary school where local kids gathered after hours on the ample playground. Harry lived on the other side of that school. One day Harry spotted a handful of us playing baseball, stopped, and offered to hit some ground balls to us.

Harry was in high school at the time and played on the Sumter American Legion team. My hometown has long taken pride in its American Legion teams, so you can imagine how thrilled we boys were to have a high schooler *and* an American Legion player join us on the playground.

Harry was someone I already looked up to, because I had watched him play second base when Dad took me to American Legion games in Riley Park. I was so excited to learn that Harry Stokes—*the* Harry Stokes—lived two blocks from my house and was actually willing to play with kids my age.

One of Harry's favorite stories was about a summer morning after he had played an American Legion game the night before. He awoke to find me standing next to his bed, baseball cap on, ready to go outside and play. It was seven o'clock.

"I want to play baseball," I told Harry.

Harry said he'd be happy to play with me sometime.

"I want to play *now*."

Harry said he couldn't play then because he needed more sleep.

Three and a half hours later, Harry woke up again. I was still standing next to his bed, still ready to play. Harry got up, changed clothes, and took me outside to play baseball.

Some time later, Harry came to watch me in one of my youth-league games. Afterward, Harry hung around the park, and I wasn't ready to go home yet.

"You want to catch a few fly balls?" Harry asked.

"Sure!" I said.

Harry took a fungo bat and started hitting pop-ups to me. He hit the flies progressively higher and higher, and I kept catching them. Harry was impressed.

"Why don't you come out a little earlier tomorrow, and we'll play some pepper," Harry said. "I want to see you field ground balls."

I was there the next day, eager to play. I wasn't about to miss out on that invitation.

When we were a little older, Harry started coaching my team. He took a real interest in me, to the point that hardly a day went by during baseball season when we weren't playing catch or field-ing flies and grounders. When he had a job, he would meet me after work at the elementary school between our houses. We had a routine in which Harry would hit ground balls to me, and I would have to field one hundred in a row without missing one. If I made an error, Harry would start the count all over. If I reached one hundred, we would stop for the day.

The problem was, I didn't *want* to stop for the day. I wanted to keep playing. So when the count reached into the nineties, I would miss a grounder on purpose.

It didn't take long for Harry to catch on to my scheme. "I saw you do that," he'd say. "But okay—one more time." Then he would hit me one hundred more grounders.

I never got tired of playing baseball with Harry. Rain or shine, I was always up for our sessions together. When there was *really* bad weather and we couldn't meet at the schoolyard, I would stay home, heartbroken.

I wasn't the only player Harry helped, of course. Harry loved baseball and loved sharing his knowledge of the game with young players. But I always knew our particular baseball bond was special.

Together, Harry and my dad represented a proud and capable baseball-mentoring partnership for me. On the occasions when they would sit together at my games, I would look over at them from my spot on the field and feel so fortunate to have both of them there.

My dad was a great baseball dad. His quiet nature carried over to the ballpark. He often chose to sit alone and watch, sometimes in the left field bleachers away from everyone else. He wouldn't yell or cheer or anything like that; he just quietly took note of me and the game. Afterward he would offer me a short, encouraging word—something like "Good game" or "You played well"—and that would be it. He didn't criticize me or pick apart everything I had done, and he didn't try to coach me when we got home. He believed that was the job of my coaches, and he wasn't going to interfere with what they were doing.

Even though Dad didn't say much, he said enough for me to never doubt that I had his full support. Harry also was a great encourager. When he corrected me—and all players need correction—he did it in a positive way. From when I first began watching Harry play American Legion ball, I understood that he knew what he was talking about, and I put complete trust in what he told me. If Harry said I needed to do something differently, I made the change.

After Harry completed high school, he was able to play semipro ball until he was drafted and spent two years in the service. I missed Harry when he was gone, but he stayed in touch through letters. Harry had a knack for knowing when I was in a batting slump or struggling in the field, and he always seemed to come up with just the encouraging word I needed.

When I reached the majors, I made sure Harry had opportunities to come watch some of my games. I wanted to do the same for my dad, but his emphysema had worsened to the point that he couldn't travel very far. Harry would often come up to New York with his older brother—another fine baseball player who once led a lower-level minor league in batting average—and watch some of my games.

Harry looked like he could have been a major leaguer. When he was with me and other Yankees, he was frequently mistaken for a player. Always the prankster, Harry would just play along. A couple of times when someone asked who he was, he claimed to be Al Kaline, the famous Detroit Tigers outfielder.

After I retired, I invited Harry to go with me to New York for an Old Timers' Game at Shea Stadium. I took Harry into the dugout with me during the game, and he sat next to Art Howe, who was then the manager of the Houston Astros. One of the hardest balls that ever came my way in an Old Timers' Game was hit to me that day. There were runners on second and third, and the ball was hit on a line toward me so that the runners had to hold their places to see if I would catch the ball before it hit the dirt. I shuffled to my right and fielded the ball on a short hop, looked the runners back to their bases, and threw to first to retire the batter. It might have been the best play I made in the Old Timers' Games.

Knowing who Harry was, Art looked over to him and said, "None of my players on the Astros could have made that play." Then Art added, "I understand you taught him about baseball."

That one statement from Art made Harry so proud. He couldn't wait to tell me what Art had said, and he told me that story again many times over the years. Just that one moment on that bench with Art was worth the entire cost of taking Harry to New York for that game. I am so glad I had the means to pay for Harry to experience a taste of life in the majors. I'm sure he'd had his own major league dreams, and with all the time he devoted to working with young dreamers back home, he deserved to have a major league manager compliment his work.

When we won the pennant in 1960, I gave Harry my American League pennant ring. He wore that ring just about everywhere he went. "When did you play for the Yankees?" someone would ask him. "Well," the jokester would answer, "it's been a long time ago now. It seems like yesterday, but it's been a long time."

Harry wore that ring until he developed dementia late in his life. He didn't have a son of his own to pass it along to, so his daughter, Sherri, graciously returned it to me so I could give it to my children.

I learned the fundamentals of baseball—and their importance—from Harry. Following his lead, I always took pride in my ability to make the routine plays. Every major leaguer can make those plays, but not everybody works on them as much as they should. It takes commitment and focus to recognize the importance of basic plays and to diligently practice them daily, even those plays we think we could make in our sleep.

Outside of my dad, Harry was the person who did the most to instill in me the belief that I could become a professional baseball player. "I feel like you can play," Harry would tell me, "and one day you might even play for the Yankees." It was largely due to Harry's belief in me that in my junior year of high school, when the yearbook staff asked what I wanted to do when I grew up, I answered, "I'd like to play shortstop for the New York Yankees."

Even after I had made it with the Yankees, Harry's support helped me keep a positive outlook during the frustration of batting slumps. "Hey, listen, don't get discouraged now," Harry would write in a letter or tell me in a well-timed phone call. "Tomorrow is a new day, and I'm sure that it's gonna work out fine." Harry encouraged me like that throughout my career.

More than all that, Harry was a reliable friend. Harry loved to quail hunt. When my dad wasn't physically strong enough to take me hunting, Harry did. Harry helped me get my own bird dogs, and every off-season, when I came home, we would go hunting together.

In the late 1960s, shortly after I had retired from baseball, my friend Billy Zeoli led Harry to the Lord in my house after watching a gospel film. I look forward to spending eternity with my first baseball hero.

Every ballplayer needs a Harry Stokes in his life.

Come to think of it, every *person* needs a friend and mentor like Harry.

The Pride of the Yankees

My first close-up look at the Yankees came as a young boy when my dad took me and some of my friends to an exhibition game in nearby Columbia. A Yankees minor league team was playing against the Cincinnati Reds. Dad had been a shortstop in his playing days, and he encouraged me to study the play of the Yankees' shortstop, Frank Crosetti.

Little did we know that one day I would play for the Yankees—even playing a few games at shortstop—or that Frank Crosetti would become one of my coaches.

My path to Yankee Stadium began as a catcher for a kids' team sponsored by the Salvation Army. At tryouts, the other players were all bigger than me—that would be a theme throughout my career—and I wasn't sure I could earn a spot on the team. But one thing I had that the others didn't was the willingness to play catcher. The catcher's equipment can become burdensome, especially in the hot and humid summertime. There is a good reason we used to call a catcher's equipment "the tools of ignorance." I didn't mind wearing all that heavy gear and extra sweat, though. I just wanted to play baseball.

I continued to catch into the next level up, the Knee Pants League—a YMCA league similar to Little League. But I made the move to shortstop (and occasionally pitcher) before graduating out of that league. Shortstop and second base would be my primary positions all the way through the rest of my Sumter playing days.

As a freshman, I decided to go out for the high school team, but because I had qualified for and played in a basketball all-star game, I joined the tryouts about a week late. By then, there was only one roster spot left. It came down to me and another player who had also come out late—a catcher. A big catcher.

The coach picked the big catcher.

I jokingly told him, "You know why the coach kept you, don't you?"

"No," he said. "Why?"

"Because you're big enough to roll the batting cage by yourself."

That summer I did make the American Legion team—the

Post-15 team, or the P-15s, as we were known—as a second base-man. That team included many members of the high school team I had failed to make a few months earlier.

Sumter has a storied history in American Legion ball, which first came to South Carolina in 1929. Post-15 fielded a team that year and every year since, making it the second-longest American Legion team fielded in the world. "Hutch" Hutchinson—the same coach who would fail to launch my football career—coached that team, and we won the state championship. We did it again in 1952, and the P-15s have now won a total of fourteen state titles. My two oldest sons also played for Sumter Post-15.

A key moment for me came after we won our first state championship and advanced to the southeast regionals in Charlotte, North Carolina. We were scheduled to play a team from Richmond, Virginia, in the championship game. But before the game, our team went downtown to see a movie that would help determine the course of my life.

The film that was showing was *The Pride of the Yankees*. Babe Ruth played himself in that film. So did catcher Bill Dickey, who would be one of my hitting coaches with the Yankees. And Gary Cooper starred as Yankees legendary first baseman Lou Gehrig, who played in 2,130 consecutive games to set a major league record that stood from 1939 until 1995, when Cal Ripken Jr. broke the mark. A year before *The Pride of the Yankees* was released in 1942, Gehrig had died from amyotrophic lateral sclerosis (ALS), which became known as Lou Gehrig's Disease.

The movie helped popularize a line from Gehrig's farewell address at Yankee Stadium on the Fourth of July during the 1939 season: "Today I consider myself the luckiest man on the face of the earth." Gehrig actually spoke those words early in his address, but in the movie they were moved to the end of his speech for dramatic effect. That editing move certainly worked on me. By the time Gehrig's emotional words famously echoed throughout the Stadium—"Today (today, today) . . . I consider myself (self, self) . . ."—I was sold. I wanted to play for the New York Yankees.

I was drawn into the story line by how classy Gehrig was. I also related to the fact that his mother had wanted him to be anything other than a baseball player. Sometimes I thought my mother felt that way too, so I was glad to see baseball had turned out so well for Gehrig. Watching him and his teammates on the train trips during the movie, I envisioned the Yankees as a baseball family. *I'd like to be a part of that*, I thought to myself.

Unfortunately, the movie didn't have the desired effect on the field for our P-15s. In front of a couple thousand fans from Sumter who had driven up to Charlotte to root for us, we lost the regional championship by one run. That was the day I received my first taste of how bitter losing can be.

The score was tied at 3 in the eighth inning when a hard grounder was hit to our shortstop. The shortstop tossed the ball to me at second base, and I turned and threw to first for what should have been a double play. The umpire, however, ruled that I failed to touch second base for the force play, and he called the runner there safe. That runner wound up scoring the game's deciding run.

I knew I had touched the bag and the umpire had missed the call. But I still felt I was the reason our team had lost and would not advance to the American Legion World Series in Omaha, Nebraska. I'll never forget how hard I took that loss and how responsible I felt. In my mind, I had let down not only my teammates but also the two thousand fans who had made the trip to Charlotte, plus everyone back home awaiting the result of our game.

I told my dad that I really had touched second base, and Dad wrapped his arm around me. The man of few words again said little, but I can hear his words still to this day: "I know, Son. You've never lied to me."

That helped. So did the words of Spud Chandler, who walked up to me after the game and introduced himself as a scout for the Yankees. He explained that major league rules prevented a scout from recruiting a prospective player until he had finished high school. (Major League Baseball would not begin its amateur draft until 1965, so at the time prospects were free to sign with any team they chose.) Chandler said he would be back in touch with me when I graduated and asked me to remember his name.

I assured him I would, and I'll tell you, his was one of the easiest names I've ever had to remember. That short visit thrilled me and my dad. I couldn't believe it—a real-life major league scout liked the way I played.

And he wasn't just any scout. He was a scout with Lou Gehrig's New York Yankees!

An Easy Decision

In my sophomore year in high school, with a new coach in charge of the team, I made the Edmunds High Gamecocks as the starting second baseman. That turned out to be a busy spring for me. Not only was school in session and high school baseball in full swing, but the Norfolk Tars, a Yankees Class-B farm team in the Piedmont League, had come to Sumter for spring training. I took advantage of every opportunity I had to watch how those minor leaguers went about the business of preparing for their season. I particularly remember watching an outfielder named Bill Skowron work out with the Tars. That player would later become a first baseman more commonly known as Moose—a Yankees teammate of mine for eight seasons.

Mayo Smith was the Norfolk manager, and after the high school season, when I was back on the Post-15 team and playing shortstop, he and the Tars general manager, H. P. Dawson, would come to watch some of our games. Our team had a big, left-handed first baseman with a powerful bat who also handled himself gracefully around the first base bag. He was one of the best players ever to come through Sumter, and most, if not all, of the major league teams were taking a look at him that summer.

Back in junior high, whenever that guy came to the plate during our recess softball games, I would go stand right in front of our deep outfield fence. Sometimes the ball would fly over my head and out of our schoolyard park, but much of the time I would catch his long drives just short of the fence. He possessed amazing power even at a young age, with defensive ability to match. Sadly, he never signed with a team. A tough home life prevented him from reaching his baseball potential. I still wonder what he could have developed into as a baseball player.

Although the Tars manager and general manager were there to scout our first baseman, they noticed me, too. Mr. Smith came up to me after one game and said that when I graduated from high school, he would make sure that I had a chance to sign with the Yankees. So now I had *two* Yankees representatives saying the Yankees would want to sign me!

Immediately after my talk with Mr. Smith, the Yankees began mailing me literature about their team and organization. Based on what I read, I picked out their shortstop, Phil Rizzuto, as my favorite player. Rizzuto had been selected the Most Valuable Player of the American League in 1950, and he was a shortstop like I wanted to be. Actually, he was *the* shortstop I wanted to be. Defensively, he was about as good with the glove as a shortstop could hope to become. Scooter, as he was called, also wasn't very big—only about five feet six and 150 pounds or so. Because of his size, he wasn't a power hitter, and to make it in the major leagues he had to be excellent with the bat—adept at detailed skills such as bunting and moving runners with the hit-and-run.

The next year of American Legion ball, after my junior season of high school baseball, I was invited by the new Norfolk Tars manager, Mickey Owen, to work out with the team during its training in Sumter. I also got more attention from scouts. In all, scouts from twelve of the sixteen major league teams said they wanted to sign me when I graduated. But my heart was set on the Yankees. One Yankees scout didn't like my size—I was five feet eight and 158 pounds—and questioned whether my arm was strong enough for me to play shortstop at the major league level. I had heard similar concerns from a few others within the Yankees organization, but Mr. Dawson believed in my abilities enough to visit with my dad and make plans for the Yankees to sign me the day of my high school graduation.

Seniors like to count the days until their graduation, beginning with the first day of school. Knowing before my senior year began that I would be signing a professional baseball contract the next summer, my senior year seemed to crawl by. It felt as if graduation day were never going to get there.

The decision to sign for the Yankees was an easy one. For all intents and purposes, that decision had been made that day I watched *The Pride of the Yankees* at age fourteen. There was no financial confusion to cloud the process either. Baseball had instituted a rule regarding signing bonuses. Any prospect who signed for more than a four-thousand-dollar bonus would be required to spend the next two years on the major league club's roster. Seventeen- and eighteen-year-olds like me weren't ready to play at the major league level. Because of that rule, I had the same signing bonus offer from all twelve clubs: exactly four thousand dollars.

Of the eleven teams other than the Yankees that offered me contracts, the Brooklyn Dodgers had expressed the most interest. The Dodgers had come to Sumter and really gone out of their way to spend time with me. One of their scouts had stressed that I would have a chance to play and work my way up the organizational ladder. So the Yankees and Dodgers were clearly my top two choices, but because of *The Pride of the Yankees*, there was no doubt the Yankees were my number one.

On June 12, 1953, my graduation from Edmunds High School was only the second-biggest event of the day. My dreams—and my dad's—came true when, with my parents, my sisters, and Yankees scout Bill Harris looking on in my living room, I signed my first professional baseball contract.

I belonged to the New York Yankees!

Chapter 3

TIMELY REMINDER

IT DIDN'T TAKE LONG for me to receive my introduction to New York City. A week after signing my contract, I made my first visit to Yankee Stadium to work out with the team.

Fred Heath, a local businessman, was part owner of a baseball team in Sumter that played in a Class-B independent league. The Yankees often loaned minor league players to Mr. Heath, so he had connections with the team. Mr. Heath offered to fly me in his private plane to New York City, but I had never flown and wasn't too sold on allowing my feet to leave the ground. So Mr. Heath took me to New York City on a train instead.

When we stepped off the train in the big city, I sure was glad to have Mr. Heath with me. You can imagine how overwhelming New York City was to a not-quite-eighteen-year-old from a tiny Southern town.

The cab ride through the city was about as nerve-racking a ride as

I've ever had in my life. I was stunned by the number and height of the buildings we drove past. But my eyes kept getting pulled back to ground level every time I heard a horn honk or our cab driver made a sudden switch from one lane to another. I wanted out of that cab as soon as possible, but I was also grateful I was only a passenger. I couldn't imagine attempting to drive in that traffic. What a mess!

After we checked in to our hotel, Mr. Heath arranged for a cab to take me over to Yankee Stadium. I lost interest in the skyscrapers and traffic as the driver approached the Bronx and Yankee Stadium first came into view. This was the "House That Ruth Built," one of the most famous stadiums in the world. In fact, it was one of the first baseball venues to have *stadium* in its name. Most teams played in a "park" or a "field." But the Yankees had "the Stadium," as it was called for short.

When I first caught sight of the Stadium, it loomed large, even among the bigger buildings of the Bronx. As we got closer, I began to soak in the enormity of its exterior. Yankee Stadium was the first sports facility in the United States to have three decks, extending from the left field corner of the Stadium around behind home plate and to the right field corner.

Back home in Sumter, I had played in front of what I'd thought were huge crowds at our Riley Park. The P-15s might attract a couple of thousand fans for our big games. But Yankee Stadium, at that time, had a capacity of 67,000. As we drove up to the Stadium, I tried to imagine what it would be like shortly before game time, with that many people converging on the ballpark, buying their tickets, and working their way through the outside gates to the Stadium's interior. One day soon, I hoped, another sold-out crowd would find their seats to watch the Yankees—with Robert Richardson starting in the infield.

Among the first people I met at the Stadium were equipment manager Pete Sheehy, known as Big Pete, and his assistant Pete

Previte—Little Pete. Big Pete had been in charge of the Yankees' locker room since Babe Ruth was a player and would work with the Yankees until his death in 1985, by which time he had become known as the "Keeper of the Pinstripes." Little Pete was his assistant for about thirty of those years.

Big Pete gave me a warm welcome and made me feel about as at home as a seventeen-year-old could feel in the New York clubhouse. He began introducing me around to various members of the Yankees organization, including the manager, Casey Stengel, who had led New York to four consecutive World Series championships and was on his way to a fifth.

Mr. Stengel was busy but stopped what he was doing long enough to give me a handshake and a cordial greeting. The Yankees had a deep farm system at that time that required signing a large number of prospects to fill, so I doubted the manager knew who I was. But I hoped it wouldn't be long before Mr. Stengel was writing my name onto his lineup card every day.

After the introductions, Big Pete pointed me to a locker where I could dress and brought me a uniform to change into.

"Do you have any baseball shoes with you?" Big Pete asked.

"I have the ones that I played in high school with," I answered.

Big Pete nodded and left me to put on my pinstripes.

I couldn't help but notice how spacious the Yankees' locker room seemed compared to the smaller, cramped locker rooms of my high school and American Legion days. The floor was carpeted, too. I was used to plain, concrete floors that created a loud clickety-clack sound whenever someone dared walk on the concrete in their spikes.

Two lockers down from mine was the locker of Frank Crosetti, one of the coaches. He was the shortstop my dad had told me to watch and learn from when I was a youngster at the Yankees-Reds exhibition game in Columbia. As I was changing, I noticed that Crosetti was watching me.

When I bent over to grab my beat-up spikes, Crosetti spoke to me. "What size shoe you wear?"

"Eight and a half," I said.

"I got a pair the same size."

He walked over and handed me a pair of shiny, black spikes. I tried them on, and they fit perfectly.

"You can have those," he said. "Why don't you work out with them today? See how they do."

I thanked him, then took the spikes off and started walking across the locker room in my socks and leggings.

"Where are you going?" Crosetti called out to me.

"Out to the field."

"Well, why don't you have your shoes on?" he asked.

"In here?" I asked. "On this carpet?"

"Absolutely!" he said with a smile.

So I stopped, put my new spikes back on, then walked across the carpet—carefully, so as not to cause a snag—and out to the field.

Later that day, when I told Mr. Heath about Crosetti's giving me a pair of his spikes, Mr. Heath handed me a twenty-dollar bill and insisted I give it to Crosetti in exchange for the shoes. Crosetti scoffed at the notion of accepting twenty dollars from a seventeen-year-old minor leaguer. "I didn't sell you the shoes," he said. "I gave them to you." When I returned to Mr. Heath, he would not take back the twenty dollars, telling me to keep the money. So that day I wound up getting a new pair of spikes *and* twenty dollars.

Meeting Mickey Mantle

The tunnel from the clubhouse to the field was a straight shot. I walked through the back of the Yankees' first base dugout and up the steps.

At the top step, I stopped.

The first thing I noticed was how green the grass was. It appeared so thick and plush. Then I looked above the field to the thousands of empty seats. There were so many of them. I couldn't imagine how it would feel to step out onto the field with 67,000 fans cheering for my team. Above and beyond the seats rose the tall buildings of the Bronx that my cab had driven past, with the Bronx County courthouse standing prominent among them. Everything looked so big. But when I turned to my right to survey the Yankees' dugout, I realized that even the smallest details said "major league": the bench was cushioned.

On the field, I really wasn't sure what I should do. Yankees players were in the middle of batting and fielding practice. I tried to walk out toward second base in a way that didn't look too pre-sumptuous, yet also didn't reveal that I didn't belong on a major league baseball field. Trying not to be too obvious, I looked around to take note that I was on the same field as the likes of Yogi Berra, Billy Martin, Whitey Ford, and—my favorite Yankee of that time—Phil Rizzuto as they prepared for a game.

Man, it's good to be here, I thought. *I hope I get back here soon.*

As much as I enjoyed that moment and wanted to savor it, I realized it was a temporary experience. After a few days in New York, I'd go home to pack and then head out for the minor leagues, far from the hustle-and-bustle style of New York City and the major league feel of Yankee Stadium. I also realized that as much as I wanted to return someday soon to play in New York, and as much as I believed that was possible, there certainly were no guarantees. There were plenty of other players in the Yankees' farm system who had both my level of ability and my dream, and some had been afforded the same workout with the big club that I was experiencing.

It felt so natural, though, to be standing there on the field in Yankee Stadium.

I heard my name called, looked to the side of the field, and traced the voice to Crosetti. He was holding a fungo bat.

"Get over to second," he shouted out to me, "and I'll hit you some ground balls."

Crosetti started hitting me grounders. He hit some directly at me to start with, then some that made me move to my left, then some to my right. I did a good job of fielding the grounders. As smooth as that major league infield was, I didn't see how I could miss one.

After Crosetti finished with the grounders, he motioned me in. "Come on in and take some swings."

I took a spot next to the batting cage while the starters in that day's lineup took their hits. As much as I wanted to hop in there and swing away, there was no way I was going to cut in front of one of those guys to enter the batting cage on my own. Can you imagine a seventeen-year-old kid telling Hank Bauer, "Excuse me, Mr. Bauer. I'm just going to step in front of you and take a few cuts"?

As I stood watching alongside the cage, I saw Mickey Mantle approaching. By 1953 Mickey Mantle had already become *Mickey Mantle*. It was his third season in the majors, and he was entrenched in the center field spot that Joe DiMaggio had owned for so long. The Yankees torch that once had been passed from Lou Gehrig to Joe DiMaggio was now in Mickey's hands.

Mantle had already made one All-Star team and finished third in the American League Most Valuable Player voting the previous season. I didn't know much about Mickey personally, other than that he was from Oklahoma, but I did know that he was a great home run hitter and that he was the famous *Mickey Mantle*.

I expected Mickey to walk past me and into the batter's box, but he stopped and put his arm around me. "Come on, kid," Mickey said. "Step in here and take some swings."

As each player finished hitting, he would drop his bat outside the cage. I picked up a bat with Phil Rizzuto's name on it and gripped it real good. It wasn't to my liking, so I returned it to the ground, picked up Billy Martin's bat, and stepped into the cage.

Welcomed by none other than the Mick himself, I scratched the toes of my right shoe into the dirt of the batter's box. I didn't want to think about what might happen if I broke Billy Martin's bat, so I told myself, *Make sure you hit the ball on the good part of the bat.*

I don't remember ripping any line drives that turned the players' heads that day, but I don't think I swung and missed, either. On my way out of the cage, I passed by Mantle and said, "Thanks for letting me hit." Then I went back out to second base and fielded more ground balls until batting practice ended.

The Yankees stayed on the field for infield practice, but I returned to the locker room, changed into my street clothes, and went up into the stands to watch that day's game from the seat the Yankees had given me. The visiting St. Louis Browns defeated the first-place Yankees 3–1, with right fielder Vic Wertz hitting a two-run home run in the fifth inning off Whitey Ford. "We" Yankees would come back to win the next three games, though, and would go on to win the 1953 World Series.

After the game, Yankees television broadcaster Joe E. Brown interviewed me in a downstairs room in the Stadium that was set up for his postgame show. Brown was noted for walking into the room, removing his hat, and flipping it onto a hat rack that looked on TV like it was all the way across the room. Actually, they pulled that off by switching camera angles while another person closer to the hat rack flipped a matching hat onto the rack.

I had never been interviewed before that day, and I was nervous. To my relief, I was able to answer all Brown's questions, although I'm certain he would have preferred longer answers. I remember one question in particular: "How long do you think it will be before you actually get up here and play in the major leagues?"

"Well," I answered with a shrug, "I sure don't know that, but I hope it won't be too long."

The more I thought about that question later, the more I began to anticipate that it might take me four or five seasons. I figured I would start at the bottom of the ladder and work my way up. It turned out to be two years before I made my debut with the Yankees and four years before I was in the big leagues to stay.

Big Send-Off, Big Struggles

After four days in New York City, Mr. Heath and I returned home to Sumter. I had one day to pack up and head out to join my first team.

It was a quiet ride as my family drove me to the bus station that evening. I had mixed emotions—obviously excited about embarking on my professional baseball career, yet sad to be leaving my family and my hometown for the first time. Plus, after waiting for what felt like an eternity to sign my contract on graduation day, I almost felt like things were suddenly going too fast.

A lot of people were at the bus station when we pulled in. I looked at the crowd and tried to guess what type of a group trip would cause so many people to gather. I saw a remote unit from a local radio station. Then I spotted Harry Stokes rushing toward me and what seemed like the entire crowd following him. I turned to see my parents wearing big smiles. Immediately I was surrounded by well-wishers who had come to the bus station to see me off.

My departure turned out to be quite an occasion. The announcer from the radio station interviewed me, and Harry made a short speech. Then I was presented with a parting gift: a pen-and-pencil set, plus eighty-five dollars *in change*! Collection cans had been set up in various spots around town to raise money for me.

I couldn't believe it. Eighty-five dollars was a lot in 1953— still is, actually. Thanks to the good folks of Sumter, I was able to pay for needed items for a while out of a big pile of change. Fortunately, there were more quarters and half-dollars than pennies, nickels, and dimes.

When it came time to depart, I hugged my parents and sisters. Mom had so many tears flowing from her eyes that she needed a handkerchief to keep wiping them. All the well-wishers let out a big cheer when I stepped onto the Greyhound. I waved through the window as the bus pulled out of the station.

I didn't cry, but I sure came close. To know I was carrying the support of so many people with me made for an emotional sendoff. I really wanted to make the special people of my hometown proud.

Norfolk

Much to my surprise, the Yankees hadn't assigned me to a Class-D team, or even to a Class-C team. Instead, they were shipping me out to the same Norfolk Tars I had watched train in Sumter. The Yankees were starting me all the way up in Class B, right out of high school.

The minor league system at that time started at Class D and went up to A ball, then AA, AAA, and the major leagues. That year the Yankees had three Class-D teams, two Class-C teams, two Class-B teams, and one team each in A, Double-A, and Triple-A. Most first-year players began in D ball or perhaps with one of the Class-C teams, but I was starting out about halfway up the Yankees' system. To compare it to today's scaled-down minor league system, the Tars would have been similar to at least a High-A team.

Class B proved to be a bad place for me to start. I was over-matched there because of my inexperience, and it didn't take long for me to find that out.

Mickey Owen was still the Tars' manager, so I reported to him at the ballpark the next morning, and he began introducing me around to the arriving players. They were very friendly, and some offered to help set me up with a place to stay. Among those I met that first day was Dick Sanders. Dick was the Tars' shortstop and the reason I had been assigned to Norfolk. Because he would soon be sent to Marine reserve training, I would be taking over his shortstop spot.

The Tars were a very good team—they had easily run away with the Piedmont League championship the previous season—and Dick was a star player for them. In addition to joining a championship-caliber team at midseason fresh out of high school, I had big shoes to fill right away because Mickey immediately wrote me into the lineup.

I never felt comfortable with my new team. It had nothing to do with my teammates; they treated me great. But the truth is that I was out of my league in Class B. Most of the Tars players were in their early to middle twenties. I believe I was one of only two players on the team under the age of twenty.

On defense, I played well enough. My inexperience showed on offense, though. The pitching was by far the biggest difference between Class B and what I had faced at even the highest level of American Legion tournaments. In the Piedmont League, the fastballs were noticeably faster and the curveballs noticeably sharper. The pitchers worked the ball around the plate more too, instead of just throwing it down the middle. It didn't seem like opposing pitchers made many mistake pitches when I was at the plate, and when they did, I wasn't able to take advantage.

Segregation was still part of baseball then. The African American fans would sit down the left field line of Myers Field, where the Tars played. For some reason, they seemed to like me as a player. But among the white fans seated throughout the rest of the ballpark, I didn't have many friends. Loudly and clearly, they made it known that they would have rather had Dick Sanders at shortstop. I can't say I blamed them. I wasn't even hitting my weight, and that was before I reached the weight of—ahem—170 pounds that I carried in the majors.

After I struck out three consecutive times in one game, the booing began. I had never had to deal with any negative fan reaction, and those boos began a bad cycle for me. When the fans booed, my level of play suffered—even my normally steady defense. As my play worsened, the fans grew more vocal with their disapproval.

On top of all that, I was homesick. I had never been away from home, and I was eating into my family's finances by calling collect every night. I missed my family, I missed Sumter, and I missed playing well on the field.

I was ready to quit baseball and go home.

Then a letter arrived from Sumter. Conley Alexander had been one of my coaches in junior high school. I hadn't had much contact with him of late, and I don't know if he had heard or read of my struggles in Norfolk, but apparently he felt inspired to send me a letter of encouragement.

Coach Alexander wrote that ups and downs were a part of playing professional baseball and that I should keep in mind the words of Matthew 6:33: "Seek ye first the kingdom of God, and his righteousness; and all these things shall be added unto you."

I knew that verse well, but I really needed it now. With all the drastic changes in my life—moving into professional baseball, moving away from home—I had lost my sense of priorities, and baseball had become my sole focus. Coach Alexander's letter, and that verse in particular, reminded me that the Lord should be predominant in my life. Whether or not I played baseball, I needed to put my confidence in Him and let Him work out the details. Remembering that God, in His Word, had stated His desire for me to lean on Him removed some of the pressure I had been placing on myself to perform well.

Meanwhile, my parents, hearing in my nightly phone calls how homesick I was and knowing how much I was struggling on the field, came to Norfolk to visit me. It had to be difficult for them to hear me being jeered by the home fans around them in the stands. Hearing their son booed was a new experience for them, just as it had been for me.

As I have described, my dad was not a forceful man. He preferred to sit back and observe my baseball career. But when he saw what was going on, he visited Mr. Dawson, our team's general manager, to discuss how I was playing. After that meeting, Mr. Dawson decided I would be best served by being sent down the minor league ladder—all the way down. Mr. Dawson asked my dad and me to come to his office. That's when I learned he had talked with Dad.

"You're a good prospect," Mr. Dawson said, "but we started you too high. You need to start where the others are starting. I want you to go up to Olean, New York."

"I think you should try that," Dad said to me.

"Okay," I said. "I'm willing."

On one hand, I was relieved. I felt overmatched in the Piedmont League, and my numbers weren't good. In twenty-seven games with the Tars, I had a .211 batting average, and truth be told, I had to go on a little bit of a hot streak (relatively speaking) toward the end to get my average above the measly .200 mark. I simply wasn't ready for that level of competition.

But on the other hand, I was disappointed. Such a big deal had been made about me starting in Class B. Now here I was being sent down not one, but two classifications.

That move probably saved my career, though. The Pennsylvania-Ontario-New York League consisted mostly of rookie players like me. After I joined the Olean Yankees, I started hitting right away and didn't stop until the season ended. In thirty-two games with

Olean, I had the team's highest batting average, at .412. Baseball was easy again.

I headed home for the off-season thanking the Lord for all these things He had added unto me after Coach Alexander's letter helped me reprioritize my life. Not too long before, I had wanted to quit baseball altogether. Now I couldn't wait for spring training.

I can do this, I was thinking. *I can move up the ladder.*

Chapter 4
CLIMBING THE LADDER

THE YANKEES' MINOR LEAGUE TEAMS held spring training at different sites than the major league team did. But before the 1954 season, I was one of about two dozen Yankees prospects invited to a kind of pre-spring training where the Yankees trained in St. Petersburg, Florida. For ten days, Yankees manager Casey Stengel and his coaches put us through instructional-type workouts and intrasquad games designed to teach us the major league way of doing things and, hopefully, accelerate our development through the farm system.

It was during those extra sessions that I learned of plans to move me from shortstop to second base. I had played mostly shortstop on my high school team and had been the full-time shortstop on our American Legion teams and in Norfolk and Olean. Shortstop was my favorite position, although second base seemed to feel more natural to me and probably was my best position.

I liked the challenge of playing shortstop. A shortstop has to make the long throw to first from the hole between short and third. He also has to field the ball cleanly, while a second baseman has time to bobble the ball and still make the shorter throw to retire the runner. I believe that if a player can play shortstop well, he can play any position on the field, and I really wanted to learn to play it well. On the other hand, I preferred playing a full game at second base to spending most of the game on the bench and playing only an inning or two at shortstop. So I began working toward a move to second there in St. Petersburg.

At the end of that ten-day training session, I received my next assignment. I would be playing with the Binghamton (New York) Triplets—a Class-A team! (The team's nickname derived from the "Triple Cities" of Binghamton, Johnson City, and Endicott.) On the strength of my first season at Olean and my performance in St. Petersburg, the Yankees were bumping me up three classifications, even bypassing the Class-B Norfolk Tars I had struggled with the season before.

As a bonus, the Triplets' spring training was held in Orangeburg, South Carolina, about an hour's drive from my house. The team was housed in an old hotel downtown that nobody liked, while I had the luxury of driving home each day, sleeping in my own comfortable bed, enjoying Mom's cooking, and getting to spend extra time in Sumter.

That spring training went by in a hurry. But before we broke camp, our team played the Tars in an exhibition game in Sumter on what was declared "Robert Richardson Day." We beat the Tars easily, but I was hitless in four at bats against my old team. Ugh.

When we made the trip north to Binghamton to start the season, I followed the team bus in my off-season acquisition. It was my first big purchase after signing my first contract: a green 1954 Pontiac that didn't have air-conditioning.

During the '54 season in Binghamton, I made an important friend. Johnny Hunton was a married, twenty-seven-year-old utility infielder who had been with the Yankees' Double-A team in Birmingham, Alabama, before being sent down to join our team. Johnny was a Christian and had no qualms whatsoever about making that known. He wasn't overbearing and never tried to force his beliefs on anyone, but he was appropriately public with his Christianity. He carried his Bible with him and didn't try to hide it under an arm or set it upside down on a table. He prayed before meals in restaurants. He never missed his devotion time, and he spoke about his faith everywhere, including churches where he was invited to be a guest speaker.

Johnny also acted like a Christian on the field. He played hard, but he didn't lose his temper when he struck out or when an umpire missed a call. He always maintained an upbeat, positive attitude, not only for himself but toward his teammates.

Because he was an older player, Johnny became a mentor to me. He and his wife, Patricia, often invited me to their home for dinner. When Johnny spoke at churches during our team's road trips, I went with him to listen. Johnny was the person who modeled for me how a person could maintain an uncompromising Christian lifestyle in professional baseball.

My first season in Binghamton turned out to be Johnny's last one in professional baseball, so 1954 was the only season we played together. Yet our close friendship lasted through the years, and after our playing days were over, we would work together on the coaching staffs of two different colleges.

Another lasting friendship that began at Binghamton was with outfielder Sam Suplizio. Later on, Sam and his wife, Caroline, would become good friends of ours.

Sam had signed his first contract with the Yankees the same year I had. The first All-American baseball player at the University of

New Mexico, he was highly thought of by the Yankees organization. The plan was to bring him up to play center field with the big club and move Mickey Mantle to another outfield position or possibly to first base, to save wear and tear on Mickey's legs.

But late in the 1956 season, about a week before the Yankees were going to bring him up from the minors, Sam badly fractured his arm while breaking up a double play. Sam could not fully recover from the injury and never played in the majors, but he remained active in baseball after being forced to retire because of his injury. He worked as a coach and instructor for several major league teams and later went into business in Grand Junction, Colorado. He helped Grand Junction become the host site for the Junior College World Series—the stadium there is named for him—and also was instrumental in helping Denver secure the Colorado Rockies franchise.

Sam survived two strokes. After the second, he made a wonderful decision for Christ. When Sam passed away in 2006, I was privileged to be asked to be a part of his memorial service, along with Paul Molitor and Robin Yount, two of the many major league players Sam had mentored.

My '54 season with the Triplets was a fine one for many reasons. I played in all 141 games—every inning of every game. The transition to second base went smoothly, and I led our team with a .310 batting average, which was high enough to rank me near the top of the Eastern League's leaders. I also made the league's All-Star Game.

The highlight of the season, though, was probably a game that didn't count in the standings or in the statistics: an exhibition in Binghamton against the parent-club Yankees, who brought with them Mickey Mantle, Yogi Berra, Phil Rizzuto, and Billy Martin, among others. Our fans were excited about having the big Yankees visit, and the game received a lot of publicity. Despite Mickey hitting a homer against us, we beat the five-time defending World Series champions. I hit a double and made a couple of nice defensive plays.

After the game, Casey Stengel told me, "I'll see you in spring training next year," inviting me back to St. Petersburg for another year of his pre-spring training. Casey didn't throw words around much, especially compliments, so I was ecstatic that, first, he knew who I was, and second, he thought I was climbing the ladder.

A "Chance" Meeting

After the 1954 season, when I was back in Sumter, I met the young lady who would become my wife, Betsy Dobson.

We attended the same church, which had a semicircular seating arrangement. I had noticed a stunning brunette sitting across the way with her mother every Sunday morning. We both were fairly shy. But we obviously had an interest in each other because we would look across the congregation, and when our eyes met, we would both quickly look away in that "Oh, no! I hope he/she didn't see me!" sort of way.

After several weeks of exchanging glances, I came up with a plan to meet her. When the service ended, I would cross over to exit out her door instead of the door closest to where I sat among the other youth, thus creating a "chance" meeting at the back of the church. Clearly that was a great idea because Betsy had it too. She came up with the same plan for the same day and decided to exit out my side of the church, which meant our paths crossed sooner than we had planned. Surprised, we offered an awkward "hi" to each other and continued on our journeys out each other's doors.

I knew very little about Betsy at that point, but I did some checking around and learned that she played softball. Shortly after our not-so-grand introduction on the way out of church, I spotted her at the Sumter County Fair. I knew her softball coach well enough to ask him to introduce me to Betsy that day. He did, and we exchanged a cordial greeting.

Man! I thought as I watched her walk away. *I want to date that girl. I'm going to ask her out.* I gave myself a brief "you can do this" pep talk and set out to find Betsy again. But by the time I caught up with her, she was boarding to ride the Loop-O-Plane ride. I stopped in my tracks. The Loop-O-Plane turned its riders upside down—and fast.

I am not going to ride that thing, I said to myself. I would have followed her onto the Ferris wheel, but I wasn't about to get on any ride that would spin me upside down. So I temporarily called off my pursuit.

The next time I saw Betsy was at a football game. Her brother-in-law, whom I knew, had two extra tickets and offered them to a friend and me. Betsy and I talked a little during the game, but not much.

Finally, a few days later, I worked up the courage to call her and ask her out on a date. She accepted, and on our first date we played miniature golf. As we neared the end of the course, we added up our scores. Betsy was leading by seven strokes. As she tells the story, she thought to herself, *I shouldn't beat him on our first date. He's an athlete!* She also likes to tell how from that point, she began purposely hitting bad shots. But despite her best efforts to sabotage her own score, she still beat me by two strokes.

Betsy was a very good athlete, so there was no shame in losing to her in miniature golf. In addition to softball, she also played tennis. I couldn't tell it at the time, but she should have been playing left-handed. Back then, being right-handed was considered better than being left-handed. Betsy's mother, a schoolteacher, trained her around age two to do everything right-handed. I wish I could have seen what kind of athlete Betsy would have developed into if she had been allowed to play from her natural side.

At the end of our first date, Betsy told me that she was a Christian and asked whether I was too. I didn't know then how bold a move that was for her. Much later she told me that she feared I might not go out with her again if she asked that question. But the truth is, her question made me like her even more.

One of the many things I didn't know about Betsy at first was her age. She was not quite fourteen, and I was five years older. She looked mature for her age, and I figured her to be about sixteen or seventeen. But even after I did learn her real age, it wasn't much of a problem. Betsy looked much older than she was, for one. She had been raised by a single mother and had older sisters, so she had always been more grown-up than most girls her age. Besides, in the South in the 1950s, it was very common for a girl her age to be dating. Her mother approved of me, too, so that helped.

Betsy was a load of fun and a strong Christian. When the spring of '55 rolled around, as much as I was looking forward to getting back into baseball, I found it difficult to say good-bye to Betsy.

For the 1955 season the Yankees shipped me westward, having me bypass Class AA to play for their top minor league team, the Triple-A Denver Bears of the American Association. Joining the Bears meant I was only one step from the major leagues. And I would be playing for Ralph Houk, who was in his first season as a manager after spending eight seasons as a backup catcher with the Yankees.

As a piece of trivia, it was in Denver where the name etched into my Louisville Slugger bats began reading "Bob Richardson." I had been Robert growing up in Sumter, but that somehow was switched to Bob during my minor league career. I don't know how I became known as Bobby, either, but that was the name that stuck throughout the rest of my baseball career.

Betsy and I kept a steady stream of letters flowing back and forth during that season. I would send her letters on hotel stationery from the cities where we stayed. (She still has two rather large boxes filled with those letters.) Betsy knew our team schedule well. She had to, in order to make sure her letters to me wound up in the right places.

As soon as one of us received a letter, we would write a reply and drop it in the mail to go out as soon as possible. Often Betsy would get a letter, pen her response immediately, and hurry to the post office to make sure it was postmarked by midnight and thus ensured of reaching me. If she knew I would be leaving a city soon, she would mail the letter ahead of us, so I often arrived in the next city with the special treat of a letter from Betsy waiting for me at the hotel front desk. I really looked forward to having a letter greet me when we arrived.

Even though Betsy's letters were great, I sure did miss talking to her in person. "Unchained Melody" was our song. The line "Time goes by so slowly" was certainly true for us while we were apart.

I continued to play well in Denver and was selected to the league's All-Star team. We were in the middle of the play-off race in early August, and I was hitting .296, with a career-high twelve triples, six home runs, and fifty-nine runs batted in, when Ralph said he needed to talk to me. "The Yankees want you to report to them tomorrow," he said with a big smile.

I was stunned. I had expected to spend the entire season in Denver. The Yankees were set in the infield, with Gil McDougald and Jerry Coleman at second, Phil Rizzuto and Billy Hunter at shortstop, and Andy Carey at third. (Billy Martin, who had been the starting second baseman, was serving his second year of military service.)

Ralph told me that McDougald had been hit by a line drive during batting practice. Until he got better, the Yankees planned to put me in his lineup spot. And they wanted me to begin the next day.

I called Betsy first. "New York is a lot closer to Sumter than Denver is," I told her hopefully. Next I called my dad. Even though it was only a temporary call-up, he was thrilled that I would be joining the Yankees.

On my flight to New York, I sat next to Ruth Pesky, the wife of Bears coach Johnny Pesky. Johnny had played for the Boston Red Sox, Detroit Tigers, and Washington Senators, and the right field foul pole at Boston's Fenway Park was named Pesky's Pole as a tribute to him. Mrs. Pesky and I spent the flight talking about what it would be like playing in my first major league game.

Welcome to the Big Leagues

I felt slightly timid joining the Yankees. I didn't know if Mickey Mantle would remember me, but he did. He reached out to me when he first saw me and made me feel welcome again.

I have a picture from that day of Mickey and me in the dugout. I'm sitting on one of the steps and Mickey is next to me, with one foot on the dugout floor and the other a step higher. Mickey is pointing toward the field, and I'm looking out toward where he is pointing. It looks casual and unrehearsed, but Mickey planned the whole thing. He knew that a photographer was likely to snap a picture of him anywhere he was. So he told me, "Come over here, and they'll take this picture if we sit together. I'll be pointing things out." Sure enough, a photographer saw us and snapped the picture of the star and the rookie together.

That was the kind of person Mickey was, always thinking of and looking out for others. He never sought out attention for himself, preferring instead to find ways of deflecting attention onto his teammates. Mickey was a superstar—one of the biggest superstars ever in baseball—but he was always a team player.

The day I joined the Yankees, my name was indeed in the starting lineup. I was hitting second, just before Mickey Mantle and

Yogi Berra. On the field, I took McDougald's spot at second base, between Jerry Coleman at short and Joe Collins at first.

That was Friday, August 5, 1955. The Yankees were playing the Detroit Tigers at Yankee Stadium and were one game out of first place, trailing both the Chicago White Sox and the Cleveland Indians. The Tigers were in play-off contention too, so I was stepping directly into the midst of a good pennant race.

A familiar face was on the mound for us the day of my first game: Don Larsen. The Yankees had traded for Don during the off-season, and after a few starts at the beginning of the season, he'd been shipped down to the Bears. He'd been fantastic for us in Denver and had been called back up to New York about a week before my call-up.

Casey put me second in the batting order, behind right fielder Hank Bauer and directly in front of Mickey. After Hank grounded out to third to start the bottom of the first, I stepped into the box against Jim Bunning, a rookie right-hander who would wind up being elected to the National Baseball Hall of Fame and be just as successful during a long political career. I grounded out on a routine ball to Tigers shortstop Harvey Kuenn.

In my next at bat, leading off the fourth inning, I reached base for the first time on a walk off Bunning. Then I stole second base. Mickey walked behind me, and I scored on Yogi's two-hundredth career home run. Not a bad way to score my first major league run—ahead of Mickey Mantle and Yogi Berra.

My first hit came in my final at bat, in the seventh inning off relief pitcher Babe Birrer. I would love to say that my first major league hit was a real smasher, but in truth it was an infield single to the first baseman. But hey, a hit's a hit, especially in the major leagues. We won that day 3–0, with all the runs being scored on Yogi's milestone homer, and moved into a tie for first place in the league.

What stands out most for me from that first game is that I didn't have a single ball hit to me at second base. No grounders, no pop-ups—the only time I got to touch the ball was when we threw it around the infield after someone else had recorded an out. It's true what they say about a professional ballplayer's nerves calming a bit once he's been involved in a play. Not having a ball hit to me meant I battled a case of the nerves on defense for the entire game.

I got my second big league hit the next day. We were trailing the Tigers 7–5 going into the bottom of the ninth, and I had been held hitless in my first four at bats. Leading off the inning, I reached on another single—another infield single. Mickey singled me to third with one out, but we weren't able to score and lost to Detroit. I had only one ball hit to me in my second game, and I made an error.

We concluded the series on Sunday by splitting a doubleheader, and Casey had me leading off during the first game. I finally made my first play on defense, as the middle man in a 5-4-3 double play in the first inning, but I went hitless in eight at bats in those two games. After we had Monday off, McDougald was back to starting at second and Carey was at third for the next game on Tuesday. I played in three more games as a substitute without getting to bat again before being shipped back out.

I had known going into New York that my stay would be short, and I wasn't surprised to be returned to the minors. I was, however, surprised with where I was sent: Richmond, Virginia. The Virginians were the Yankees' other Triple-A team, in the International League, but they weren't as good as the Denver Bears. In fact, when I joined the team along with veteran relief pitcher Jim Konstanty, who'd also been sent down, the Virginians were a dismal forty-two games out of first place.

My being shipped to Richmond instead of Denver wasn't a demotion. The regular season was winding down, and the Yankees wanted to keep me closer geographically. A player was required to be on the roster on September 1 in order to be eligible to play in the postseason. If the Yankees needed to bring me back up quickly to meet that deadline, it would be easier to have me nearby in Richmond instead of farther away with the Denver team.

I understood all that and was glad the Yankees wanted to keep me that close. But after being in a playoff race with Denver, then joining the American League pennant chase with the Yankees, hooking up with a team whose season was in the tank sure felt like a demotion. Not surprisingly, morale was low on the Richmond team. Few fans were coming to their games. Players were skipping pregame batting practice and infield practice. It was as though everyone in the clubhouse couldn't wait for the season to end. It wasn't an enjoyable situation, but at least I had the chance to play every day—and hope the Yankees would need me again.

I spent almost a month with the Virginians. We finished in last place, thirty-six and a half games behind the first-place Montreal Royals. After our season ended, the Yankees did call me up as part of the expanding of rosters late in the season. But that was after the September 1 deadline for postseason eligibility, and mostly I was there "just in case." With the pennant clinched, Casey started me in both games of a doubleheader on the final day of the regular season to give his starters a day off before the World Series. I got two hits that day, and both were to the outfield, not of the infield variety. In my two stints with the Yankees that season, I played in eleven games and had four hits in twenty-six at bats for a .154 batting average.

While the Yankees went on to the World Series, losing in seven games to the Brooklyn Dodgers, I returned home to Sumter to start my dove-hunting season. Imagine my surprise later when I opened a copy of *Sporting News* magazine and learned that, even though I had been with the Yankees for about a month, I had been voted by the players to receive one-third of a share of their World Series earnings.

Players in the World Series receive a financial reward for reaching the postseason, with players from the winning team receiving larger amounts. Players who had played in the World Series could vote to give players from the season who were not part of the Series a portion of the bonus money. I received a one-third share, or a third of what a full-season player would receive. I think my share came to about eighteen hundred dollars. Getting to spend about a month in the majors had been bonus enough for me. But receiving that extra check gave me an introduction to the Yankees players' generosity and sense of family.

Chapter 5

WEDDING BELLS AND BASEBALL

BETWEEN THE 1955 and 1956 seasons, my relationship with Betsy grew more serious. I took a job over the winter working at the Gulf service station in town. One day Betsy drove up in her family's big, blue Buick Roadmaster.

"What can I do for you?" I asked. "Want gas?"

"Fill it up!" she said.

So I filled it up with gas, and when it came time to pay, all Betsy had was two dollars. That Roadmaster's tank held a lot more than two dollars' worth of gas, but she had never purchased a full tank of gas before and had no idea how much it could cost.

I paid for her tank of gas. I can't remember the amount, but I do recall figuring that it amounted to almost what I would make in a full week of work at that service station. Betsy later admitted that the only reason she came to get gas was so she could see me. It turned out to be an expensive little visit for me, but she certainly was worth it.

Just about all my spare time that off-season was spent with Betsy, attending football games, playing miniature golf (by that point I was more competitive and was able to win without her throwing the match), and attending church together. I wanted to marry her and found subtle ways to broach the topic to see how receptive she would be to the idea. I had been dropping hints in my letters to Betsy, saying that Ralph Houk had told me, "You ought to marry that young girl back home," or that our pastor had been saying, "Betsy is pretty mature for her age." I could tell that Betsy loved me and that marriage appeared to be in our future.

All too soon the off-season came to an end, and I was headed to St. Petersburg for the third consecutive year to take part in Casey Stengel's pre-spring training. Then, for the first time, I stayed in St. Petersburg to take part in the Yankees' major league spring training. And I did well enough there to be included on the big league roster for the start of the regular season.

We headed north by train with the Philadelphia Phillies, who were also just out of spring training, and we stopped in Savannah, Georgia, to play an exhibition game. Not only was my dad there, but so was a large group of family and friends from Sumter. I didn't start the game but was substituted in, and I hit a triple. That was especially exciting to me because, even though it was just an exhibition game, it was still my first game as a major leaguer in front of my dad.

The Phillies' third baseman in that game was Willie Jones, who went by the nickname of "Puddin' Head."

"You're from South Carolina, aren't you?" Puddin' Head asked me as I stood on third, waiting for the next play.

"Yeah," I said.

Puddin' Head told me he was from a small town that I recognized as being near my hometown.

"I'm from Sumter," I told him.

"Glad to see you," he said. Puddin' Head and I were quickly

becoming best friends right there at third base. "How about you move your foot and let me get the dirt off that bag there."

"Sure," I said and stepped off the bag.

Puddin' Head still had the ball in his glove, and he reached over and tagged me.

The umpire at third base was also from South Carolina.

"I can't believe you did that," the umpire told Puddin' Head. "He's safe. I will *not* call him out."

Then the umpire looked at me. "Don't you ever do that again."

I learned my lesson, and never again did I step off the bag like that without first calling time-out.

Starting in New York

Back then, clubs started the season with expanded rosters before having to cut down to the number of players they would carry throughout the season, until rosters expanded again in September. For Casey, having a larger roster was like playing with a deck that had sixty-five cards: it just gave him more options to manage.

Casey had to be one of the most unconventional managers in modern baseball history when it came to platooning and substituting players. He loved to put in pinch hitters at unexpected times. "Hold that gun," he would say to summon the scheduled batter back to the dugout in favor of a pinch hitter. Sometimes it seemed like he had drawn a number out of his cap to determine when he would do it. Casey didn't care if it was the first inning; if he wanted to bring in a pinch hitter, he would. I never understood why Casey put in pinch hitters at such odd times, though it's difficult to argue with Casey's managerial record.

When I arrived in New York to start the regular season, I didn't expect to stay long. Despite Casey's substituting ways, the infield seemed set. Gil McDougald was back at second base after starting the most games at second of anyone in 1955. Also, Billy Martin had returned from his military service for the final month of that season and had now had a full spring training to work out the rust. I figured I would spend the bulk of the season in Denver.

Knowing I probably wouldn't be with the Yankees for long, I asked Betsy and her mother to come up early in the season for a visit. I had told Rizzuto that I wanted to marry Betsy, and he'd recommended I buy a ring from a jeweler friend of his who could give me a good deal. One day when Betsy and I were walking in the city, I suggested we stop at the store Rizzuto had told me about "just to look" at rings. I wasn't going to ask Betsy to marry me until I was certain she would say yes. But watching her check out the rings in that store, I knew the time was right to propose.

After dinner at a restaurant close to the Concourse Plaza Hotel near Yankee Stadium—and having obtained the blessing of Betsy's mother—I proposed, and Betsy accepted. We decided to marry that fall after the season ended.

Betsy and her mother planned to follow the team on our trip to play the Baltimore Orioles. Then they would ride the train back from Baltimore to Sumter. The day before they were to leave for home from Baltimore, Betsy went with me to the ballpark while her mother stayed at the hotel. Betsy and I arranged to meet in the seating area after the game.

After the game, though, I was delayed because Casey called me into his office. I was being sent down to Denver.

"Don't get discouraged," Casey told me. "We'll call you back up. Just go down there and play good."

I had played in five games at the time, starting only two of those. At one point I had gone two weeks without appearing in a game. I'd had one hit in seven at bats. I just hadn't been given an opportunity to play and show what I could do.

Even though I'd expected that the move down was coming eventually, it was still disheartening to leave the majors. A player just couldn't assume that everything would go as planned and he would be back. A bad injury could happen. There could be an extended hitting slump at the wrong time. Some fast-rising prospect could climb past him on the ladder.

The meeting with Casey didn't last long, but my equipment had to be packed, and I had to get my travel arrangements from the team's traveling secretary. Meanwhile, poor Betsy was all alone in the stadium, waiting for me. The seats around her emptied. Then a policeman walked over and told her that the stadium was closing and she would have to leave.

An idea came to Betsy. The workers in the concession stands were still there cleaning up, so she went to a nearby concession stand and tried to blend in with them so she could stay in the stadium. She told me later that she began praying about what she should do next. While she was praying, I saw her standing there and walked over to her, much to her relief. (It's always nice to hear the person you love say that you are an answer to prayer!)

I apologized for taking so long and shared what Casey had just told me. Betsy was probably just as disappointed as I was. I was leaving the majors, and Betsy had to say good-bye for who knew how long. Betsy and her mother headed south, and I headed north to New York to pack up my belongings and then get back to Denver.

Newlyweds

Once I joined the Bears, I really started missing Betsy more than ever. Waiting until the off-season to marry seemed too far away; I wanted to get married now, during the season. So did Betsy.

I asked Bears owner Bob Howsam for permission to leave the team long enough to return home and marry Betsy, then rejoin the team.

Howsam's response was short: "That's the silliest thing I've ever heard. Wait until the end of the season." End of conversation.

Then I went to our manager, Ralph Houk. We were close, and I knew I could tell Ralph what I wanted to do. He had encouraged me to marry Betsy, probably because he had witnessed too many ballplayers during his playing days marry girls who were interested in them only because they were ballplayers or for their money. He knew what Betsy and I had was different.

"Absolutely—go home," Ralph said. "Take as long as you want. Don't worry about it. I'll cover for you."

Ralph's permission set the planning hurriedly in motion. We picked the date of June 8 at our church, Grace Baptist. The Bears would be playing in Indianapolis right before then, so I would fly home from there. Of course, I wanted to look good for my wedding, so before I left for South Carolina, I got a haircut in a hotel barbershop. In my letter to Betsy that day, I told her that I'd had "my ears lowered."

Because Betsy had grown up without her father around and had only sisters, she had never heard that phrase. When she read that letter, she ran to her mother and said, "Mom, Robert said he had some kind of surgery on his ears! I think they looked fine!"

"Betsy," her mother explained, "that's a haircut."

We married on a Friday and immediately started the drive to Denver to join the team. I don't think we had what would be considered a real honeymoon until after our fifth child was born.

For our wedding gift, Betsy's mother gave us a full set of new tires for my car so we could safely make the drive to Denver. Our first night, we stopped in nearby Columbia. The next day we drove all the way to Tupelo, Mississippi, before stopping to spend a night there.

That drive was hotter than it was long, and it was plenty long. The car's heater knob was stuck in the on position. Not only did we not have air conditioning, we had a heater we couldn't turn off. It might be the heat still influencing my memory, but I remember that first day we headed out toward Denver as the hottest June day in the history of South Carolina.

That was before there was an interstate highway system, and I also wasn't too good with maps and navigation, so I didn't plot out the best route for us. From Mississippi, I took us through northern Arkansas, where I got us lost somewhere in the Ozark Mountains. I called Ralph and said, "I think we're going to be a couple of days later than I planned."

We did make it to Denver—a little later than expected, but after the adventures of our first road trip, it was a relief just to get there.

I pulled a little joke on Betsy when we got to Denver. I parked the car outside a run-down house and announced, "This is where we're going to live." Betsy didn't know what to say. The look on her face, though, said enough. I quickly informed her I was kidding.

I had arranged for us to rent a small apartment near Bears Stadium (later renamed Mile High Stadium) from an elderly couple named the Ellises, who were as nice as could be. It was an upstairs apartment with a private entrance.

"*This* is where we're going to stay," I told Betsy when we pulled into the driveway. The look on her face was much more approving of that house.

A photographer from the *Denver Post* newspaper was there. Betsy had started helping me unload the car when the photographer suggested that me carrying Betsy across the threshold would make a good photo. I picked her up, and he took the photo of us arriving at our new home.

When I got to the field, my teammates teased me about being a couple of days late, saying I'd deliberately taken extra time to report back from our "honeymoon." Actually, though, the delay made bad timing even worse, because my first game back with the Bears was the final game of a home stand. We hadn't even unpacked all our suitcases, and I had to leave with the team on a two-week road trip.

On one of my first calls to Betsy from our trip, I told the operator my call was for Betsy Dobson. "I'm sorry, she doesn't live here," Betsy playfully told the operator. "There's no Betsy Dobson here."

When she said that on the other end of the line, I realized my mistake.

"Oh—Betsy Richardson!" I quickly corrected. "That's my wife!" Needless to say, as a newlywed, that was the longest road trip of my playing career.

There was no call-up from the Yankees during the '56 season. Other than the time off for my wedding, I didn't miss a game with the Bears, hitting .328 with twelve triples. That season I seemed to hit a lot of line drives into the outfield gaps, and I had the speed to turn those into triples. I made the league All-Star team again. We had a good team, finishing second in the regular season to an Indianapolis Indians team that included a young, power-hitting outfielder named Roger Maris. We defeated the Omaha Cardinals in the first round of the postseason, but then, in the championship, we were swept in four games by Indianapolis.

That season was the beginning of my friendship with shortstop Tony Kubek. Tony and I were roommates before my wedding, and we would eventually become roommates on the road for most of our major league seasons. My average had me up among the league leaders, and Tony hit three points better than I did, at .331. That was a lot of offensive production from the middle infielders.

Ralph Terry was also on that team, and he would become a key part of the Yankees' pitching rotation. Another pitcher for the Bears that season was Tom Lasorda, who would of course become known for managing the Los Angeles Dodgers to two world championships. Before Tom began to "bleed Dodger Blue," he was my teammate in the Yankees' system.

I received a phone call not too long ago.

"I bet you can't tell me who this is," the caller said.

"Give me some help," I said.

"We go back fifty years," he said.

"Teammate?"

"Yeah. Denver. Denver Bears."

I started running through names in my mind, trying to match one to the voice. Then came a clue that gave away the answer.

"I'm the one that started the fight. We were playing Omaha."

"Tom Lasorda!" I said.

There's only one Tommy Lasorda, that's for sure.

Tom was eight years older than me, and his wife, Jo, was one of the team wives who stepped in while we were in Denver to help Betsy adjust not only to married life but also to being married to a ballplayer.

After the season, Betsy and I made the drive back to Sumter— without getting lost in the Ozarks—and in our first off-season as husband and wife, we lived with Betsy's mother.

Back home, I kept up with how the Yankees were doing in their World Series rematch against the Brooklyn Dodgers. The '56 Series is known as the one in which Don Larsen, in Game 5, threw the only perfect game in World Series history. After Larsen struck out Dale Mitchell for the game's final out, Yogi ran out from behind the plate and toward the mound, then leaped into Larsen's arms. I've seen that in game highlights many times, but I'm pretty sure I was watching that game live on television with Dad at my parents' house.

The Yankees won the World Series that year in seven games. I wanted that to be the last time I would *watch* the Yankees play in a World Series. I wanted to be playing in the next World Series my dad would watch on his television.

When I evaluated my season in Denver, I told myself, *Okay, next year is my year to go to New York and stay.*

Chapter 6

MIXED EMOTIONS

WHEN THE 1957 SEASON OPENED, I didn't know if Dad would be watching me play in that year's World Series. But if he did, he would be watching me on a new color TV.

That was the season I posed for my first bubblegum card. The Topps Company presented me with two offers. I could sign a one-year contract giving permission to use my image on a card and receive a $125 gift certificate, or I could sign a two-year contract and choose from among three or four higher-value payment options. I opted for the second and chose a television to give to my dad. The fact that delivery was free helped sway my decision, because the TV in question was one of those big, heavy console models that took up floor space in the living room. After I signed my Topps contract, a brand-new color television was delivered directly to my parents' home.

Dad wouldn't be able to pick up the Yankees' regular-season

games—they weren't broadcast in Sumter—but he would be able to watch me when we were featured on *Game of the Week* broadcasts.

As I had in 1956, I headed north out of spring training to start the regular season with the Yankees. While in '56 I had expected I would move out to Denver when the roster was cut down, this year I hoped to stay on with the big club. Though I wouldn't say I *expected* to remain in the majors, I thought I had a realistic chance. But the deadline for roster cuts was in mid-May, a month into the season, so until that time I wasn't going to assume anything about securing a spot on the team.

The first week of the 1957 season, I was limited to a substitute's role. Billy Martin, who for good reason was one of Casey's favorite players, started the season at second base. Third baseman Andy Carey sprained an ankle in one of our first games, so Casey slid Billy over to third and inserted Jerry Coleman at second. Jerry was a veteran player who could play second, third, and short with equal skill. My early appearances in games were as a defensive replacement in the late innings.

Late in the second week, Casey gave me back-to-back starts at second for weekend games against the Boston Red Sox. I went 0 for 2 in the first game before being lifted for a pinch hitter in the seventh inning. The next day I was 2 for 4 and drove in a run. Carey returned from his injury the next game, and I returned to the bench. I didn't play in another game for a week and a half, and then I made a few more late-game defensive appearances.

That stretch took us right up to the deadline for roster cuts. I wondered whether my inactivity was an indication that the Yankees could get along without me—and that I would soon be on my way back to Denver.

I don't know if Casey wanted to give me one more look before the decision or not, but right before the deadline he started putting me into the starting lineup. I had two hits in my first two games and survived the roster cuts. I then went on to hit in six consecutive games. Casey even moved me from the bottom of the order—I had been hitting mostly seventh or eighth—to the leadoff spot.

Even after my hitting streak, there still was a stretch at the end of May when I was in and out of the starting lineup. By early June, however, I had become the regular starting second baseman.

I had also become a dad, because June was when our first son, Robert Clinton Richardson III—Robby—was born. When the season had started, Betsy had stayed in Sumter to have the baby instead of joining me in New York. After a Sunday doubleheader at Yankee Stadium, I received a phone call informing me that Betsy had given birth to a boy.

Monday was a day off for us, so I immediately flew home and rushed to the hospital. I was so excited to see Betsy and my son that I hurriedly walked through the hospital hallway and into Betsy's room. I gave her a hug so big that it set off the buzzer to call for a nurse. When Robby was brought into our room, I was able to hold our son for the first time. Words cannot describe the love and joy I felt as I held that gift from God in my arms.

I had hoped for a son, and now I had one. But just as quickly as I had arrived in Sumter, it was time to go again to join the team for a series in Cleveland. I hated to leave Betsy and Robby, but I knew they would be joining me in New York as soon as they were able.

The Billy Martin Trade

Less than two weeks after Robby was born, the Yankees cleared out a little more room for me at second base by trading Billy Martin to the Kansas City Athletics.

The Yankees and the A's had an interesting relationship in those days. The "big market" and "small market" distinction prevalent in baseball today was not recognized then, but that would have been a fitting way to describe the contrast between the two teams.

Connections between the franchises' ownerships made them convenient trade partners. Because of the teams' different needs, the Yankees seemed to get the better end of most trades.

The Yankees needed players who would keep them in championship contention; the A's needed marquee players to draw fans. The Yankees would identify up-and-coming young players (whose biggest paydays were still ahead of them) and acquire them from Kansas City, often in exchange for aging players (who didn't have the skills they once did but still had the fan-attracting name). Some of those trades were met with such complaints from other teams that the A's became derisively referred to as a Yankees farm team.

In addition to Billy, Kansas City received starting pitcher Ralph Terry and minor leaguers Woodie Held and Bob Martyn. The A's sent us relief pitcher Ryne Duren, outfielder Jim Pisoni, and outfielder/first baseman Harry Simpson. It was a seven-player trade, but it obviously centered on Billy. And it's widely believed that his trade had something to do with an incident that happened a month earlier in New York, on Billy's birthday.

Billy, Mickey, Whitey, Hank, Yogi, and a few others players, along with some of the players' wives, had gone to the famed Copacabana nightclub to celebrate. Some drunks made crude racial comments toward Sammy Davis Jr. as he performed there, and our guys stepped in to try to calm down the drunks. As could be expected considering the environment, things got out of hand, and one of the drunks who had razzed Davis claimed he had been punched by Hank. Hank denied hitting the man, but the incident made ugly headlines in the New York newspapers.

The altercation remains one of the more infamous off-field incidents in Yankees history, and it's often said that Billy was traded because general manager George Weiss blamed him for what happened.

A subplot in that story is that the players ran up quite a tab that night at the Copacabana, to the tune of several thousand dollars. The birthday celebrants didn't have enough money on them to cover the tab, and Billy said, "I'll sign the owner's name to the check!" So Billy signed Yankees owner Dan Topping's name on the bill. Mr. Topping was none too pleased when it arrived. This presented a problem for Yankees' management. They couldn't do anything to Mickey, Whitey, or Yogi because of their status with the team, but they also couldn't just let the incident slide. They needed a scapegoat, and Billy became that guy.

The big trade went down on June 15, while we were in Kansas City for a series. After the game, we dressed and boarded our bus to go back to the hotel. When we realized the bus wasn't leaving, we looked around to see if anyone was missing.

"Martin's not here yet," someone said.

"Stengel's talking to him," someone else said. "He'll be here in a minute."

We waited about an hour until Billy and Casey finally came out and boarded. Casey took his seat at the front of the bus. Billy walked up the aisle and plopped down in the seat next to me.

"Okay, kid, it's all yours," he said. "I've been traded to Kansas City."

I was stunned. Billy was far more collected than I was.

Billy had been my main competition at second base, and we had been going back and forth in terms of who got the most playing time there. But on a personal level, Billy never felt like competition. We'd had a good relationship all along.

As the story about the nightclub bill suggests, Billy was a big joker. He could even make light of our competition for the second base job.

When Betsy came down to spring training to visit, Billy had asked her, "Is Bobby still here?"

"What do you mean, 'Is Bobby still here?'" she asked.

"Well," Billy said with a straight face, "I wrote a letter to Bobby's draft board about six weeks ago. You haven't heard anything yet?"

Or, aware of my clean-living lifestyle, Billy would say to Betsy, "Didn't somebody put something in Rich's milk last night? He must not have drunk it."

Billy's jokes were always good-natured, though. He was never mean as far as I could see. I just couldn't believe that we would trade him away.

Billy Martin was Casey's type of ballplayer—always hustling and focused on team first. He would be the first player on our team to sacrifice his batting average to hit a grounder that would move a runner up a base. Billy was also a big rah-rah guy, always encouraging his teammates. When we were down, he would be the one to get us going by walking up and down the dugout, hollering and slapping guys on the knees. Then he'd turn toward the field and target the opposition with not-so-encouraging words. Billy never hesitated to make an opponent mad and would look for any way he could to get under an opposing player's skin. Casey liked that about Billy.

Billy and Casey's relationship went back to the minor leagues, where Billy had played for Casey on the Oakland Oaks. After Casey became the New York manager, he was instrumental in the trade that brought Billy to the Yankees. Billy looked at Casey like a father. He loved being a Yankee, too, and Casey knew that.

It had to be difficult for Casey when Billy was traded. That's probably why he and Billy talked for an hour. I'm sure that decision was handed down to Casey from George Weiss and Casey had nothing to do with it, but it was his job to deliver the bad news.

The trade hurt Billy, and I don't think Billy ever understood why he was traded. He must have believed that Casey either wanted him traded or didn't go to bat for him with the general manager, because it would be a number of years before Billy would speak with Casey again.

Not only did I take Billy's spot at second base, but I also eventually took his jersey number—the coveted number 1. That decision was made by Big Pete Sheehy, who hung the jersey in my locker before the start of the next season and said, "You wear this."

I had worn number 17 during my short stays with the Yankees in 1955 and 1956. When Enos Slaughter came over by trade in '57, he'd taken the number 17 and I'd been assigned 29. I liked wearing the 1. Saying you are number 1 sounds much better than saying you're number 29. Plus, even then single-digit numbers with the Yankees were becoming difficult to come by. By that time, numbers 3 (Babe Ruth), 4 (Lou Gehrig), and 5 (Joe DiMaggio) had been retired, Mickey was wearing number 7, and Yogi wore number 8.

Number 1 was mine for the rest of my career, and Bobby Murcer wore it after me. He was the last Yankees player to wear that number, although Billy wore it later when he managed the Yankees and Gene Michael wore it for one season when he was a coach. Now, though, it will always be Billy's number with the Yankees. They retired the number in 1986 in Billy's honor.

When the number was to be retired, Billy granted me permission to continue to wear it in Old Timers' Games. "Number 1 is something I am proud to have had in common with you," Billy wrote me in a letter that he signed, "Your friend in God always."

An All-Star

When the All-Star break rolled around in July, we held a two-and-a-half-game lead in the American League over the Chicago White Sox. As manager of the American League All-Star team, Casey selected me as backup second baseman behind the White Sox's Nellie Fox.

The game was at Sportsman's Park in St. Louis. I didn't play, but the American League won 6–5 in an exciting game—both teams scored three runs in the ninth inning. I enjoyed being a part of my first All-Star festivities and being able to share a field with the compilation of the game's best players.

I came out of the All-Star break confident, feeling solidly in place at second base and having been added to the All-Star team by my own manager. To me, being chosen as an All-Star meant Casey must have been pleased with how I was playing. But the thing with Casey Stengel was, just when you thought you had things figured out, he would throw you a changeup.

In late July I gave way to Gil McDougald, who moved over to second from shortstop when my roommate, Tony Kubek, started getting more playing time at short. (Tony was named American League Rookie of the Year after that season.)

A week later, I was back to starting at second.

Another week later, I was out again.

Needless to say, the changes frustrated me—to the point that I did something way out of character for me. In an August game at Yankee Stadium against the Washington Senators, I started at second and batted eighth. When it came time for my first at bat, in the third inning, Casey called me back to the dugout and sent in Tommy Byrne to pinch-hit. When I walked by Casey in his spot at the edge of the dugout, I said, "If you're going to pinch-hit for me the first time I'm up, why did you start me?"

I kept walking through the back of the dugout and into the clubhouse, where I began to take off my uniform. Casey followed me into the locker room. "Get your little glove," he ordered, "and go down to the bullpen and warm up Ryne Duren."

That was my punishment for my attitude. It might not sound like much, but it could have been a pretty harsh punishment.

Duren had been part of the Billy Martin trade. He wore Coke-bottle glasses and threw about a hundred miles per hour. He threw a lot of his pitches in the dirt, too, because he had yet to gain control of his fastball. I could have gotten beat up catching for Duren in the bullpen, but he took it easy on me, throwing just a few pitches and never really getting up to full speed.

My playing time remained inconsistent through the remainder of the regular season, and a late-season pulled hamstring that I reinjured hampered me too.

We won the pennant by six and a half games over the White Sox to advance to the World Series against the Milwaukee Braves, who had won the National League for the first time since moving from Boston in 1953.

We split the first two games in Yankee Stadium before the Series moved to Milwaukee, where the fans were almost salivating at the thought of winning their first World Series by beating the Yankees. We won Game 3 in Milwaukee, but the Braves came back to win the next two games for a 3–2 lead, with the final two games scheduled for New York. We won Game 6 to force a seventh and deciding game, but Lew Burdette shut us out. The Braves won the game 5–0 and the Series 4–3. Burdette pitched three complete games in that series, shutting us out twice and allowing only two runs over his twenty-seven innings. My playing time in the Series had been limited to pinch-running in Game 2 and serving as a late-inning defensive replacement in Game 5.

The end of the season was doubly disappointing for me. As a team, we had failed to successfully defend our world championship of 1956. As a player who had hoped to establish myself in the major leagues in 1957, I hadn't really succeeded. Back in June, I'd thought I was in the process of securing my role as a starter. But then my playing time had grown frustratingly inconsistent late in the season. So even though I had been part of the All-Star Game and the World Series, I couldn't say I was satisfied with the way the season had played out. But I was happy to be going home to spend time with my wife and my new little son. And next season, I told myself, would have to be better.

Chapter 7
STAY OR GO HOME?

MY FAVORITE STORY from the 1958 season comes from off the field, if that offers any indication of what kind of season it was for me.

We started 23–5 and had already built up an eight-and-a-half-game lead by late May. Our lead was in double digits throughout most of the summer, and that allowed us to clinch the pennant by mid-September.

After we had wrapped up the American League championship in Kansas City, Yankees management commissioned private detectives to follow players around and make sure we weren't doing anything or going anywhere that could distract us from the upcoming World Series.

Unfortunately for management, we found out about the detectives, and Mickey, Whitey, and some of the other guys turned the situation into a game of chase. They would hail a cab and climb into the backseat. While the detectives were getting into their own cab behind the players, Mickey, Whitey, and company would slide out the other door and get into another cab headed in the opposite direction. The detectives couldn't keep up with them.

Tony Kubek and I were a different story. The detectives had no trouble keeping up with us. Since the detectives knew they had to turn in something to Yankees management to justify their expense, they submitted this report on the two of us: "They went to the movie theater and didn't go in. They bought popcorn and then went to the YMCA and played Ping-Pong. Then they left to get milkshakes." After that, the media began calling Tony and me the "Milkshake Twins."

There wasn't much else to laugh about that season for me individually. In 1957, my first full season in the big leagues, I had played ninety-seven games. That had felt like too few to me. Yet in 1958, I played only seventy-three games all season. My at bats also dropped to 195, down from 320 the year before.

After going 1 for 6 in a doubleheader on May 11, my batting average sat at .203. My playing time really began to diminish from there. I did have a string of starts in June during which I had a five-game hitting streak, but other than that I didn't feel I received enough consistent time in the lineup.

Casey would say of me, "Look at him. He doesn't drink, doesn't smoke, and he still can't hit .250."

My reply to Casey: "To hit, you have to play."

(A couple of years later, as my batting average improved, Casey amended his quote to say ".260.")

There were a few days when I would be sitting in the dugout, out of the lineup again, and feel tears forming. We had a great team, but I didn't feel like I was contributing anything.

I was out of the lineup for both games of a July 13 doubleheader against the White Sox. By now we were renting a house in Ridgewood, New Jersey, each season, and Betsy was pregnant with our second child, due any day. She had awakened me at five o'clock that morning and said she needed to go to the hospital because she thought our baby was on the way. I took her to the hospital, but then I had to leave for the ballpark.

I was sitting on the bench when Dr. John Glasser called the Yankees to say that Betsy had delivered our baby. I received the news that I had a second son via the Stadium scoreboard. Right after that, the scoreboard announced that teammate Enos Slaughter's wife also had given birth that day, to a daughter.

After I learned I had another son, our doubleheader seemed to drag on and on and on. It didn't end in time for me to make it to the hospital before visiting hours ended, but the doctor arranged for me to get into the hospital that night and see Betsy and my new son, Ron. I learned then that before Ron was born, Dr. Glasser had prayed for a safe delivery, and after Betsy gave birth, he had prayed to dedicate Ron to the Lord. Dr. Glasser, who delivered a good number of other Yankees' babies, was one of the many blessings God afforded us while we lived in New Jersey. We were also blessed with the kindness and support of many others, including Betsy's cousin Lula Mae, who looked out for her while I was on the road; the Kilgos, our next-door neighbors who were like parents to us; Dave Marshall, our pastor in Ridgewood, and his wife, Lorraine; and the many friends in our church there.

If Ron had come one day earlier, he might have been born at Yankee Stadium. The previous day had been Family Day, and our trainer had told a very pregnant Betsy that he had the trainer's room set up just in case our baby decided to make an appearance. Ron still wishes he had arrived a day earlier so he could claim to have been born at Yankee Stadium.

My batting average was still in the low .200s when the calendar turned to September. With the Yankees leading the American

League by a large margin, I began to play more in September and responded by hitting well enough to raise my batting average to .247 by the end of the regular season. That still wasn't the average I wanted, but at least it looked more respectable.

The Milwaukee Braves won the National League that year, setting up a World Series rematch. The Series began in Milwaukee, where we lost the first two games. We won Game 3, then lost Game 4 in Yankee Stadium to fall into a 3–1 deficit. Only one team, the 1925 Pittsburgh Pirates, had overcome such a deficit in a best-of-seven format to win the World Series.

Lew Burdette, the pitcher who had shut us down three times in the '57 Series and defeated us again in Game 2, started Game 5 opposite our "Bullet Bob" Turley. This time it was Bob who threw the shutout, and we got to Burdette for six runs in the sixth inning to win 7–0. Spared watching the Braves celebrate on our field, we returned to Milwaukee needing to win Games 6 and 7 in order to take back the world championship.

We did it.

We won a tense Game 6 in ten innings, 4–3. In Game 7, Moose Skowron hit a three-run home run in the eighth inning off Burdette, and we won 6–2 to secure the Yankees' eighteenth World Series title.

I saw more action in that World Series than in the previous one, although still not much. I entered both Games 2 and 3 in the eighth inning to play third base.

I started Game 4 at third base. That was the only time, other than a preseason exhibition game in Georgia, that my dad was able to see me play a major league game in person. Dad's emphysema made it extremely difficult for him to make the long trip to New York, but he and Mom came up with my sisters because he wanted to watch me play at least one time.

Lefty Warren Spahn started pitching for the Braves that day.

I flied out to left field in my first at bat against the future Hall of Famer. Leading off the fifth, I popped out to first base. When it was my turn to bat next, in the bottom of the seventh with the Braves leading 2–0, Elston Howard was sent in to pinch-hit for me. To that point, I hadn't even had a ball hit to me in the field. So the only time my dad watched me play, I went 0 for 2 and didn't make a play on defense. I would have liked to have done better for him.

Game 5 was my final appearance of the Series, again as a late defensive replacement at third base.

I felt better at the end of the 1958 season than I had the previous year when I hadn't played much *and* we'd lost. But I was still extremely disappointed I hadn't played more—and someone back in South Carolina felt the same way.

Not many people in the little village of Alcolu, where Betsy lived as a child, had televisions at the time. But Betsy's grandmother had one and opened her home to those wanting to watch the World Series (and their local boy). In the games when Casey didn't start me, however, Betsy's grandmother would get mad, turn off the TV, and not allow anyone to watch the game. When that happened, Betsy's aunt Jennie would have to leave and find another TV set to watch.

It's nice to have that kind of support from an in-law. I just wished I hadn't needed it.

Playing under Casey's platoon system for two full seasons had disheartened me to the point that I once again considered quitting baseball. Since the discouraging start to my first season in the minors, when that letter from Coach Alexander helped me reprioritize my life, I had been mindful that my serving the Lord was more important than playing baseball. Now I was thinking that I might be of better service to God if I returned home to Sumter to stay. I had attended some college classes during previous off-seasons, and I began to wonder whether the time had come to put baseball behind me and go earn a college degree.

I sought the counsel of Ralph Houk, my manager with the Denver Bears, who had moved up to the Yankees as a coach. "Don't be discouraged," Ralph told me. He advised me to stick with baseball, reminding me of the number of youth groups I had enjoyed speaking to, and shared his belief that staying in baseball would open up more opportunities to talk about my faith than I might expect. If I gave up baseball, he said, I would be giving up the platform that God was building for me in New York.

I gave weight to Ralph's advice because he had become a trusted advisor. I returned home for the off-season and prayed about whether I should remain in baseball or quit. The more I prayed, the more it became clear that I should keep playing.

Chapter 8

.300

THE YEAR 1959 turned out to be a complete reversal of the '58 season. While I had the finest season of my career to that point, it was the worst season for the team that I had experienced. With the talent we had and the depth within our farm system, I thought at the beginning of every season that we would win the world championship. In 1959, that was not to be, much to the chagrin— and delight—of baseball fans across the country.

Our Yankees were a polarizing club. We were a national team, not merely a New York franchise. I never played for any other team, so I don't know what it was like to be on their road trips, but with the Yankees, passionate fans greeted us everywhere we played. But we also seemed to attract a large number of people who, with equal passion, desired to see us fail. The more miserably we failed, the happier they would be. Baseball fans were either very much for us or very much against us, and there just didn't seem to be any middle ground.

When I say I thought we would win the world championship every season, I don't mean that in an arrogant way. We all knew that winning the championship would require hard work from each of us and a commitment to playing the fundamentals throughout the long grind of the 154-game schedule. But we could enter each season with a high level of confidence because we knew that we would have the pieces in place to compete in the World Series. We never had to wonder during the off-season whether management would be able to assemble a championship-worthy roster. And with our depth, we never had to go into a season thinking we would be in serious trouble if one particular player got injured.

But even with all that, there were no guarantees—and 1959 proved that.

Our title in '58 had marked the Yankees' fourth consecutive World Series appearance and the ninth in ten seasons. The only season during that time when the Yankees had missed the playoffs was in 1954, when New York had won 103 games. That represented a winning percentage of .669, a number that in most seasons would win the American League pennant and put us in the World Series. In fact, that was the Yankees' best record for any season of the 1950s. In '54, though, the Cleveland Indians had fashioned a remarkable 111–43 record to defeat the Yankees by eight games. So even that one time during that ten-year stretch when the Yankees had not advanced to the postseason, it took an incredible season by another team to keep them out.

However, that was not the case for our 1959 team.

We barely produced a .500 record, finishing 79–75 for the Yankees' worst showing since all the way back to 1925. That was the year of Babe Ruth's "bellyache heard 'round the world," when he missed the first two months of the season because of surgery for an abdominal abscess caused by his diet of too many hot dogs and— depending on which sources you prefer—too many sodas or beers.

We finished in third place in the eight-team American League, fifteen games behind the pennant-winning White Sox.

Mickey Mantle, Moose Skowron, Gil McDougald, and Andy Carey were among the position players who either missed stretches of games because of injuries or were hampered by them. With those players in and out of the lineup, our offense never seemed to get clicking, and we struggled to score runs. That put a strain on our pitchers, who also had to battle injuries, and they just couldn't shut down the opposition like they had in recent seasons.

By late May of 1959, we were in last place in the league, nine and a half games out of first. Before then, the Yankees hadn't spent one day in last place since 1940. A hot streak helped us climb to within one and a half games of the first-place Cleveland Indians heading into the first day of summer, June 21, but that was as close to the top as we would get. By the end of July we had plummeted to a double-digit deficit behind the leader, and for the first time in a long time, the Yankees spent the parts of the calendar usually reserved for a pennant race merely playing out the string.

One of baseball's unique aspects, and one of the many reasons I love the sport so much, is that it is a series of individual matchups within a team competition. When I was at the plate, it was me against the pitcher. There was no one setting a pick or throwing a block for me. It was up to me to beat the pitcher. There were nine of us hitters each night in the same situation, but in the big picture we were all contributing to our team. Our motivation to succeed as individuals was for the greater cause of our team, and that could be very satisfying.

Occasionally, though, it could lead to awkward feelings.

In 1958, for example, we were world champions, and I celebrated our team's great accomplishment along with my teammates. Yet solely on an individual basis, that season would have to be classified as discouraging for me. We were the best team in baseball, but I left that season wondering whether I should even continue to play.

The 1959 season, on the other hand, was a major disappointment from a team standpoint. When we heard things such as "This is the first Yankees team to be in last place since 1940," that stung. Yet '59 was the best season I'd had individually.

The first week of the season I was starting at shortstop. The second week I was at second. The third week I was back at shortstop. The fourth week I was on the bench.

On May 5 my batting average was at .232. After that, other than an occasional spot start, I was back to playing as a late-game defensive substitution until the middle of June, when Casey decided to insert me back into the starting spot at second. I started there every game through the rest of the season.

Provided with what I felt was my first real opportunity to show what I could do as a regular starter, my average soared to above .300 at the start of July, and I picked up my second berth in the All-Star Game, although again I did not get to actually play.

After the All-Star break, my average dipped into the .260s in August. Then, steadily, my average began to rise again. With two weeks left to play, my average was at .291. Entering the final week, it was at .295. Heading into the final day, it was at .298. A .300 batting average is a magical number for players, but there was added significance to my average because at that point I was the only Yankee with the chance to hit .300 for the season. No one could imagine a Yankees team without at least one .300 hitter.

Before we closed out the season against the Baltimore Orioles in an otherwise meaningless game, Casey told me I needed two hits to raise my average to the .300 mark. If I could get those two hits, he would then pull me out of the game so the team would have a .300 hitter.

Billy O'Dell was starting on the mound for the Orioles that day.

Billy was from Newberry, South Carolina, and was a good friend I sometimes hunted with back home. The day before our final game, Billy had sent word over, "Tell Bobby I'll be throwing it right in there for him tomorrow." Orioles third baseman Brooks Robinson was another good friend. He also sent a message: "Tell Bobby that I'll be playing real deep if he wants to bunt." Joe Ginsberg was the Baltimore catcher, and I didn't know him too well, so I was surprised when he told me he would let me know what pitch was coming. First base umpire Ed Hurley told me on the field before the game, "Just make it close. You'll be safe."

My first time at the plate, leading off the bottom of the first, Ginsberg said, "Fastball." I was shocked and immediately wondered whether he was just messing with me when a curveball was actually coming. Confused, I didn't swing at the pitch, and it was indeed a fastball. The catcher appeared to be shooting straight with me.

Before the second pitch, Ginsberg again said, "Fastball." I looked for a fastball, and Billy threw one right down the middle of the plate that I hit for a double. Trust me when I say I wasn't doing this exact math on the field at the time, but that hit raised my average to .2997. That would have officially been rounded up to .300 if that had been my final at bat, but no player wants to hit .300 by having the numbers rounded up.

I came to the plate again in the third inning, one hit shy of the milestone average. I was confident, too, knowing that the pitcher and catcher were working with me, the third baseman was in my corner if needed (although I had no intention of bunting my way to .300), and the first base umpire was in a generous mood too.

Notice that the right fielder wasn't a member of that group. In my second plate appearance, I smashed a line drive toward right field. Albie Pearson, one of my closest friends in baseball, made a diving catch to rob me of a hit!

My spot in the order came around again with one out in the

sixth. The score was 0–0, and if we happened to take the lead on a solo home run and not bat in our half of the ninth, my third at bat would be my last chance to reach .300. That probably wouldn't happen, but it wasn't a chance worth taking.

With O'Dell still pitching, I hit a grounder up the middle and into center field for a clean single.

Casey used the dugout phone to call the Yankees' statistician and get my updated batting average. It was .301. As he'd said he would, Casey pulled me from the game so I would finish the season above .300.

The people of Sumter have always treated my family so graciously. After that season, because I had topped .300, they held a special day in my honor. They presented me with shells to go with a shotgun they had previously given me, provided Betsy and me with a washer and dryer and some furniture, and gave little Robby and Ronnie each a small fire truck with pedals that they could ride around in.

It felt strange, though, being back in Sumter while the World Series was being played.

Chapter 9

A SERIES TO REMEMBER

IT IS AMAZING HOW one week of swinging a hot bat can forever determine how a ballplayer is viewed.

Although the 1960 regular season was far from a standout year for me, it is the one year most associated with my name. I was chosen Most Valuable Player of the World Series that year, even though we lost the Series in seven games to the Pittsburgh Pirates. That honor has made me the answer to a trivia question. I'm the only player ever selected World Series MVP from a losing team.

Nothing during the regular season indicated that I would have that type of postseason success.

I played in 150 of our 154 games in 1960 and started 138, including 134 at second base. I batted first or eighth in almost all those starts. With Casey's emphasis on platooning and the way he liked to play hunches, I never allowed myself to think I had settled permanently into the second base position. But though there was always a chance I might be moved in and out of the lineup or bounced around the batting order, that never actually happened. The relative stability allowed me to focus on assuming a role that I thought could serve the team best: playing solid defense at second base and, on offense, either setting the table for the heart of the lineup from my leadoff spot, or moving runners and getting on base from my spot at the bottom of the lineup.

My numbers in 1960 didn't match what I had done the year before. I hit .252, drove in twenty-six runs, and stole six bases. I was never much of a home run hitter, and I hit only one that season. In fact, as far as I was concerned, I had an unproductive regular season. At least that was happening during a year when our injuries were minimal and it seemed that just about everyone in the lineup was playing well.

Moose Skowron was back to his old self at the plate, hitting .309 during the regular season to finish among the American League leaders. Roger Maris, whom we had acquired in the off-season in another trade with Kansas City, won the regular season MVP award, and Mickey Mantle finished second. Mickey hit a league-leading forty home runs, and Roger set a career high to that point with thirty-nine. He also led the league with 112 runs batted in. And our pitching was dominant again, with Whitey Ford, Art Ditmar, Bob Turley, and Ralph Terry all finishing among the league's top ten in earned run average.

We needed their performances that season because we were locked in a tight pennant race with the Baltimore Orioles and the Chicago White Sox. The Orioles swept a three-game series from us in Baltimore in the first week of September to take a two-game lead over us and a three-and-a-half-game lead over Chicago. The next time we played Baltimore, on September 16, we were coming off back-to-back losses at Kansas City that had dropped us into a tie for first, two games ahead of the Sox.

Whitey was on the mound to start the four-game series with the Orioles in Yankee Stadium. From all my years as a Yankee, Whitey was the pitcher that I would want holding the ball to start a big game. As expected, he was outstanding for us that day. Whitey took a shutout into the ninth inning, Roger hit a big two-run homer in the fifth, and we won the first game of the series 4–2 to take back sole possession of first place.

That game started one of the great closing stretches in baseball history. We swept that four-game series from the Orioles and led both them and the White Sox by four games, with eleven games remaining. We won all eleven of those, too, ending the regular season on a fifteen-game winning streak and claiming the pennant by a deceptive-looking eight games over Baltimore and ten over Chicago.

It was on the heels of that winning streak that I experienced one of the more embarrassing moments of my career. I had been elected as the Yankees' player representative for the first time. A player rep back then would be somewhat similar to a team captain today, with the biggest difference being that a player rep had more business-type responsibilities in the clubhouse.

One of my duties was to organize the team photograph late in the regular season that would be used in the World Series program, in Yankees history books, in baseball yearbooks, and other such publications. It would serve as the official team photograph for that year. I set up the team photo to be taken before a day game in Yankee Stadium. The day beforehand, I kept reminding all the players, "Everybody be here at nine o'clock tomorrow for the picture."

My sister Inez's husband, Heyward Strong, flew in for a visit the night before our team photo. He stayed at our in-season home in Ridgewood, New Jersey, and we were up late that night talking and laughing and having a good time. Heyward had an early flight the next morning, and I dropped him off at the airport at six o'clock. I drove by the Stadium about an hour later, but I thought, *Man, it's so early. I'll just go on back to Ridgewood.*

I forgot all about the team photo.

When I arrived at the Stadium later that morning, Big Pete Sheehy asked, "Where have you been?" That's when I realized I had missed the photo.

Casey was really steamed at me about that—and rightfully so, considering I had set up the photo and reminded everyone to be there, then been the only no-show. I can still point to the spot on the right-hand side of the front row where I was supposed to be, sitting with arms and ankles crossed like everyone else on that row.

So here's another trivia question: Which World Series Most Valuable Player was not in his team's official photo in the World Series program?

Me.

Grand Slam!

While we had qualified for the World Series for the tenth time in twelve years, it was a different story over in the National League, where the Pittsburgh Pirates had won a pennant for the first time since 1927. Their World Series opponent in '27 had been the Babe Ruth–led Yankees, who swept the Pirates in four games.

Because of our postseason experience and the momentum we carried from our season-ending winning streak, we were tabbed as heavy favorites to defeat Pittsburgh in 1960. But the Series got off to a bad start.

The environment at Pittsburgh's Forbes Field was much like what we had faced in 1957, when the Braves were making their first World Series appearance since moving to Milwaukee. Pittsburghers had waited thirty-three years to see their team return to the World Series, suffering through some lean seasons in the process. Pirates fans had plastered "Beat 'em, Bucs" signs every-where. The entire city was excited for the start of Game 1.

Going into that first game, Casey Stengel made a decision that I believe wound up costing us the Series and, ultimately, cost him his job: he didn't start Whitey Ford in the first game. There had to be an underlying reason, but to this day I have not heard what that might be. I've heard some rumors and much speculation, but noth-ing I could ever substantiate.

Instead of going with Whitey, Casey gave Art Ditmar the first postseason start of his career. Art was a fine pitcher and had led our team in victories during the regular season, but Whitey had been given the nickname "Chairman of the Board" for his con-trol in high-pressure situations. Whitey was our best postseason pitcher, but Casey decided to hold him back until Game 3 at Yankee Stadium. He told the media that he thought we could win in Pittsburgh without using Whitey and that Whitey could then pitch at our park, where there was a short fence in right field. That explanation didn't make sense, though. Whitey could have both started the important first game on the road and then been available to pitch three times in the Series instead of two, including once at Yankee Stadium with the short porch.

In the top of the first, Maris homered off Vern Law to give us a 1–0 lead. That lead didn't last long. Art faced only five bat-ters, retiring one and leaving the game with a 3–1 deficit. Law, a twenty-game winner that season, was tough on us, holding us to two runs through eight innings. By the time Law left the game, the Pirates had stretched their lead to 6–2. In the ninth, Elston Howard belted a pinch-hit, two-out home run to make the score 6–4, and Tony Kubek singled to bring the potential tying run to the plate. But a double play ended our comeback. Pittsburgh had grabbed the first game.

I am convinced that the Pirates' winning Game 1 was the key

to their winning the Series. And I remain convinced that if Whitey had pitched the opener, we would have won that game.

Games 2 and 3 would symbolize our frustration with how the Series played out. We plastered the Pirates 16–3 in the second game, pounding out nineteen hits. Mickey hit two home runs—one to right center, where it was 436 feet from the plate to a twelve-foot wall. Mickey was the first right-handed batter to hit a home run to that part of Forbes Field, and that ballpark had opened in 1909, so it had a lot of history even then. That homer has been estimated as traveling 475 feet. I witnessed Mickey hitting longer home runs during our time together, but to see the ball leave that part of the field and clear that high wall makes it one of the most memorable home runs I ever saw.

After going hitless in four at bats in the opener, I went 3 for 4 in Game 2 with a double, two RBIs, a walk, and three runs. As most of us felt that day, I was comfortable in the batter's box. But I had no idea what was coming in Game 3.

Back at Yankee Stadium, Game 3 was another runaway victory for us, 10–0. That was Whitey's start, and not surprisingly, he was almost untouchable. He pitched all nine innings and held the Pirates to four hits.

We took control of the game early, scoring six runs in the bottom of the first. With one out, Moose singled in one run. Then Ellie Howard's dribbler down the third base line for a base hit scored another run and kept the bases loaded—with me up next.

To be honest, I was expecting Casey to put in a pinch hitter for me there in the first inning—perhaps Enos Slaughter—because with Whitey pitching we had a chance to pretty much put the Pirates away with an extra-base hit. I wasn't going to look back over my shoulder to the dugout and perhaps give Casey an idea he hadn't considered, but I was listening for that familiar voice to bark out, "Hold that gun!" I never heard those words, though.

Before I stepped into the batter's box, I looked down to third base coach Frank Crosetti as he flashed through the signs. I almost did a double take when I saw the bunt sign. With the bases loaded and the pitcher batting next in the ninth spot, I was more stunned to see Crosetti telling me to bunt than I'd been that day in '53 when he walked over and handed me a pair of his spikes. I replayed the signals in my mind just to make sure I had read them correctly.

Clem Labine had replaced Pittsburgh starter Wilmer "Vinegar Bend" Mizell, a close friend of mine, before Ellie Howard's at bat. Labine started his delivery to the plate, I squared to bunt, and I fouled the ball off.

Surely he'll have me hitting now, I thought.

But again, Crosetti gave me the bunt signal.

Again, I squared and fouled off the bunt attempt.

With two strikes I was sure the bunt signal wouldn't come again. It didn't.

"Hit the ball to right field!" Crosetti shouted down the baseline to me. "Try to stay out of the double play!"

A double play would have brought us to three outs and ended the inning. But with the bases loaded, even a ground ball out would have given us a 3–0 lead.

As instructed, I intended to hit a grounder to the right side that would be difficult for the Pirates to turn into a double play if it didn't get through the infield. But Labine threw a high fastball that was in on me a little bit. Because of that, I had to bring my hands through the swing quickly. That's a pull swing instead of a go-the-other-way swing. The ball jumped off my bat and soared toward the left field corner, where it was 301 feet to the fence.

Man, oh man, I hit that pretty good!

I took off running right away, anticipating an opportunity for extra bases, and didn't look to see where the ball was until I was rounding first. Pirates left fielder Gino Cimoli was standing at the short wall in the left field corner and looking at his glove. My heart sank a little, thinking he had caught the ball and I had lost a double that would have scored two, maybe three, runs. Then I caught sight of second base umpire Dusty Boggess, who was twirling his index finger in the air—the signal for a home run.

I knew it was a home run, but I didn't truly *realize* I had homered until I reached home plate and Ellie, Moose, and Gil McDougald were there waiting after scoring ahead of me.

"Good bunt!" Casey teased me when I walked past him and into the dugout.

I had hit only one homer during the regular season, and that had been all the way back in April, in the eighth inning of a game we were leading 15–0. The Stadium scoreboard posted a note: "Richardson 1 of 7 to hit World Series grand slam."

(As a humorous sidebar, my home run was included in a nice short film about me called *The Bobby Richardson Story*. The film shows my swing on the grand slam, but after the ball leaves my bat, the footage switches to Mickey's mammoth home run in Game 2. How can I tell? First, Mickey's home run was to right center, and mine was to left. Second, Mickey's happened at Forbes Field, and mine came at Yankee Stadium. Third, Mickey's soared out of the ballpark, and mine snuck into maybe the third row. Bill Virdon was the Pirates' center fielder, and about twenty years later, when he was manager of the Houston Astros, he mentioned to me that he had seen the film but hadn't remembered my hitting a home run at Forbes Field.)

Our 6–0 lead with Whitey on the mound was enough at that point, but it was one of those days when everything was going right for our offense and we knew we would keep scoring runs.

I struck out in the third, and by the time I came up to bat again in the fourth, Mickey had homered for an 8–0 lead. Moose, Gil, and Ellie had all singled, and for the second time that day, I batted with the bases loaded. With Red Witt pitching, I lined a single to straightaway left that scored Moose and Gil and gave us a 10–0 lead. The scoreboard provided Yankees fans with another statistical note: "Richardson's 6 RBIs today set all-time Series record." In only the fourth inning, I had broken the record for the most RBIs in a World Series game.

Memorable Finish

With us leading the Series 2–1, Pittsburgh gave the ball back to Game 1 starter Vern Law for Game 4 at Yankee Stadium. This time Casey chose Ralph Terry to oppose Law. Game 4 was a good one. Once again, Law was tough to hit, holding us to two runs in six and a third innings. Ralph pitched well too, and the Pirates were able to get to him in only one inning, the fifth. But they scored three times that inning and beat us 3–2 to even the Series at two games apiece.

During Game 4, I continued to swing the bat well, going 2 for 3 with an RBI before Casey told me to hold my gun. There were two outs in the ninth with us down a run when Casey made that call. With right-hander Elroy Face pitching for the Pirates, the left-handed batter Dale Long pinch-hit for me and flied out to right to end the game.

Naturally, I would have liked the opportunity to bat with the game on the line. Before being pulled, I was thinking that all I would need to do was get on base, then Casey could pinch-hit for the pitcher's spot to tie or win the game. But that was my thinking, not Casey's.

With the Series tied 2–2, Art Ditmar came back to start in the final game scheduled at Yankee Stadium. Unfortunately, Art wasn't able to come through for us the way he had in the regular season. Taking advantage of a defensive error, the Pirates put up three runs in the third, knocking Art out of the game early.

In the bottom of the second, Kubek scored Howard on a ground-out to make the score 3–1. The Pirates answered with another run, driven in by Roberto Clemente. Then Maris homered off Pirates starter Harvey Haddix in the bottom of the third, but Pittsburgh still led 4–2. That score remained until the Pirates added a run in the top of the ninth. I led off the bottom half of the ninth by grounding out to short. That made me 0 for 4 on the day and started an inning in which we all went down in order. That 5–2 loss put us down 3–2 in games, with the Series heading back to Pittsburgh.

Despite the deficit and the fact that we were returning to Forbes Field, where Pirates fans were supercharged by the prospect of ending their long world-championship drought at home, I believed we were in great shape because Whitey would be pitching Game 6. And sure enough, Whitey dominated from the start. We jumped out to an early lead and kept pulling away. We won that game 12–0, with Whitey tossing another complete-game shutout.

Whitey pitched shutouts in both of his World Series starts, and I have no doubt that if the rotation had been set up so that he started three games, he would have thrown three shutouts.

I probably hit the ball better that afternoon than in any other game in the Series, going 2 for 5 with two triples and three more runs batted in. Both triples were hit very, very hard, with one going over Gino Cimoli's head and off the scoreboard in left field, and the other reaching the ivy-covered wall left of deep center field.

Our Game 6 victory to even the Series set up what would prove to be one of the most memorable Game 7s in postseason history.

Once again the Pirates turned to Vern Law as their starter, and we countered with Bob Turley, who had won Game 2. In a curious move, Casey had two relief pitchers warming in the bullpen before Bob had even thrown a pitch. That had to make Bob wonder how much confidence Casey had in him.

Pittsburgh scored two runs off Bob in the bottom of the first, and after he allowed a single to start the second, Casey pulled him for Bill Stafford. Stafford allowed Bob's runner to score, plus one of his own, and we were down 4–0 after two innings.

Law had been mowing us down since early in the game. Casey had moved me into the leadoff spot, and I'd started the game with a line out to shortstop. Then I flied out to left to end the third. Through four innings, Law had held us scoreless and had allowed only two singles.

Moose finally got us on the board in the fifth inning with a leadoff home run. Then, in the sixth, we were able to get to Law. I led off with a single, and Kubek walked. That ended Law's day, as he gave way to Elroy Face. After Roger Maris fouled out, Mickey singled to center to score me. Yogi Berra followed with a three-run homer, and we led 5–4.

Bobby Shantz, who had entered the game in relief in the third inning, was pitching great, holding the Pirates scoreless through the seventh inning. In the eighth, we went ahead 7–4 on RBIs by Johnny Blanchard and Clete Boyer.

With a three-run lead, we were six outs from winning Games 6 and 7 on the road to claim the World Series. Then things began to unravel.

Pinch hitter Gino Cimoli started the Pittsburgh eighth with a single into right center. Bill Virdon followed with a routine grounder to Kubek at short. When the ball was hit, even with the Pirates' leadoff hitter at the plate, I immediately thought, *Double play!* and raced toward the bag for a flip from Tony. But right before the ball reached Tony, it hit a clump of dirt in the chewed-up infield and bounced directly up and into his throat. The ball caromed toward second as Tony spun and fell in the opposite direction. I raced over and picked up the ball, signaled for a time-out, and knelt next to Tony, who was still lying on his side.

Our trainers and Casey sprinted out to check on Tony. "Give him room!" Casey ordered. "Maybe he'll be all right!"

"I can't breathe," Tony said in a husky voice.

After a few minutes, Tony rose to his feet and struggled to talk. He insisted he wanted to stay in the game, though his windpipe had already begun to swell. Casey and the trainers knew that Tony was not okay and removed him from the game. Joe DeMaestri stepped in at shortstop while Tony, holding an ice bag to his throat, was loaded into the Pittsburgh team doctor's car for a run to the hospital.

If the ball hadn't hit that clump of dirt, we would have turned the double play. Virdon told me some time later that he knew when he hit it that it was a sure double play ball. That was the first of two missed opportunities that inning.

The second came after the Pirates had scored to pull within 7–5 and Jim Coates had replaced Shantz on the mound. With runners on second and third and Roberto Clemente batting with two outs, we still had a chance to get out of the inning with a two-run lead. Clemente reached for an outside pitch and tapped a weak bouncer toward first. Moose fielded the ball wide of first, expecting Coates to cover the base as usual. But Coates, instead of heading directly to first, had made a move to try to field the ball himself. Moose was too far off first to beat Clemente to the bag. If Coates had covered first, we would have retired Clemente. Instead, Clemente was safe, one run had scored, and the inning kept going.

With runners on first and third, Hal Smith, the right-handed Pirates' catcher who had come into the game in the top of that inning, cleared the bases with a long home run to left center that landed in the trees beyond the 406-foot marker on the wall. The Pirates suddenly led 9–7. There was nothing cheap about Smith's home run. But as he rounded the bases, I couldn't help but think that, with the bad hop that ruined the double play and the missed out at first, we had given the Pirates three extra outs in an inning in which they had scored five runs.

Invigorated by the turn of events, Pirates fans were cheering expectantly as relief pitcher Bob Friend came in to start the ninth. I led off and looped a single over the shortstop's head. Dale Long, pinch-hitting for DeMaestri, singled to right, and I stopped at second instead of trying to take third on Clemente's strong arm. That knocked Friend out of the game, with Harvey Haddix taking his place.

Haddix, a starter making a relief appearance because it was Game 7, was staring into the heart of our order: Maris, Mantle, Berra, and Skowron. He retired Roger on a foul pop-up, but Mickey singled to right center to score me and send Long to third. It was 9–8 with one out, and Gil McDougald went in to pinch-run for Long at third.

Yogi then hit a hard shot down the first base line. I mean, Yogi smashed that ball. But first baseman Rocky Nelson snared it and stepped on first to retire Yogi, then turned to throw to second to try to get Mickey for a double play. But Mickey had stopped still just off first after Yogi hit the ball, not knowing if Nelson would catch the ball before it hit the ground. As Nelson raised his arm to throw to second, Mickey dove back to first. Nelson couldn't react in time to tag Mickey, and McDougald scored.

During postgame interviews, reporters told Mickey he had made a great play, because if he had been thrown out at second, he could have been tagged before McDougald scored, and the game would have ended at 9–8.

"It wasn't a great play," Mickey told the reporters. "I froze. I didn't know what to do."

But we had tied the score, 9–9.

Moose then hit a grounder to shortstop, and Mickey was forced out at second to end our half of the ninth.

Ralph Terry started the bottom of the ninth for us. Ralph had come on with two outs in the bottom of the eighth inning and retired Don Hoak on a fly to left. Ralph was in a difficult spot, though, because he had already warmed up three or four times in the bullpen during the game. Getting up and down repeatedly in the bullpen is tough on a pitcher, and nowadays there are managers who either will bring a reliever in after he's warmed up once or won't bring him in at all.

Bill Mazeroski was first up for the Pirates. Like me, he was a second baseman, and as I had for most of the Series, he was batting eighth. Mazeroski took Ralph's first pitch high for a ball. Any Pirates fan from that era can tell you exactly what happened with the next pitch—at 3:36 on the afternoon of Thursday, October 13, 1960.

Ralph wanted to keep the pitch low, but instead he got it up around Mazeroski's belt. And that pitch landed in the history books, because when Mazeroski hit it, he became the first player to hit a game-winning home run in the final game of a World Series. Only one other player has done so since—Joe Carter of the Toronto Blue Jays in 1993.

When the ball left Mazeroski's bat, I looked over to Yogi in left field. As soon as I saw Yogi's body language as he faced the outfield fence, I knew the game was over. While Mazeroski rounded the bases, Pittsburgh fans started pouring onto the field—so many of them that he could barely get back to home plate.

I removed my cap so no fan would try to grab it, put it in my hand with my glove, and worked my way through the onrushing crowd into the safety of the dugout, then back into the solemnity of our clubhouse. Mickey came in behind me, sat at his locker, and wept.

Tony would later talk about how he was resting in the hospital when Mazeroski homered. Tony didn't have the game on television or radio, but when he heard car horns honking outside and noticed how happy the nurses were, he knew the Pirates had won.

That, by far, was the toughest loss I ever experienced. Mickey summed it up well for the rest of us afterward when he said, "I just hate to lose when we're a better team. I feel like we had a better team and deserved to win."

Wheeling and Dealing

None of us Yankees publicly questioned Casey's decision to hold Whitey until Game 3, but it was widely believed among the players that we would have won the Series with Whitey making three starts. Casey was fired after the World Series—which was his record tenth to manage—because of how we lost.

That's not to say the Pirates shouldn't have won that World Series. Even five decades later, I try to be careful not to sound as if I'm saying that. The Pirates beat us, and they deserved to win. The outcome shows that they had the better team for the Series, though I still firmly believe that we had the better team that season. If there were such a thing as a do-over in baseball, I think the Yankees players from that era would unanimously vote to try that Series again.

The awful feeling we experienced after Game 7 never goes away. Even while watching the World Series in 2011, those feelings came rushing back at me when the Texas Rangers twice came within one pitch of winning Game 6—and the championship—against the St. Louis Cardinals and then wound up losing the Series. I watched on television as Rangers players sat on the bench after the final game, dejected because they'd had the chance to win and didn't. That's the way we felt in Pittsburgh.

Contributing to our feelings was the fact that we had absolutely dominated the three games we'd won, by scores of 16–3, 10–0, and 12–0. In that seven-game World Series, we had outscored Pittsburgh by a combined total of 55–27. We'd scored more than twice as many runs as the Pirates, yet they had won the close games—and won one more time than we did.

That goes to show how important it is in tight games to do the little things, like moving a runner from first to third or scoring a runner from third. That's what Pittsburgh was doing in the close games that Series, and that's why they won the championship.

There were reporters in our locker room while we changed out of our uniforms, but it was pretty quiet in there. Ed Fitzgerald, editor-in-chief of *Sport* magazine, came in and announced that I had been chosen Most Valuable Player of the Series.

His announcement surprised me because I had never heard of an MVP coming from the losing team. Indeed, it hadn't happened before in a World Series, and it hasn't happened since. It's also only happened once for the Super Bowl (Chuck Howley of the Dallas Cowboys) and the NBA Finals (Jerry West of the Los Angeles Lakers).

"What are you talking about?" I asked Fitzgerald when he brought me the news. "We lost. How can that be?"

Fitzgerald said I was the player who had contributed the most to his team over the seven games; thus the MVP had been awarded to me. I'd hit .367 in that series, scored eight runs, doubled twice, tripled twice, hit a grand slam, and driven in twelve runs. And I know records are made to be broken, but two records I set in that World Series have not been broken yet. Since my six RBIs in Game 3, two other players have tied that record: Hideki Matsui (a Yankee!) in 2009 and the Cardinals' Albert Pujols in 2011. My twelve total RBIs still stands as a single-Series record.

The MVP award included a new Corvette. Among the many telegrams I received after the Series was one from Tony Kubek: "Congratulations on the MVP. Send car care of my house." Pittsburgh pitcher Elroy Face mailed a letter joking that he should have been selected MVP and added, "You're driving my car."

I received my Corvette—white with red-leather interior—in downtown New York City two days after the World Series. A long-time friend from Sumter, Dan Lyles, came up to New York, and while I rode home with the family in our station wagon for the off-season, Dan followed us in my new sports car.

As we neared Sumter, we were stopped at a highway-patrol roadblock and given a police escort into Sumter, where about ten thousand people were waiting to welcome us home. After making a short speech, I was named honorary mayor, honorary chief of police, and goodwill ambassador for the city. Then we were paraded in a convertible down Main Street, where a big banner reading "Welcome Home Bobby (Grand Slam) Richardson" spanned the street.

My new Corvette was a big hit around town, but we didn't have it long.

At the time, Betsy and I had two sons and a third child on the way. A two-seater Corvette didn't exactly make for a family car. So after I got back home to Sumter, I made a two-for-two trade with a local car dealer—my Corvette and our old station wagon for a new station wagon and a Jeep. But people kept asking me why I'd traded in the Corvette, and not everyone bought my explanation.

Some time later a friend who owned an Oldsmobile dealership in Sumter called and told me that a high school–aged girl from a nearby town had brought my Corvette in as a trade-in. It had nine thousand miles on the odometer and was in perfect shape, he said. So I bought the car back for $2,800. If I remember correctly, that type of car wasn't selling for much more than $3,000 brand-new at the time.

Betsy didn't particularly care for the Corvette, and I didn't have much use for it with our growing family. As one friend joked, I couldn't take my bird dogs in it to go hunting, either. Then there was the time when I was driving home from Columbia in my

Corvette. I topped a hill and saw that there were no other cars in sight, so I stomped the gas pedal and got up to about eighty-five or ninety miles per hour in no time. (I hope the statute of limitations for traffic violations has expired by now.)

Frightened by the power that car possessed, I quickly slowed to a safe speed. *Man,* I thought, *I need to get rid of this thing.*

I had a friend who was traveling around the country, preaching and giving his testimony, so I let him use the car for a while. I also loaned it to Youth for Christ in Columbia, and they offered rides in the MVP car as a promotion. Finally, I decided to get rid of it for good.

Johnny Sain, our pitching coach, owned a Chevrolet dealership in Walnut Ridge, Arkansas. On a road trip, Johnny asked how I liked the car.

"I'm ready to trade it again," I said.

"I'll trade with you," he said. "What do you want?"

"Another station wagon."

"I'll trade you even up," Johnny offered.

Right there on the plane, we agreed to the trade, and I don't know what happened to the Corvette after that.

Maz and Pirates Fans

The 1960 Series remains a fascinating one for conversations. In 2010 I had a big thrill when sportscaster Bob Costas called and asked if I would take part in a special night to celebrate the fiftieth anniversary of that Series with a showing of a long-lost recording of Game 7.

For years it had been believed that all copies of the original television broadcast of that game were lost or destroyed. Then in 2009 a near-perfect black-and-white copy of the broadcast had been found in the wine cellar of the late Bing Crosby.

Crosby, who was a part owner of the Pirates, had believed his presence at the games would jinx his team. Instead of attending, he and his wife had traveled to Paris, keeping up with the Series by radio. But in the event that his Pirates won, he'd had the television broadcasts recorded on kinescope.

When the reels were found, it was like discovering a baseball treasure. I was invited to represent the Yankees at the first public showing of that treasure at Pittsburgh's Byham Theater. Among the Pirates players there were Dick Groat, Bill Virdon, Hal Smith, Vernon Law, and Elroy Face. Roberto Clemente's widow, Vera, also attended. We all watched together, with Costas moderating discussions at various points in the game, and we shared our memories of key moments.

I took my youngest son, Rich, with me to the showing. Richie was born in 1968, bringing much joy to the Richardson household. That was two years after I retired. My two older sons have memories of my playing days, but Richie doesn't. I thought that night would be the closest Richie could come to the experience of watching me play in person.

Richie had to be the only Yankees fan among the 1,300 people in that theater. When Costas asked, "How many Yankees fans are here today?" Richie let out a loud, "Yeaaaaah!" His was the only voice that responded.

As the only Yankees player present, I had to absorb a few jabs. All were good-natured, though. And I will say this about the 1,299 Pirates supporters there that night: they were unbelievably gracious. When I was introduced, they gave me warm applause that I very much appreciated. Although I wished we had won the Series, it was interesting to see in person how much that championship still meant to Pittsburgh.

Unfortunately, the big hero of that game, Bill Mazeroski, was unable to attend because of illness. He and I had become really good friends through our appearances in Old Timers' Games, and I'd had the honor of writing the foreword for a book about Bill. His son, Darren, had become a fine college baseball coach, and I'd had a couple of opportunities to recommend Darren for job openings.

One year Bill and I were part of a baseball clinic in Buffalo, New York, and after the clinic we were going to Toronto to play in an Old Timers' Game. Bill offered to let me ride to Toronto with him and his wife, and we had a delightful conversation the entire way about 1960, baseball, and our lives.

One thing that stands out from that Old Timers' Game in Toronto is that neither Bill nor I took batting practice before those games. Some of the old players, as they did in their playing days, liked to step into the cage and try to hit the ball out of the park as many times as they could. Bill and I preferred to hang out in the outfield and chat with the other old-timers. During that game in Toronto, after skipping batting practice, Bill hit a home run.

Bill is a good man—a very good man. I am happy for the attention that his game-winning home run continues to shine on him and his career. The reverence that remains for him in Pittsburgh is well deserved.

Betsy and I spend about four months of the year on the South Carolina coast, and there seem to be a lot of Pittsburgh fans who come into the area restaurants. I'll strike up conversations with them and start talking baseball. They have no idea who they're talking to, and I'll say something like, "That was some World Series back in 1960." Of course, being Pirates fans, they'll agree. Then I like to ask, "Who was the Most Valuable Player in that World Series?"

Almost every time, they'll answer, "Mazeroski."

So if you ever want to stump a Pirates fan, I have a good trivia question you can use.

Chapter 10

SIXTY-ONE IN '61

TWO EVENTS BEFORE Opening Day of 1961 resulted in a greater sense of permanence for me, both on and off the field.

First, during that off-season, construction began on a new home for Betsy and me in Sumter. The first off-season after we married, we had lived with Betsy's mother. After that we'd rented a place in Sumter during the off-season. Betsy and the kids would join me for spring training, then head north for the season to a place we rented in New Jersey.

We picked out a lot in an undeveloped area on the west side of town, and a friend who was a builder started working on our home. The total cost was $28,000. I had signed a contract for $22,500 for the 1961 season, and I clearly remember thinking, *Man, I won't ever be able to pay for this.*

Well, we were able to pay for that home, and we still live in it. We've enclosed the garage and added on to the back a little, but today Betsy and I occupy the same home we paid $28,000 to build after the 1960 season.

That turned out to be a busy off-season because of the construction and the attention I received during the World Series. I started fielding more requests for appearances and speaking engagements. Then, right before the New Year, our first daughter, Christie, was born. I was so excited to have a little girl that I told everyone I met about her.

We didn't really get to enjoy our new home right away because it was completed just as it was time to head back to St. Petersburg for spring training. That's where the second event happened, which gave me a new sense of permanence on the field.

With Casey out as the Yankees' manager, Ralph Houk—who had been my manager when I played with the Denver Bears—took over our team. Ralph had come up from Denver before the '58 season to be our first base coach. During the '60 season, when Casey missed thirteen games because of a bladder infection, Ralph had served as interim manager. Now he was in charge.

For Casey's sake, I hated that he had been fired. (At Casey's farewell press conference, it was first portrayed as a retirement, but that didn't last long once the reporters starting asking questions and Casey saw an opportunity to reveal what had really happened.) Casey was a good man. However, his platooning, his constant lineup shuffling, and his love of pinch-hitting had become frustrating to me.

Ralph didn't believe in platooning and changing the lineup as much as Casey did. The first week of spring training he told Tony and me that we would be his full-time shortstop and second baseman. And he didn't just tell us. He announced it publicly so that everyone—players, media, and fans—would know that we had his full support.

"Okay, it's a new era," Ralph told me. "I don't care if you hit

.200, .300, .400, or .100. You're going to be my second baseman. Know that you're in there every day, and just have a good time. Enjoy yourself."

Whew! What a relief that was.

I wasn't the kind of player who was going to take it easy or start coasting when I knew I had a permanent place in the lineup. But for the first time since coming up to the Yankees, I felt that I didn't have to prove myself, that I could just play baseball without having to look over my shoulder all the time.

Hearing Ralph say those words was like receiving an extra-large injection of confidence. Building up his players was a key part of Ralph's managerial style. With Ralph as manager, the atmosphere in the clubhouse and on the field immediately became more relaxed. Ralph was a player's manager. He was positive, always trying to encourage players to do their best.

Casey's style had been to keep the players from getting too relaxed. I think sometimes he wanted us to be a little unhappy or on edge. He had a habit of using the media to communicate with his players; it wasn't unusual to find out what Casey thought of how you were playing by reading the newspaper.

Ralph, though, would come over to a player and talk to him one-on-one. It would be a gentle conversation, and it would be constructive. He communicated in a way that made you believe that he was pulling for you and that, as your manager, he wanted to put you in situations where you could do your best.

Yet Ralph was no pushover. His nickname was "the Major" because he had entered the Army during World War II, become an Army Ranger, and worked his way up to the rank of major. Ralph had received the Bronze Star, the Purple Heart, and the Silver Star for his military service. Ralph had the respect of the clubhouse, both as a baseball man and as a person. He definitely had mine.

Once the season began, Ralph proved to be a man of his word. I started every game at second base except for three—one in July and two in late September after we had clinched the pennant. From about the middle of June on, Ralph also committed to me as the leadoff hitter. Being in the lineup every day and usually at the top of the order instead of near the bottom, I produced some of the best statistics to that point in my career.

My 662 at bats in 1961 were almost 200 more than my previous high. I scored 80 runs (53 in '59 had been my best), drove in 49 runs, and even set a new high mark in home runs—three. My .261 batting average was my second best, behind the .301 of two years earlier. I also earned the first of my five consecutive Gold Glove awards for being voted the best defensive second baseman in the American League.

I clearly benefited from Ralph's managerial style, and it all began with that spring training conversation when he said the second base job was all mine. It's interesting how when a manager tells a player that he's sticking with him no matter what type of statistics he puts up, that player will usually produce the numbers they were both hoping for in the first place. That's the impact expressing confidence in someone can make.

I wasn't the only player who thrived in Ralph's first season, and that's the reason fans today ask for my memories of 1961 more than any other season. That year, of course, was the year of the historic chase after Babe Ruth's hallowed record of sixty home runs in a season, and the two players chasing the Babe were my teammates Mickey Mantle and Roger Maris.

For the 1961 season the American League expanded from eight teams to ten with the additions of the Minnesota Twins and the Los Angeles Angels. (The Washington Senators moved to Minneapolis–St. Paul to become the Twins and were replaced by an expansion team also named the Washington Senators.) To keep the schedule balanced with the expanded number of teams, the regular season was stretched from 154 games to 162.

With the addition of the Los Angeles team, our transportation changed for that season as well. Before 1961 the westernmost franchise had been Kansas City, and we rode the train everywhere. We were the last team in the league not traveling by plane. Why? Because our traveling secretary, who made all travel arrangements, was afraid of flying. "We have too valuable a team for all of them to die at once," he would say. "In a train wreck, they probably wouldn't all die."

Beginning in '61, however, with the exception of a short train trip like New York to Boston or Washington, DC, we finally became the flying Yankees.

Best Ever?

Our '61 team is usually included in discussions listing the best baseball teams ever. In my completely biased opinion, I think we deserve that consideration.

Granted, we played in the first season of the longer, 162-game schedule. But our 109 wins that year were the second most in franchise history behind the 1927 Yankees team that featured the Murderers' Row lineup with Babe Ruth and Lou Gehrig in the middle. Even today, only one other Yankees team has won more games than our 109—the 1998 team, with 114 victories.

The Detroit Tigers with Al Kaline, Norm Cash, Rocky Colavito, and Jim Bunning were our closest competition that year. The Tigers ended up tying their franchise record with 101 wins, yet the pennant race was effectively decided the first week of September.

On September 1 the Tigers came to Yankee Stadium to start a three-game series. By then it was down to a two-team race, and we led the Tigers by one and a half games. We won the first game 1–0 when Moose Skowron drove in Ellie Howard with two outs in the bottom of the ninth. We came back the next day to win 7–2 and finished off the sweep with an 8–5 victory on Sunday. The Tigers left town four and a half games back. Five days later our lead had grown to ten games. Our sweep started an eight-game losing streak for Detroit and a thirteen-game winning streak for us.

Our taking such a comfortable lead relatively early in the pennant race created room for Mickey and Roger's pursuit of the home run record Ruth had set at sixty back in 1927.

When the Detroit series began at the start of September, Roger had hit fifty-one home runs and Mickey was at forty-eight. Both clearly had a chance at breaking Babe's record. But both felt the pressure, too, not only because they were pursuing baseball's most sacred record, but also because baseball commissioner Ford Frick had announced in July that if either were to break Ruth's record, he would have to do so by the 154th game. If a sixty-first home run came after that, Frick said it would be noted in the record books with a distinctive mark due to the expanded season.

The commissioner didn't actually use the word *asterisk*. But eventually popular conception was that if the record were broken after the 154th game, it would be marked with an asterisk—and somehow deemed "inferior" to Ruth's. The commissioner's ruling deserved an asterisk itself. Mr. Frick had previously served as Babe Ruth's ghostwriter and was out to protect Ruth's legacy.

We all saw the pressure Mickey and Roger were under. Mickey could adjust to it better than Roger since he'd had more experience with being in the spotlight and having his every move scrutinized. It has been well documented that Roger had patches of hair falling out and rashes breaking out on his body as he approached the record.

Roger didn't like the constant media attention. He was shy to begin with, and the press kept asking him the same set of questions over and over and over. It was a big story that was covered on a daily basis, but there wasn't much different that could be reported. Either Mickey or Roger homered, or they didn't. What else could they really say? But there were still stories to file about *something* every day, so the press kept asking.

That grated on Roger especially, and sometimes, out of frustration, he would answer a reporter's question in a way that made him sound arrogant. But Roger wasn't arrogant at all. He was just a shy person who wanted to play baseball in relative peace. Unfortunately, that wasn't going to happen as the home run chase heated up. That's too bad, because that was a momentous time in baseball, and I don't think the key figure involved enjoyed the end of that season.

Our public relations director later admitted that the situation could have been handled better. If the same situation occurred today, Mickey and Roger would be taken into an interview room each day for an organized question-and-answer session with the media. Instead, the interview process was treated just like any other normal day at the ballpark—except by then, there was no such thing as a normal day. When the home run race really heated up, there would be between fifty and seventy writers in our locker room for every game.

Of course, a press corps that size could not gather around Mickey or Roger at one time. A group of ten or so would encircle Roger, ask their questions, and move on to Mickey. Then another small group would move in and ask their questions—typically the same questions as the first group's. The groups kept rotating with Mickey and Roger. There was no protection for the players that way.

Some members of the press tried to stir up trouble too. There were reports—and some still try to claim this today—that Mickey and Roger didn't get along. Nothing could be further from the truth. They were both very supportive of each other and spent time together in the clubhouse and away from the Stadium. My observation was that both players benefited from the friendly competition between them, and I think they would have agreed. It wasn't merely one person chasing the ghost of Babe Ruth. They were two teammates, next to each other in the outfield and in the batting order every day, and they could go head-to-head in a healthy, competitive way.

One advantage Mickey had was that he had hit fifty-two homers in 1956, so this wasn't the first time he'd experienced a big home run year. Roger's best had been thirty-nine home runs in his first season with us, and he had topped that number in 1961 before July ended.

An advantage for Roger was that he hit directly in front of Mickey, so he had Mickey's protection in the lineup. Roger did not have a single intentional walk that season. That statistic still amazes me, but who would put Roger on base and then have to face Mickey?

Truthfully, most of us were pulling for Mickey to beat Babe's record. We weren't anti-Roger at all. It's just that we had known Mickey longer. He had come up through the Yankees' system and stepped in to replace Joe DiMaggio as *the* Yankee, whereas Roger had just joined the team the year before. But again, we had nothing against Roger. When Mickey eventually fell out of the home run race, all of us—including Mickey—threw our full support behind Roger.

On September 10, Mickey homered during a doubleheader against Cleveland to reach number fifty-three. Roger was at fifty-six.

Nagging injuries, though, began to take their toll on Mickey— he had injured a muscle in his left forearm in the sweep of Detroit but kept playing—and he didn't hit another home run for almost two weeks. He also came down with flu-like symptoms during that time. Broadcaster Mel Allen recommended a doctor who could give Mickey a shot to take care of the flu. The doctor, however, hit

Mickey's hip bone with the needle. The shot bruised Mickey's hip, and the bruise developed into an abscess that sent Mickey to the hospital with a high fever.

Mickey tried to keep playing, but he was in obvious pain. I don't think people realized how bad that abscess was. It was big enough that I think a person could have put his fist into it. I would see Mickey's hip in the locker room and wonder how he was suiting up, much less playing. He did end up missing some games in the final two weeks of the season, and the doctor's shot wound up having ramifications not only on the home run race but also into the postseason.

Roger had fifty-nine home runs after our 155th game on September 20, so according to the commissioner's declaration, the record was safe from being beaten without some type of distinctive mark. Roger hit number sixty in game 159 and went into the final day of the regular season tied with Babe Ruth's mark.

When Mark McGwire and Sammy Sosa engaged in their pursuit of the single-season home run record in 1998, the crowds for their final games of the season were enormous. But it wasn't that way in '61. The action Ford Frick had taken to protect Babe's record took the glamour out of Roger's bid for sixty-one once the 154-game mark had passed. When we hosted the Boston Red Sox in the regular season finale with Roger sitting on sixty, the attendance that day was only 23,154, and that was the largest crowd for the three games in which Roger had a chance to break the record.

Roger reached sixty-one in his second at bat, in the fourth inning, off Tracy Stallard. Roger turned on a knee-high fastball and dropped it into the right field seats of Yankee Stadium as he had so many times that season.

The response was different than most would probably imagine. If that had happened in today's baseball, Roger's teammates would have raced out of the dugout and mobbed him in celebration as soon as he touched home plate. Back then, though, it wasn't considered appropriate for teams to leave the dugout and greet a home run hitter at home plate. We stayed in the dugout and waited for Roger.

After Roger had completed his trot and stepped into the dugout, the fans were yelling loudly for him. Two or three of the guys near Roger pushed him back up the dugout steps to acknowledge the fans with a tip of his cap. We all congratulated Roger with handshakes and pats on the shoulders. Then Roger sat on the bench, leaned back against the dugout wall, and released a big sigh.

There was a strange silence in the dugout, I think for two reasons: First, as baseball players, we realized the enormity of what he had just accomplished. And second, seeing Roger's posture on the bench afterward, we realized just how much the pursuit of sixty-one had taken out of him.

Mickey was not in the dugout that day. He was back in the hospital after his infection had flared up again. I wish Mickey could have been there, though. Knowing how he always looked out for his teammates, especially younger ones, I believe Mickey would have been the one person who would have gone over, sat next to Roger on the bench, and said something simple like, "Well, you did it." Then, because Mickey always had to crack a joke, he would have added, "At 296 feet to right field, it shouldn't have taken this long!"

I know there have been individuals since who have hit more home runs than Roger's sixty-one in a season. But sadly, each of those has either admitted to using some type of performance-enhancing drug or has been strongly tied to PEDs. And I know the argument that hitters on steroids were facing pitchers on steroids. It still saddens me that Roger's record has been broken, because I know he made his mark on natural ability alone. I need to add, though, that I was very impressed with the way Mark McGwire treated the Maris family and honored them at the game the night he broke Roger's record.

I have learned not to get too heavily involved in debates about what the single-season home run record should be. I still recall the time when I was speaking at the Babe Ruth World Series in Jamestown, New York, and began talking about how Roger hit sixty-one home runs and broke Ruth's record. A woman in the audience jumped up and added, "But it took him 162 games."

I was told she was Babe Ruth's daughter.

But I'll never back down from saying Roger Maris's sixty-one homer season truly was an amazing accomplishment, and I appreciated the opportunity as his teammate to be a front-row witness to his sixty-one in '61.

Strong to the Finish

In the year of the "M&M boys," we played the '61 World Series with about an M and a half. It's an indication of the depth our team enjoyed that we were still able to defeat the Cincinnati Reds in five games.

Mickey missed the first two games at Yankee Stadium while still battling the aftereffects of his infection. Roger slid over from right field to center to take Mickey's place, while Héctor López or Johnny Blanchard started in right.

This was Ralph's first World Series as a manager, and he didn't repeat Casey's mistake of the year before: He started Whitey Ford in Game 1. Whitey was in his full Chairman of the Board mode in the opener. He allowed only three base runners—two on singles and one on a walk—in pitching his third consecutive World Series shutout going back to the previous year. We won 2–0, with Ellie Howard and Moose Skowron hitting solo home runs.

The Reds evened the series by taking Game 2 by a score of 6–2. Joey Jay pitched very well against us in that one. That wasn't surprising considering that Jay had tied Milwaukee's Warren Spahn for the most National League wins that season, with twenty-one.

After a day off for traveling to Cincinnati, Mickey wanted to give it a go for Game 3. He still wasn't in good shape, and he went 0 for 4 with two strikeouts and didn't do anything noteworthy in center field. But just having him in the lineup provided a huge boost for us. I know for me, just turning around on the field during the game and seeing our leader in center made everything feel normal. We all knew how bad Mickey's hip was, and it's an emotional inspiration when a teammate who you know shouldn't be playing is out there anyway, trying to help any way he can.

The Reds took an early lead with a run off Bill Stafford in the third inning. The score stayed 1–0 until the seventh, when we scored an unearned run on Yogi Berra's single that brought Tony Kubek home from second. Cincinnati regained the lead, at 2–1, in the bottom of the inning. But in the eighth, Johnny Blanchard's pinch-hit home run retied the score at 2.

In the ninth inning, Roger Maris won the game for us when he homered off Cincinnati starter Bob Purkey. That was one of only two hits Roger would have in that World Series, but it was a key one. After losing the second game at Yankee Stadium, we had gone to Crosley Field in Cincinnati and taken the first of the three games scheduled there. We now held a 2–1 advantage in the Series.

Whitey was back on the mound for Game 4, and we won easily, 7–0. Whitey retired the first seven batters before Darrell Johnson singled in the third. The inning ended when leadoff hitter Elio Chacón grounded out to me. That out gave Whitey a streak of twenty-nine and two-thirds consecutive scoreless innings pitched in the World Series, breaking the record Babe Ruth set during the 1916 and 1918 World Series. In 1961, two of my teammates broke a big hitting record and a big pitching record, both set by Ruth.

Whitey's streak would reach thirty-two innings by the sixth

inning, when he left with an ankle injury. Jim Coates would replace Whitey and keep the shutout intact.

Even before that, in the fourth inning, Mickey had to leave the game. Roger walked, leading off the inning, and Mickey followed with a hit to left center. Roger ran around to third, but Mickey pulled up at first. His abscess had opened and begun to pour out blood. The blood seeped through the gauze and bandages wrapped around his leg and stained his uniform pants from the hip down to his knee.

Mickey immediately left the game and didn't play again in the Series. But Roger scored to give us a 1–0 lead.

In the bottom of that inning, the Reds mounted the best chance they would have to score against Whitey. Eddie Kasko led off with a single to left field. One out later, Frank Robinson was hit by a pitch, putting runners at first and second. Then Wally Post hit a double play grounder to Tony at short. Tony's throw was a little lower than usual. I caught the toss, made my pivot, and threw to first. But because of the low throw, I wasn't able to make my usual jump over the runner sliding into second.

The throw to first was in time to complete the double play and end the inning. But Frank Robinson's spikes caught me right on the ankle. By the time I had hobbled to the dugout, my sock was stained red, and I could feel blood that had run to the bottom of my shoe. I thought of Mickey limping past me in the dugout, his pants coated in blood. *If he played with a hip that bad, there is no way I'm coming out of this game over a spike.*

After the game I needed stitches to close the gash. That was one of only two times in my entire career that I got spiked at second base. Both came on slides by Frank Robinson.

We scored a second run in the fifth inning. I had a single in the middle of that rally, right after Whitey had walked with two outs. Whitey scored the run on a single by Tony. We scored twice more the next inning for a 4–0 lead, then put the game away in the seventh with three runs. I led off that inning with my third hit of the game. It was my second three-hit game of the Series, to go with my 3 for 4 in the opener.

Even though we had a 3–1 Series lead, with Games 6 and 7 back home if we needed them, I thought the fifth game was important going into it because of injuries on our side. Mickey hadn't been ruled out from playing, but it certainly appeared doubtful that he would. Whitey had hurt his ankle, and it was too early to know if he would be able to come back if the Series went to seven games. Also, Yogi Berra would miss the fifth game with a stiff shoulder.

As the leadoff hitter, I wanted to get us off to a good start and set the early tone in our favor. I singled off Joey Jay to start the game. That was my one hit in six at bats that day, but if someone had told me before the game that I would get only one hit, that's the spot I would have picked for it to come. Tony and Roger followed with fly outs, then Jay had me dead to rights at first on a pickoff. First baseman Gordy Coleman misplayed the ball, though, and I wound up safe at second. That turned out to be huge because Johnny Blanchard, starting for Mickey, immediately homered to right field for the game's first two runs. After that error at first that should have ended the inning, we wound up scoring five runs and knocking Jay out of the game.

We won that game 13–5 to wrap up the world championship. Whitey was named Most Valuable Player, as well he should have been, although Blanchard had a fine Series filling in for Mickey.

Whitey's MVP award was a fitting cap to a year in which he led the American League during the regular season with a 25–4 record. Ralph had decided to go with a four-man pitching rotation instead of five during the regular season—a shrewd move that gave Whitey about ten extra starts over the course of the season. Consider that we won the pennant by eight games over an outstanding Detroit club, and the easy math tells the importance of Whitey's ten extra starts.

Of the seven World Series that I played in, 1961 is my favorite because it was a world championship I felt I contributed to. We had won in '58, but I played only an inning or two in most of my appearances. I had an MVP Series in '60, but we didn't win that one. In '61 we won the Series, and I hit the ball as well as, if not better than, during the '60 Series. My batting average was .391, and my nine hits set a World Series record for a five-game series that has been tied but not broken.

The funny thing is, after driving in a record twelve runs in the '60 Series, I had absolutely zero in '61 despite having a higher batting average. I was batting leadoff that year instead of in the lower third of the order, so there were fewer runners on base when I was batting. That shows how much a player's records are impacted by his teammates.

I've talked with Yogi and Tony many times about how we thought our 1960 team was just as good as the one in 1961. We probably had even more depth off the bench in '60. The biggest difference between how those teams are viewed is Bill Mazeroski's home run.

Chapter 11

THE TRUTH ABOUT
THE CATCH

BEFORE THE FINAL GAME of the 1961 World Series, Tony Kubek was greeted in the locker room by a man in a military uniform. The man handed over an envelope that contained a letter informing Tony, a member of the United States Army Reserve, that he was being called into active duty.

As a result, we played the first four months of the 1962 season without my double play partner. Tom Tresh, a rookie whose father had been a catcher in the majors, stepped into Tony's spot and played well enough to earn American League Rookie of the Year.

By the time Tony returned from military duty in early August, we were in first place, five games up on the Minnesota Twins and five and a half games ahead of the Los Angeles Angels. After playing for about a week in left field, a position he had played at times under Casey, Tony took over again at shortstop, and Tresh moved to left field to keep his bat in the lineup. With Moose Skowron still at first and Clete Boyer still at third, our infield was back together for the pennant stretch.

We spent the rest of the summer looking into the rearview mirror as the Twins and Angels tagged closely behind us. With two weeks to go in the season, we led the Twins by three and the Angels by six and a half. The Angels slipped back slightly from there, but the Twins wouldn't go away. Minnesota never managed to get closer than three games back, but they kept battling. We captured the American League flag by five games, winning five of our final six games to once again head into the postseason with momentum.

Wally Moses was our batting coach in 1961–62, and he had really taken a special interest in me as a hitter. Wally had produced a 200-hit season in his playing days and was widely respected around baseball for his hitting knowledge. Wally worked with my swing and stance, but for the most part he fine-tuned those skills. The biggest impact he made was in another area: my confidence. He instilled in me that I should go to the plate each time expecting to get a hit—and not just expecting, but confidently expecting.

The fruit of our one-on-one sessions came during the '62 season, when I had the best offensive year of my career. I hit a career-high .302 for the second of my two .300 seasons. Batting first or second almost exclusively, I led the American League in at bats, with 692. I also had a league- and career-high 209 hits—the eighth player in Yankees history to reach the coveted 200-hit mark. The last had been Phil Rizzuto in 1950.

Sacrifice hits aren't a much-touted statistic, but my twenty sacrifice bunts that season was the highest in both leagues. From my days as a young player in Sumter, I took great pride in being able to lay down a bunt when called upon by the manager. It's rare to find a player who looks forward to seeing the bunt signal, and I certainly would have preferred to drive in a run with a hit or to advance a runner from first to third with a single rather than bunt him over. There's little glory in a sacrifice bunt. But in a one-run game—and we seemed to find ourselves involved in many of those that season—a good bunt can help a team win.

Bunting is not difficult. In fact, I consider bunting to be more about attitude than ability. Every big leaguer lays down at least a couple of bunts during batting practice before games. But the good bunters are the ones who are actually willing to bunt. They're the ones who put effort and concentration into their bunting practice instead of having the approach, *I'll lay down a couple of bunts real quick so I can start hitting the ball out of the park and impress people.*

I was a good bunter because I wanted to be one, and I wanted to be one because I knew that was a way I could contribute to the team. I liked to bunt for hits, too. If I saw a second baseman playing deep, I'd push a bunt past the mound to where the pitcher couldn't get it, yet not far enough to where the second baseman could field it in time to throw me out at first. If I saw a third baseman playing deep, I'd drop a bunt down the third base line and hustle my way to first for a hit.

Because of my bunting ability and because I wasn't a power hitter, it was rare to glance over my left shoulder from the box and see the third baseman playing deep. More often than not, the third baseman played me a little closer than he would most hitters to defend a possible bunt. Bringing a third baseman in like that opens a bigger hole between shortstop and third to hit through. So my advice to any young player reading this—and any old one too, if it's not too late—is to put serious work into your bunting. Bunting is an underrated weapon for a player to possess. Remember, bunting is more about attitude than ability.

Now that I have stepped down from my bunting soapbox, I would like to add that '62 was a season of power, at least for me. I had career highs in doubles (thirty-eight) and home runs (eight), and my five triples were one shy of my career high. My fifty-nine RBIs also were the most of any season in my career.

That was the year of my other major league grand slam. Up until then, the 1960 Series had been my only home run with the bases loaded, but I hit another at Minnesota in August. I played more than fourteen hundred games during my career, so I have to work my memory pretty hard to call up the details of games, especially from the regular season. I don't, however, need help recalling that one. When you hit two grand slams in a twelve-year career, those two games tend to stand out.

The Twins were in third place, six and a half games behind us. We had won two of the three games in the series, and it was the last time we would face Minnesota that season. August 16 is probably a little early for a must-win game, but for the Twins, that was about as close to a must-win game as they could have had at that point in the schedule.

It was the top of the ninth, we were trailing 7–4, and the bases were loaded with two outs. Dick Stigman was pitching for the Twins, and manager Sam Mele went out to the mound to talk with Stigman before he pitched to me.

I can imagine what Mele likely told his pitcher: "Whatever you do, don't walk him. Look over there at who's on deck: Maris." I didn't walk much anyway, hitting ahead of Maris and Mantle. But I knew that in that situation, of the next three batters Stigman could face, I would be his first choice. He was not going to pitch around me.

During their conference, I walked back over near the dugout to the on-deck circle, where Maris was loosening up in case I kept the game going. Mickey, who was next after Roger in the lineup, came out of the dugout to me.

"I don't feel very good," Mickey told me. "See if you can hit one out of the park."

Of course, I wouldn't be telling this story if I had struck out. After taking the first two pitches for balls, I knew Stigman would have to throw me a fat strike. He could not afford to fall behind 3–0 to me. I deposited that fat strike into the seats for a grand slam and an 8–7 lead.

After I rounded the bases, touched home plate with the go-ahead run, and jogged toward the dugout, I heard Mantle laughing.

"Why are you laughing?" I asked when I met him on his way to the on-deck circle.

His reply: "I didn't think you could do it!"

The joking was short-lived, though, because the Twins tied the game at 8 in the bottom of the ninth on Rich Rollins's single— a broken-bat single, at that. They went on to win it in the tenth when Bob Allison scored on a hit by Bernie Allen. We lost our chance to put the Twins in an even deeper hole, and they wound up being the team that pushed at us all the way into the final week of the season.

Once we did clinch the title during the final week, Ralph Houk shuffled the lineup for Mickey's benefit. Mickey had missed a month of the season with a leg injury. Because of that time off, his numbers were down. Mickey had struck at least thirty homers in seven consecutive seasons, but he was in danger of falling short in '62.

Mickey had homered twice on September 18 to reach twenty-nine, but that had been his last homer as we entered the final week of the season at the end of September. For our final four games, Ralph moved Mickey from cleanup into the leadoff spot to give him more at bats. That way Mickey could have as many chances as possible to belt homer number thirty and keep his streak of thirty-homer seasons going.

Mickey didn't ask for that, because that statistic probably didn't mean that much to him. Most of the time we players weren't too aware of what milestones and records we were approaching unless it was particularly significant. But the team statisticians kept up with those things, and they kept the managers informed of what numbers were within the players' reach.

Late in the season, when the league's postseason spot was clinched, it was common for a manager to be statistics-conscious when he made lineup decisions. After our playing days, when we look back and evaluate our careers, those numbers do mean something to us, so we're grateful someone was mindful of our statistics at the time.

Mickey went homerless in the three games before the season-ender. But on the last day of the season, against the Chicago White Sox, Mickey hit number thirty in the fourth inning. Because I was in the unusual spot of batting behind Mickey, I was the on-deck batter and got to be the first player to congratulate him. I should have remembered the line he had used on me in Minnesota and said, "I didn't think you could do it!"

Despite the amount of time he missed, Mickey was voted American League MVP for the third time, by a wide margin. I finished second, with Harmon Killebrew third. Mickey had been out of the lineup from mid-May to mid-June, and we'd had a more difficult time winning games when he was out. When he returned, we won at a more frequent rate, and I think that proves right there that Mickey was "most valuable" to our team.

I'll admit that when asked about the biggest thrill of my career, I will give different answers. There are so many great moments I was able to enjoy that it's difficult to pick just one and stick with it. One of my responses to that question, though, is that when Mickey was announced as the MVP winner in 1962, he said, "Bobby should have won it."

I was thrilled just to finish second to Mickey, but it meant a great deal to me when Mickey acknowledged my season in that manner.

My sisters, Inez (left) and Ann (right), claimed I was spoiled because I was the only boy. I suppose there might have been some truth to that.

I may have been only five feet eight and 158 pounds my senior year, but I was still able to catch the eye of Yankees scouts H. P. Dawson and Mayo Smith.

My stance got a little better by the time I hit the big leagues. Still—not bad for a six-year-old.

A photographer took this shot of Betsy and me the day we arrived at our first apartment in Denver in June 1956. Unfortunately, our honeymoon was cut short when I had to leave for my first road trip before we'd even unpacked. Betsy has always been a great sport.

Starting a Family

This is a shot of my dad, Clint Richardson, and me in 1956. I played 1,412 games in the majors, but only one with my dad in the stands. (At least it was a World Series game.)

It's always nice to celebrate great moments with family. Here I am on September 17, 1960, holding my boys, Ronnie (left) and Robby (right), along with the bat I used to hit a two-run single in the eighth that helped us beat the Orioles 5–3.

My youngest son, Rich, was born after I retired, but he was still part of the Yankee family. Here he is with Mickey in 1969.

My daughter Jeannie was there to help me cut the cake on Bobby Richardson Day at Yankee Stadium in 1966.

Here I am amazing my daughter Christie with my bubble-blowing skills after a game in 1961.

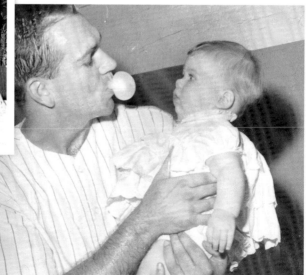

Just before my first game with the Yankees, Mickey (who was constantly followed by photographers) said, "Come over here, Rich. They'll take our picture if we sit together." Sure enough, a photographer saw us and snapped a picture of the star and the rookie together. That was the kind of person Mickey was—always thinking of and looking out for others.

Here I am trying to turn a double play as Dick Groat slides into second during the 1960 World Series against the Pirates.

See? I told you my swing got better by the time I got to New York. (circa 1962)

This is me sliding into home, just ahead of the glove of Cleveland catcher Johnny Romano in 1961 while Moose Skowron looks on.

Contrary to popular opinion, it can get pretty rough at second base. (circa 1964)

With the bases loaded in the first inning of Game in the 1960 World Series, Casey Stengel told n to lay down a bunt. But Clem Labine threw in a h fastball on me, and I hit it 301 feet to the fence. didn't even realize I had homered until I reached home plate and Moose, Gil, and Ellie were the waiting after scoring ahead of me.

◀ I love this shot of Moose Skowron, Elston Howard, Ralph Terry, Tony Kubek, and me celebrating the final out of the 1962 World Series after we beat the Giants 1–0 to become world champions.

In my entire career at ▶ second base, I only got spiked twice—both times by Frank Robinson (20). This shot was snapped seconds before Frank's spikes caught me in the ankle in Game 4 of the 1961 World Series.

Mickey and Whitey were both great teammates. Here they are helping me celebrate after my grand slam in Game 3 of the '60 World Series.

…e guys even grabbed some grease paint to decorate the bat I used to drive in …RBIs in Game 3.

…ere I am accepting the title for the 1960 …orvette convertible I was given for winning …orld Series MVP that year. It was a beautiful …r but not very practical for a guy with a wife …d three kids, so I ended up trading it for a …ation wagon a couple of weeks later.

I consider it a tremendous honor to have played on the Yankees with such greats as Elston Howard, Whitey Ford, Mickey Mantle, Tony Kubek, and Yogi Berra.

◄ In 1962 I was the runner-up to Mickey for the American League MVP Award, and I have to say, it couldn't have gone to a more deserving guy. Mickey was a good friend, a great teammate, and a true warrior.

▲
Moose Skowron, Tony Kubek, Clete Boyer, and I made up the infield in 1961.

Even though I was still in my prime, I decided to retire from the game in 1966 so I could spend more time with my family. On September 17, 1966, the Yankees celebrated Bobby Richardson Day at Yankee Stadium. What made the day even more special was the fact that my wife, Betsy; my kids, Robby, Ronnie, Christie, and Jeannie; my mom, Willie; and my mother-in-law, Mary, were all there to celebrate with me.

 Finishing Well

Over the years God has blessed Betsy and me with three wonderful sons, two beautiful daughters, and fifteen grandkids. We treasure every minute we get to spend with them.

◄ After I retired from the Yankees, I took a job coaching baseball at the University of South Carolina. I coached the Gamecocks from 1970 to 1976. During that time I got to work with some extremely talented kids, including Whitey Ford's son Eddie, who was just as fine an athlete as his dad.

In 1976 President Ford asked me to run for Congress. Even though I lost (by less than 4 percent), I received a tremendous amount of support from the state of South Carolina. Three years later I helped campaign for Ronald Reagan during his run for president. Betsy and I are pictured here with Reagan during his stop in South Carolina in 1979.
▼

After Baseball

I loved playing in the Old Timers' Games. They were a great way to keep in touch with old teammates. This is me with Tony Kubek in 1987.

Yogi Berra and I decided we were a little too "mature" to play at the Old Timers' Game in 2009, but we still enjoyed catching up in the clubhouse.

...ly Martin and I caught up with each other again in 1985 at a golf tournament ...Coastal Carolina University.

...'e had a pretty spectacular infield back ...the '60s, and it's great to see guys like ...erek Jeter keeping the winning tradition ...ing.

My aim in both baseball and in life is simple: to make an impact by being used by God in the lives of others. I don't know how many more innings of life I have yet to play, but I plan to use whatever time I have left to make an impact for Christ. If my relationship with Mickey taught me nothing else, it was that it's never too late to make "the decision." As my dear friend Yogi Berra (#8) once said, "It ain't over till it's over."

Rain, Rain, Go Away

Typically the regular season would end on a Sunday, and the World Series would begin on a Wednesday. In 1962, though, we had an extra day off because the San Francisco Giants and the Los Angeles Dodgers had tied for first place in the National League and needed a three-game playoff to determine the pennant winner. Although we didn't know our opponent after the final Sunday of the regular season, with San Francisco and Los Angeles playing each other, we at least knew we would be making a cross-country flight.

The Dodgers had led the Giants by four games with seven left to play. But the Dodgers won only one game in the final week, and San Francisco won on the last day to move into the first-place tie. The Giants won the first and third games of the three-game playoff, clinching the pennant in Los Angeles on the day before the Series was to begin. In keeping with the way they forced the best-of-three playoff, the Giants came from behind to win the clincher, scoring four runs in the ninth inning to win 6–4.

Our West Coast destination was decided. The 1962 World Series would open the next day at Candlestick Park. But it would take a while to finish. In fact, "delay" became the theme of the Series, which required thirteen days to complete because of rain. The first four games all went off as scheduled, over five days, but it took a full week to play the final three games.

Because we had had those three days off while the Giants were playing Los Angeles, we started the Series with a pitching advantage. Ralph was able to go with our best pitcher—Whitey, of course—while San Francisco manager Al Dark had to go with his most rested pitcher, Billy O'Dell. That meant we didn't have to start the Series against San Francisco ace Juan Marichal, a future Hall of Famer who had started the final game against Los Angeles.

We jumped out to a quick 2–0 lead. Tony Kubek struck out

leading off, but I singled and Tom Tresh singled after me. After Mickey struck out, Roger Maris doubled to right to score me and Tresh.

The Giants scored a run in the second, ending Whitey's record streak of thirty-three and two-thirds consecutive scoreless innings in the World Series. They scored again in the third to tie the game at 2. Whitey and O'Dell then locked into a pitcher's duel that lasted until the seventh inning. Clete Boyer got us going again with a solo home run in the seventh, and with Whitey still putting up zeroes on the board, we scored twice more in the eighth and once more in the ninth for a 6–2 win.

Game 2 was dominated by the pitchers. Ralph Terry had won twenty-three games for us during the regular season, and the Giants started a twenty-four game winner in Jack Sanford. Ralph pitched great, but Sanford was a little better that day, holding us to only three hits as we lost 2–0 for a split of the first two games in San Francisco.

In what would be a seesaw Series, we won Game 3 in New York 3–2, a game that was scoreless until the seventh. The Giants won 7–3 the next day in a game started by Whitey and Marichal. Marichal pitched only four innings, though, because of a hand injury, and San Francisco's winning pitcher was Don Larsen, my former Yankees and Denver Bears teammate who had been traded to Kansas City in 1959, then on to the Chicago White Sox, and after that to San Francisco.

Rain pushed Game 5 back from Tuesday to Wednesday, and we won that game 5–3 thanks to a three-run homer by Tresh in the eighth that scored Kubek and me. Then we boarded another cross-country flight, needing one more victory to wrap up the Series.

It would take a while to get it.

We arrived in the Bay Area on Thursday, October 11. So did the effects of Tropical Storm Freda, which made landfall in the

Pacific Northwest. Between Thursday and Sunday, more than six inches of rain fell down the coast in San Francisco. It rained so heavily that games were being called off before we even left our hotel for the park. The rain ended Saturday, but there had been too much rain for us to play Sunday on the poorly draining field at Candlestick Park, even though helicopters were brought in to hover just above the outfield in an attempt to dry it out.

Counting the scheduled off-day for travel, we didn't play for four straight days. That was a day-longer break than we'd had between the end of the regular season and the start of the World Series, waiting for our World Series opponent to be determined. Then, however, we'd been at home. During the weather delays, we were stuck in our hotel in San Francisco. Guys were getting together to go out and eat, go watch movies, play card games, or come up with whatever else they could to battle boredom.

The extra time off created a different type of problem for me. I'd agreed to write a daily column about the World Series for *The State* newspaper back home in Columbia, and I was having a difficult time coming up with column ideas each day. I would go to my teammates and practically plead with them to tell me something interesting or share a story that I could use to fill my column.

Tony Kubek came up with several good ideas I could use, and I'm still grateful to him, because I was really struggling. I never thought the rainouts would end so we could get back on the field and I could have games to write about. That Series saw the start and end of my brief newspaper-columnist career, although it didn't seem so brief when I was scrambling for column ideas.

The Giants, of course, had to sit through the same delay, although they had the advantage of being at home during the break and could go about their normal schedules. But in our favor, Ralph Houk could once again bring a fully rested Whitey back to start Game 6. With the Chairman of the Board on the mound, I liked our chances of finally ending that Series right then, but it didn't happen. San Francisco scored five runs off Whitey in less than five innings, and veteran pitcher Billy Pierce held us to only three hits.

The Giants won that game 5–2, to force a Game 7. It would be one of the most memorable seventh games not only in World Series history, but also in all professional sports.

Game 7, like most games in that Series, was masterfully pitched. For the third time in the Series, our Ralph Terry started opposite Jack Sanford. We had split the two previous games those two had started, and based on the way they had gone, we expected runs to be at a premium in Game 7.

They certainly were.

We led 1–0 going into the bottom of the ninth, with the only run scored in the fifth inning, when Kubek grounded into a double play with the bases loaded, scoring Moose Skowron from third. Terry was pitching incredibly. He had retired the first seventeen batters he faced, and the only time the Giants really had threatened to score was in the seventh, when big Willie McCovey tripled with two outs. But Ralph had struck out Orlando Cepeda to end that inning and protect our 1–0 lead.

We'd had a chance to increase our lead in the eighth when we loaded the bases. I'd reached first on an error leading off, and Tresh and Mantle had followed with singles. My friend Billy O'Dell came in to replace Sanford. Maris faced him first and hit a grounder to second baseman Chuck Hiller, who threw home to force me at the plate. Ellie Howard then hit into a double play, and we failed to score.

I have to admit, I was a little concerned at that point. I had played in too many games in my career when one team had a chance to pad a lead late, failed to do so, and wound up losing because of the missed opportunity. I hoped that wouldn't be the case in this game.

With Terry still pitching, Matty Alou pinch-hit, leading off the Giants' half of the ninth inning. He reached base on a bunt single placed so well past the pitcher's mound that I could only field the ball and not make an attempt to throw to first. Terry struck out Matty's brother Felipe and Hiller—both after they failed to sacrifice-bunt Matty to second. (Practice those bunts, kids.) But Terry was still looking at the heart of the San Francisco order: Willie Mays, McCovey, and Cepeda. Any one of them could have ended our championship hopes with one swing.

On an inside-out swing, Mays lined a ball down the right field line toward Roger Maris. With the fast Matty Alou at first base, I instantly knew I would be making a relay throw to home plate with the game possibly on the line.

It's been said that the still-soggy grass of Candlestick Park prevented Mays's hit from getting all the way into the right field corner. I don't know if that's true; field conditions weren't that bad by the end of the Series. But even if that was the case, I think it needs to be considered that right fielder Maris would have been running on the same soggy grass that slowed the ball. Either way, Roger made a great hustle play by racing into the corner, picking up the ball before it rolled onto the warning track, and throwing it quickly to me.

Roger had been playing with a sore arm for a couple of months, so I'd been going out a little deeper than normal to serve as his cut-off man. I set up several feet inside the right field line to position myself in a straight line between Roger and home plate so I'd know exactly where to throw the ball. Roger's left foot slipped just a tad as he came up, and his throw short-hopped me slightly. Just as I had all those times fielding a tennis ball bouncing off my chimney back home, I cleanly scooped the short hop with both hands, then immediately turned and threw to Ellie Howard at home plate. San Francisco third base coach Whitey Lockman threw up a quick stop sign and halted Alou at third.

My one-hop throw to home was accurate, but it took a surprisingly high bounce—chest-high to Ellie and into his mitt.

As happens with any play like that, there was intense speculation in the days after the Series as to whether Lockman should have sent Alou home. Even today that decision is occasionally discussed, although the general consensus is that Alou would have been tagged out at the plate if he'd continued around third. I've always believed Alou would have been out by about five feet, but the fact that my throw took such a high hop would at least have made a play at the plate more interesting.

With McCovey coming up, Ralph Houk went to the mound to talk to Terry. Alou was at third with the tying run, and Mays with his great speed was standing at second as the winning run. Houk asked the right-handed Terry whether he wanted to walk the left-handed McCovey to load the bases for a righty-righty matchup against Cepeda with a force-out at any base.

While they were discussing strategy, Tony and I met near second base. "I sure hope he doesn't hit the ball to you," my longtime roommate said.

"Why?" I asked.

"Well, you've already made one error this Series, and I'd hate to see you blow it now."

Mays, standing on second, laughed.

Terry told Houk that he would rather pitch carefully to McCovey than walk him. He didn't like the idea of having the bases loaded and running the risk of walking Cepeda, who had hit thirty-five homers that season, to force in a run.

I returned to position on the back of the infield dirt, but it wasn't my normal position. McCovey was known for hitting balls up the middle, just to the second baseman's side of the bag. But there had been a couple of plays in that Series when I'd thrown McCovey out at first from the hole between first and second.

One of those times, I'd fielded the ball so far toward first that I had to wait on the first baseman to get to his bag before I could make my throw. So I moved a little bit into the hole between first and second, expecting McCovey to pull the ball.

"Hey, Rich." A voice came from behind me and to my right. It was second base umpire Al Barlick. "Can I have your cap for my little cousin?" he asked.

"Sure," I answered, although surprised to hear such a question from an umpire at that time.

His request stuck with me as Terry looked in to Ellie for the signal.

Give him the cap.

The next thing I heard was the ball meeting McCovey's bat. He pulled a ball down the right field line that Roger gave chase to, but it landed several rows back in the seats. I edged slightly closer to first.

I saw Terry looking at me from the mound. He later told me he noticed I was playing out of my normal position and started to walk out toward me and tell me to move back to my right a few steps. But then he reconsidered, thinking I had played hundreds of games at second base and must have had a good reason for positioning myself as I had.

If a gut feeling telling me that McCovey would pull the ball qualifies as a good reason, then I guess I did have one.

McCovey took the following pitch for a ball, then hit the next pitch. It was a screamer, too. Willie smoked that ball. And I caught it.

Over the past fifty years I have heard or read all kinds of adjectives for that catch—*miraculous, incredible, amazing, sensational, tremendous,* and on and on and on. I believe it was Felipe Alou who wrote in his autobiography that I made a leaping, one-handed catch that no other second baseman in major league baseball could make.

I wish it had been that spectacular, but in all honesty, it wasn't. I simply took one step to my left, reached about shoulder high, and snared the ball. McCovey had hit the ball so hard, that was *all* I had time to do. Even if I had needed to step and leap, there would have been no time to do it.

The ball came off Willie's bat with a lot of topspin, so it was dipping as it neared my glove. I caught the ball with my bare hand near my glove and secured the ball as the momentum from following the ball's flight carried my glove and bare hand to just above the ground. I took two or three more off-balanced steps to my left, still clutching the ball tightly in my glove as my teammates started racing toward the pitcher's mound to celebrate. Kubek ran to join me where the infield grass meets the dirt, and when I got a few steps from Tony, I removed my cap and handed it to the umpire for his cousin.

We celebrated briefly on the field and hurried into the locker room, where I gave the game ball to Ralph Terry. He was named World Series MVP for his super pitching and deserved the award. (I wonder what he did with his Corvette.) I was especially happy for Ralph, because he'd been the pitcher who gave up Bill Mazeroski's homer when we lost Game 7 in 1960.

We didn't do much celebrating after the game because Ralph, Tony, Johnny Blanchard, Jim Bouton, and I were hurrying to shower, get dressed, and leave the ballpark. With all the rainouts in the Series, we were eager to get home and had bought commercial tickets to fly back to New York City instead of flying later on the team charter. We had arranged for a policeman to take us to the airport, and naturally the policeman got caught in traffic on the way to the airport. Even with his siren on, we weren't moving for a while.

Man, I thought, *we've paid all this money for these special arrangements, and we're going to miss our flight and not get home any earlier!*

We did catch our flight—barely. Once we got home, my family

and I started our drive down to South Carolina and made it to Sumter the next day.

About two months later someone handed me a copy of the comics section in the newspaper and pointed to Charles Schulz's *Peanuts* strip. Schulz was a big Giants fan. In the first three panels Charlie Brown and Linus sat speechless, chins in their hands. In the final panel Charlie Brown stood and screamed out, "Why couldn't McCovey have hit the ball just three feet higher?"

Another month later, there was a second reference to that game in *Peanuts*. Charlie Brown and Linus sat for three panels slightly less disconsolate, but still silent. In the fourth panel Charlie Brown spoke again: "Or why couldn't McCovey have hit the ball even *two* feet higher?"

Well, Charlie Brown, if McCovey had hit that ball two feet higher, or even three feet farther to my left, it would have flown past me for a single into right field. Would Mays have scored from second to win the game? He could fly on the base paths, and with two outs he would have been off at the crack of the bat. But McCovey's ball was hit hard and would have gotten to Maris in right field quickly. There would have been a play at the plate, I'm sure, although Roger had that sore arm that would have affected his throw home. Would Mays have been safe? I'm just glad we didn't have to find out.

When Willie McCovey was inducted into the National Baseball Hall of Fame in 1986, I gave a prayer as part of the program. When asked how he wanted to be remembered, McCovey replied, "I'd like to be remembered as the guy who hit the line drive over Bobby Richardson's head."

The next time I recall being with Willie was in 2007. That year interleague play brought the Yankees back to San Francisco for their first regular-season or postseason game there since our Game 7 in 1962. San Francisco hosted some of us as part of a

'62 World Series reunion, and McCovey and I had been invited to throw out a joint first pitch.

Willie broke into a big smile when he saw me.

"I bet your hand's still hurting," he said.

I nodded and returned the smile.

"You did hit it hard."

Chapter 12
TOO MUCH KOUFAX

IN NOVEMBER OF '62 I received word that the Yankees had traded our first baseman, Bill "Moose" Skowron, to the Los Angeles Dodgers for pitcher Stan Williams. Joe Pepitone, the next can't-miss prospect rising through the Yankees system, had spent about half of the '62 season up with us, and the decision was made to turn first base over to him and let Moose go. I hated to see that happen—for both personal and professional reasons.

Moose, who had come over to the Yankees from Kansas City in 1954, was thirty-one years old and still productive. We knew we could expect at least twenty home runs and eighty RBIs from Moose every season. He was also an integral part of our tight-knit infield group—Moose, Tony Kubek, Clete Boyer, and I—which I believed was the best in baseball. And Moose could always make us laugh. Even today, thinking of Moose brings up something he did or said that still makes me chuckle.

When Hank Bauer was playing with us, he and Moose had been inseparable. They were known for being ridiculously early to airports. If they had a flight at six in the evening, for example, they would sometimes arrive at the airport before noon and wait there until six. And even if there were flights they could take during that time and arrive at their destination hours earlier, they would still wait for their scheduled flight for no better reason than the fact that their reservations had already been made.

Moose owed me money when he left for the Dodgers, and I knew that once he left the Yankees, my chances of collecting were gone. Moose didn't trust himself when it came to catching pop-ups, especially really high ones, so before the start of each season, we struck a deal whereby he would give me five hundred dollars to catch all the pop-ups around first that I could.

When a pop fly was hit in his direction, instead of calling "Mine!" to let me know he'd take it, he would immediately yell, "Bobby!" and move out of the way.

Whenever Moose told that story, he would say, "I paid Bobby five hundred dollars to catch my pop-ups." Well, the part about paying me wasn't correct, and Moose knew it. Even in recent years, Moose would tell me, "I know I haven't paid you yet, but I'm still gonna do it." Then we both would laugh.

Betsy thought my arrangement with Moose was especially funny because she didn't share his confidence in my ability to catch pop-ups. Shortly after Betsy and I arrived in Denver as newlyweds, I dropped a couple. After that she closed her eyes when I was about to field a pop-up. She couldn't believe Moose would actually pay me—or at least intend to pay me—for doing that.

Moose and I had another arrangement—one that didn't involve money. I liked to tip him off when one of our pitchers was throwing a changeup to a left-handed hitter, because that was the type of pitch a lefty was most likely to pull in Moose's direction. My signal was saying something with Moose's name, such as, "Come on, Moose." When the batter would hit a ball to Moose that he fielded, after the play he would look at me and say, "Thank you."

Keeping Things Light in Spring Training

I started missing Moose, both on the infield and in the locker room, the very first day of spring training in 1963.

Spring training was always an interesting time of the year for us. We had to get our work in and make sure we were focused on our purpose for being there—getting ready for the regular season. However, we didn't want to take things too seriously.

Baseball's regular season is accurately described as a long grind. If we treated spring training like the regular season, the grind would probably get to us in the final month of the regular season and negatively affect us during a pennant race and the postseason. So we players tried to keep things a little loose during spring training. Our managers, who were concerned with making sure we were ready to *start* the season, tended to be more serious during spring training than the players were.

Ralph Houk usually kept a good balance of loose and serious, but there was one point in 1963 spring training when he thought we weren't being serious enough. Ralph didn't put much emphasis on our spring win-loss record, but he was concerned about how we were playing. And we'd hit a stretch of several days when we didn't play well.

As a penalty for our lackadaisical performance, Ralph called for a special intrasquad scrimmage on one of our scheduled off-days. He told us the game would last longer than nine innings too. Spring training games against other clubs seemed to drag on long enough, so we weren't thrilled at the idea of playing an even longer game against each other.

There were no umpires for the game, so pitcher Steve Hamilton, who was scheduled to rest his arm that day, was appointed as umpire. Steve stood behind the pitcher's mound and umpired from there.

As we'd anticipated, it didn't take long for the scrimmage to begin to drag a little, so Steve and I came up with an idea.

"Listen," I told him between innings, "if we have a play at second base that's obvious, call it the wrong way. I'm gonna come up and get in your face and start yelling at you. Then I'll turn my back to the dugout, put my hand up near my face, and you slap my hand as though you're slapping my face."

Steve didn't just like the idea—he loved it. And sure enough, we soon had an obvious play at second. I can't remember what it was, but I do remember that Steve completely blew that call, as planned. So I sprinted over to him and started screaming in his face about how he'd missed the call and how he was a terrible umpire and whatever else I could think of to scream about.

Steve was a big guy. At six feet six, he was almost a foot taller than me. Before pitching in the majors, he had actually played basketball for the Minneapolis Lakers. It had to be a comical sight—me looking up almost directly under Steve's chin and yelling at him.

While I was right in the middle of my fake tirade, Steve joined in and began yelling back at me. At that point, when we were cap to chin yelling at each other, some members of the ballpark grounds crew apparently thought Steve was going to start beating on me. They headed out onto the field to rescue me. But before they could reach us, we executed the second part of our scheme. I turned to walk away, and Steve stepped around as we had planned and delivered a loud, cheek-high slap to my bare hand.

Thwap!

I had positioned myself so that only the center fielder could tell that he had hit my palm instead of my face. I fell to the grass, grabbing my face on the way down. Things got quiet in a hurry when I hit the ground. But only for a second or two, because Steve and I could not keep straight faces. We burst out laughing. When we did that, everyone else on the field and in the dugout did too—even Ralph Houk.

"That's it!" Ralph yelled. "Practice is over!"

For Dad

My dad's health had been deteriorating, and he suffered a stroke in May of '63. I flew home after a Sunday game to visit with Dad and flew back before our next game on Tuesday. My sister Ann was an excellent nurse and had moved into my parents' home to help take care of him.

The stroke left Dad paralyzed on his left side, and he was no longer able to speak. Although I couldn't talk with him, I stayed in constant contact with my mom and sisters over the next few weeks. From those phone calls, I knew that Dad was close to going on to be with the Lord. After a call when I was clearly discouraged, Betsy would want to talk to me about it, but I wasn't up for much talking. "I'm just concerned about my dad right now," was all I'd say.

And that was true. He was always on my mind, at home and on the field. I hit safely in twelve of the first thirteen games after I'd flown home to see Dad. I really wanted to play well for him.

Dad died on June 17 at the age of sixty-seven. I flew home for the funeral, but the next day I rejoined the team to continue playing. There still was a lot for the family to take care of, especially his business, but I thought I could handle the business affairs just as well by telephone as I could in person. My sister Ann and close friends were there to help comfort Mom, and she knew that Dad would have wanted me to get right back to baseball. Mom also was in good health—and would remain that way and stay actively involved in her church XYZ Club for years. So I thought the best way I could honor my dad was to get back on the field with my teammates.

In my first game back, I had three singles and scored a run as we beat the Washington Senators 3–2. I know Dad would have been pleased with how I played that day, but I don't think he would have been any prouder of my baseball career than he already was. His support for me went all the way back to the first game I'd played in my Knee Pants League uniform. And Dad was especially thrilled that I was able to play baseball professionally, as he had wanted to do— and for the Yankees.

"We Want Mickey!"

To me, 1963 was one of our more impressive seasons. We finished 104–57 and won the pennant by ten and a half games over the White Sox. More impressive than what we accomplished is what we had to overcome to accomplish it.

Our lineup was hit hard by injuries that season. Mantle played in only 65 of the 162 games. Maris played in 90. Tom Tresh, our left fielder, played in 145 games, but he missed a stretch of games in September. Because of their injuries, we did not start a game with Tresh in left, Mantle in center, and Maris in right from June 6 until September 24, when there were only four games left in the regular season. Injuries also affected Tony Kubek, who missed 27 games.

Even before the injuries began piling up, we spent all of May out of first place. A key stretch during that month came from May 11 to May 26, when we won eleven of thirteen games. But during that same time, the Baltimore Orioles won fourteen of fifteen games to move from fourth place to first.

Despite the Orioles' torrid streak, we were able to hang with them and were only a game back heading into June. We took over first place late in the month and stayed there for the final ten weeks of the regular season. Even with the M&M boys missing for long stretches, our lead never dropped below seven games.

Mickey missed two months, and even when he returned he was able to do so only as a pinch hitter. But just the news that

Mantle was nearing a return created an exciting sense of anticipation among Yankees fans. In situations that might call for a pinch hitter, they would chant, "We want Mickey! We want Mickey!"

Mickey made his return on August 4 at Yankee Stadium. It was the bottom of the seventh, and we trailed Baltimore 10–9 when Mickey stepped out of the dugout to a thunderous ovation. Mickey homered to tie the score, 10–10. As he rounded the bases, his chin down as always during his modest home run trot, our fans somehow found a way to cheer even louder than when he'd first stepped out of the dugout. Tears came to my eyes as I sat on the dugout bench that day, and I looked down to see goose pimples on my arms.

Midsummer Nightmare

I was selected to seven All-Star teams in my career, but I started only once, largely because Nellie Fox played second base for the Chicago White Sox, and he was the American League starter year in and year out.

I always appreciated the recognition that went along with the All-Star selections. However, while I enjoyed being around the other All-Stars and taking part in the games, I have few outstanding memories from them. If you asked me to compile a list of my five best All-Star moments, I doubt I could do it. I could probably list my five *worst* All-Star moments, though—and all five would come from the 1963 All-Star Game in Cleveland.

To begin with, I was late getting to the game. I had taken Betsy and Robby with me on that trip, and we'd stayed in Toledo with a friend, Sam Bender. But I got mixed up on the time somehow and arrived at the ballpark later than I intended. That meant I was rushed before the game, and I never liked being rushed before a game.

Nellie started as usual, and I went in for him in the top of the fifth inning with the score 3–3. Then I made an error that inning that led to an unearned run for the National League. In my first at bat, in the sixth, two men were on base with one out, and I grounded into an inning-ending double play. When I came up in the ninth, we were trailing 5–3. We had a man on first with one out, and I could have been the tying run. But I grounded into another double play to end the game.

I was frustrated after that game because I was sure I had been a big reason the American League lost. My frustration grew when I couldn't find my wife and child and we missed our plane.

I had booked a flight for us after the game so we could get back to New York, and I hurried to shower and dress because we had a tight schedule for catching our plane. I had told Betsy to meet me outside the clubhouse with Robby so we could rush to the airport. But when I came out of the American League clubhouse, Betsy and Robby weren't there. I looked all around for them and finally located them outside the National League clubhouse.

Betsy was used to meeting me outside the visiting team's locker room when she accompanied me on road trips. Because the game was in an American League city, we were the home team and used the home clubhouse, but she didn't know that.

We missed our flight and had to catch a different one that had a layover on the way to New York City. That significantly pushed back our arrival time. Then, when we finally made it back to New York, I discovered my car's battery was dead. That was just one of those days I'd like to forget.

Koufax Begins with K

Late in the '62 season, we had thought we would be matched up against the Los Angeles Dodgers in the World Series. Then the Dodgers had begun to fade, and the Giants had rallied to win the National League pennant.

In '63 the Dodgers again led their league late. But this time they finished strong to expand their lead down the stretch, win the pennant, and compete against us in the World Series. And unlike the rain-delayed Series of '62, the 1963 World Series ended about as quickly as one could end.

The Dodgers started ace Sandy Koufax in Game 1 against Whitey Ford. Sandy won both the Cy Young Award and Most Valuable Player in the National League that season, with a record of 25–5. Because our teams were in different leagues, I had never faced Koufax in a game that mattered—only spring training games and an exhibition game at the Los Angeles Memorial Coliseum.

Meeting him in Game 1 would be a humbling experience.

The game drew a crowd of 69,000 to Yankee Stadium. With that many tickets sold, the Yankees opened up the "batter's eye" portion of the center field seats. Normally, tickets weren't sold in that area, and the dark-painted seats served as a background behind the pitcher to help batters see the ball better. Having fans in those seats—all those light-colored shirts behind the pitcher in the batter's line of vision—made hitting more difficult. Koufax certainly didn't need any help baffling hitters, so the bad background was just one more problem to deal with.

Sandy struck out the first five batters he faced: Kubek, me, Tresh, Mantle, and Maris. He almost struck out the same five in a row our second time through the order. He got Kubek, me, and Tresh in the fourth inning and struck out Mantle to start the fifth. Maris made contact and fouled out on a pop-up to the catcher. I managed to walk in the sixth, and just reaching base that day against Koufax felt like a major accomplishment.

In the eighth inning, having struck out twice, I really wanted to make contact, but Sandy struck me out again. That hurt because I had always prided myself on having a low number of strikeouts during my career. I'd had eighty-nine career World Series plate appearances heading into the '63 postseason and had struck out only twice. In his autobiography, Koufax wrote that when he struck me out for the second time, he knew he had good stuff. I knew he had good stuff the first time he struck me out.

On my way back to the dugout after my third strikeout, I passed Tom Tresh, the next batter, and met Mickey as he was walking from the dugout to the on-deck circle. Mickey shook his head and said, "There's no reason for me to go up there."

Tresh actually went on to hit a two-run homer off Koufax. But that was all we got off Sandy that day, and the Dodgers beat us 5–2. Koufax had struck us out fifteen times to set a World Series single-game record.

Unfortunately, there wasn't much drop-off from Koufax to the rest of the Dodgers' staff. Johnny Podres pitched Game 2 and beat us 4–1, with our only run coming in the bottom of the ninth. Then for Game 3 in Dodger Stadium, Los Angeles gave the ball to future Hall of Famer Don Drysdale, and he held us to three hits and shut us out for a 1–0 victory. The Dodgers' only run scored in the first, when a wild pitch by Jim Bouton moved Jim Gilliam from first base to second and put him in position to score on Tommy Davis's two-out single.

Facing elimination, we drew Koufax again for Game 4. He recorded "only" eight strikeouts that day and beat us 2–1 to finish off the sweep. I didn't strike out that game and went 2 for 4 off Koufax, including a double. But that individual feat was not worth bringing up until *many* years later. For the first time in Yankees history, we had lost four consecutive World Series games.

We scored only four runs for the entire Series, and because we didn't score a run before the seventh inning in any of the games, we never held a lead against the Dodgers. A team that pitched like the Dodgers did in that Series will win every time, and probably in a sweep.

I never saw anyone pitch better than Koufax did in Game 1. His fastball was just taking off out of his hand, and he was throwing a straight changeup off his fastball. His changeup looked exactly like his fastball coming in, and we would swing so far out in front of the pitch that we were helpless to make contact. Plus, his curveball would drop off a dime, and he was throwing it precisely where he wanted to. He always seemed to be ahead in the count. As great a pitcher as he was, I don't think he could have pitched a better game than that one.

One of my sons told me about the 1975 movie *One Flew over the Cuckoo's Nest* about a man who spends time in a mental institution. The character, portrayed by Jack Nicholson, makes up a broadcast of the '63 Series in which I hit a double off Sandy Koufax, followed by back-to-back home runs by Tresh and Mantle.

My response to that was, "No wonder he's in an insane asylum."

If I had been asked to name the best pitcher in baseball at that time other than a teammate (Whitey), I would have picked Koufax. Yogi Berra apparently felt the same way. He summed up Koufax's performance against us well when he said he could see how Koufax had won twenty-five games that season but couldn't see how he had lost five.

It was odd during that Series to look out from our dugout and see Moose Skowron standing over at first base in a Dodgers uniform. Moose had a good Series at the plate, and he hit a home run in Game 2. But he told me years later, as we continued our close friendship beyond our playing days, that being traded from the Yankees was the biggest disappointment of his career, and that defeating us in the World Series that year was a hollow victory. As far as I knew, he never wore his '63 World Series ring.

But if I ever find out that Moose actually paid Los Angeles second baseman Dick Tracewski to catch his pop-ups for him . . .

Chapter 13
RALLYING UNDER YOGI

WHEN OUR FAMILY ARRIVED in Fort Lauderdale, Florida, for spring training in 1964, we had a special new Richardson with us: our second daughter, Jeannie.

The Yankees had a new manager as well, but he had a familiar face. Ralph Houk had moved into the front office to become the general manager, and Yogi Berra took over the role of running the team.

I had liked Ralph all the way back in our days together in Denver, and my best years as a Yankee had come with Ralph as the manager. I was happy to have Yogi as our manager too. He had played eighteen seasons with the Yankees, so he knew the Yankee way of doing things as well as anyone. Although Yogi had no managerial experience, I knew he was a smart baseball man and would do well.

The first obstacle for Yogi would be the transition from player to manager. We all had been his teammates, but now he would be the man making the decisions. He went from being our peer to our boss. The transition got off to a rough start.

The day before spring training was due to start, Yogi came by the house that Betsy and I were renting. "I want to try something out," he said. "Tomorrow I'll be talking to the ball club for the very first time as the manager. I'm gonna set some rules." Yogi then began listing his rules: no tennis, no swimming, no golf, no card playing, and so on. Then, Yogi said, he would tell the players, "We'll work hard on the field, but we'll have some fun, too."

He looked at us and asked, "How does that sound?"

"That sounds good," I told him, and Betsy agreed.

The next day he gathered all the players and began reciting what he had said in our living room. Yogi had made it to about his third or fourth "no" rule when Mickey threw down his bat onto the concrete floor, said, "I quit," and walked out to a chorus of laughter.

There went Yogi's big opening speech.

A Roller-Coaster Season

We lost our first three games of the 1964 season in eleven, eleven, and twelve innings, respectively. Apparently nothing was going to come easy for us that year. And naturally every difficulty we experienced sparked speculation among the press and fans as to whether the rookie manager was to blame. Yogi, though, remained resolute, assuring us and the media that we would be in our usual position at the end of the season.

It didn't help that, although Mantle and Maris were playing, both were hampered by nagging injuries. Al Downing and Jim Bouton had early injury problems too, and that strained the pitching staff.

We were slipping a bit in the standings in June before we ran off a seven-game winning streak that included a five-game sweep of the then-first-place White Sox. Just like that, we were right back among the league leaders. That entire summer was a roller-coaster ride. We would be up with a good stretch, then dip with a bad stretch, then back up, then back down.

A high point of that summer for me was receiving the Lou Gehrig Memorial Award. The annual award had been created by Phi Delta Theta, Gehrig's fraternity at Columbia University, to honor the baseball player who best exemplified Gehrig's character on and off the field. I had been named winner of the award after the previous season, but the presentation took place during the '64 season. I can't tell you how much that award meant to me.

My respect for Gehrig had only grown since I first saw *The Pride of the Yankees*, and I was deeply honored to be recognized with that award in his name. The fact that the recognition went beyond the playing field made that day all the more special. And to top it off, I also recorded my one-thousandth career hit that day—a single off Frank Baumann in a doubleheader against the White Sox.

At the All-Star break we were tied with Chicago three games behind Baltimore. I was hitting .249 and made my only start in an All-Star Game. We ended the first half of the season at home, and because the All-Star Game was slated for the next day at the New York Mets' Shea Stadium, that game had the bonus of not requiring extra travel.

I was in the American League's starting lineup with Mantle and Ellie Howard, and I batted seventh and played the complete game. In the eighth inning—with another teammate, Joe Pepitone, on first as a pinch runner—I singled off Houston Astros pitcher Turk Farrell. I would play in two more All-Star Games before retiring, but that was my only hit in eleven total at bats during the games.

When the playoff race resumed, so did our roller-coaster

ride. We were on a slight rise when we returned to Chicago in mid-August. But the Sox swept us in a four-game series, and we fell to four and a half games behind them.

As you might guess, we were all pretty down during the bus ride to O'Hare airport after that series. Then Phil Linz decided to pull out his harmonica. I need to back up a little to tell that story.

Earlier in the season, on a trip to play the Minnesota Twins, Tony Kubek and I had accepted an invitation to visit the head-quarters of Billy Graham's ministry. Tony had picked up a little chorus book there that he liked, and when we returned to our hotel, he had said, "I'd like to sing some of these songs."

I suggested he call Spud Murray, our batting practice pitcher, who I knew would rush right over with his harmonica. The three of us were up all night belting out tunes from that songbook. The next morning at the team breakfast in the hotel restaurant, some players were yawning and obviously weary. Tony and I asked what was wrong, and one answered, "Well, there were some drunks up over our room singing and playing a harmonica all night long. We didn't get any sleep."

Tony had enjoyed that night so much—not to mention the story about us "drunks"—that he'd gone to a Marshall Field's while we were in Chicago and bought four harmonicas. He'd kept one for himself and given one each to me, Tommy Tresh, and Phil Linz. Phil had his harmonica with him when we boarded that bus for the airport after being swept by the White Sox. With the bus quiet, Linz pulled out his harmonica.

Yogi, in the front where the manager sits, heard an odd but brief noise coming from the rear of the bus. He turned and looked around with a "Surely I didn't just hear that" expression, then turned back to the front.

About twenty seconds later, Linz gave another shrieking blow on his harmonica. That time Yogi jumped up, turned to face the back of the bus, and said, "Put that thing in your pocket!" Or something to that effect, because I can't use Yogi's exact words.

"What'd he say?" Linz asked those around him in the back.

Mickey was sitting across the aisle from Linz and whispered back, "He said he couldn't hear you. Play it again—louder."

Linz did as Mickey suggested.

Yogi was furious. He stomped down the aisle, grabbed the harmonica from Linz's hands, and flung it. The harmonica struck Joe Pepitone, who launched into comical theatrics about being injured and threatening to sue. Yogi fined Linz something like two hundred dollars—a heavy fine back then. It worked out great for Linz, though, because he wound up signing an endorsement contract with a harmonica company that paid him many times more than the amount of his fine.

It didn't work out nearly as well for Yogi.

There were reporters traveling with us—seven, I believe—and they got together and decided not to file stories about the harmonica incident because it could look like there was dissension on the team. But one of the reporters decided to break ranks with the rest and submitted an account to his newspaper. Once that paper printed the harmonica story, of course, all of them did, and the story made big headlines. The bad publicity was more fuel for the fire for all the Yogi critics, who already held him responsible for our up-and-down season.

Still, Yogi kept telling us and the press that everything was going to be fine by season's end. Yogi was correct.

On September 3, Baltimore led the league, and the White Sox were next, one game behind. We were three games behind Chicago. On September 17, the three of us were tied for first and set up for an exciting race to the finish. And only a week later, we were four games ahead of both Baltimore and Chicago, with only ten games left to play. Once again we had pulled everything together for a long, late-season winning streak—this one at eleven in a row—even though we'd lost Kubek during that time to a wrist injury.

We cooled off slightly after that, going 4–4 the rest of the way, but we still were able to clinch the pennant on the next-to-last day of the season.

Not in the Cards

Over in the National League, the Philadelphia Phillies held a six-and-a-half-game lead with twelve games remaining but lost ten games in a row and were passed by the St. Louis Cardinals. On October 7 we met the Cardinals at Busch Stadium in St. Louis for Game 1 of the 1964 World Series.

Whitey Ford had pitched through pain and numbness in his arm during the regular season, but our Chairman was out there toeing the rubber for us to start Game 1. Unfortunately, Whitey had more heart than arm that postseason. We scored four runs in five innings off Cardinals starter Ray Sadecki and scored another run off the bullpen to give us more runs in that game than we had scored in all of the '63 Series. It wasn't enough, though. Mike Shannon hit a monstrous homer for St. Louis, and the Cards took the first game 9–5.

Cardinals ace Bob Gibson had won his team's pennant clincher in relief, then rested until Game 2, when he made his first career Series start against our rookie, Mel Stottlemyre. Against the odds, we beat Gibson 8–3, with four insurance runs scored in the ninth after Gibson had left. Our offense was off to a good start in the Series, and I had gone 2 for 5 in each of the first two games.

Pitchers dominated Game 3 of the Series. Behind a six-hitter from Bouton, we won 2–1 to take a 2–1 Series lead.

Then in Game 4, with a chance to go up 3–1, we scored three runs in the bottom of the first. Sadecki, the Game 1 winner, lasted only five batters. Linz, who was playing for Kubek, doubled to lead off. I doubled in Linz, Maris singled me to third, and Mantle singled to score me. Mantle was thrown out trying to stretch his hit into a double, but that was the only out Sadecki recorded before being pulled in favor of Roger Craig. Ellie Howard, the first batter against Craig, singled in Maris for a 3–0 lead. The score stayed that way as Al Downing retired St. Louis 1–2–3 in four of the first five innings. But in the top of the sixth, the game—and the Series—turned.

The Cardinals had runners on first and second, with one out, when Dick Groat hit a double play grounder to me. I fielded the ball, but not cleanly. It took me a split second longer to get control of the ball, bringing it out of my glove. That would be just enough to keep us from turning two. Then I flipped the ball to Linz, who was playing shortstop, for a force-out at second. But Linz, less experienced than Kubek, came across the bag as though he still wanted to try to turn a double play instead of staying on the bag. Because of my bobble, the timing was all off on the toss, and Linz couldn't handle my flip. So in a matter of seconds we'd gone from two likely outs to one and then to none. I was given an error on the play, and deservedly so.

The bases were now loaded, with only one out. Then Ken Boyer—brother of our third baseman, Clete—followed with a grand slam that gave the Cardinals a 4–3 lead. That would be the final score.

I drove home that evening aware I had made a very costly error. Before that sixth inning we'd had a chance to take control of the Series. Instead, the Series was 2–2, and St. Louis had Bob Gibson ready to pitch Game 5.

Gibson blanked us through eight innings in the next game. Trailing 2–0 in the bottom of the ninth, we were in danger of going to St. Louis one loss away from elimination. Mantle led off by reaching on an error. Howard struck out, and Pepitone grounded out. But then Tresh homered off Gibson to tie the score and send the game into extra innings.

In the tenth Tim McCarver's three-run homer put St. Louis back in the lead, and Gibson—pitching on three days' rest—returned to the mound for the bottom of the tenth. I managed a two-out single, but I was our only base runner that inning. We lost the game 5–2, putting us behind 3–2 in the Series.

Bouton pitched great for us in Game 6, and with Pepitone, Maris, and Mantle hitting home runs, we won 8–3 to set up another winner-take-all Game 7.

Gibson again started for the Cards, this time on *two* days' rest. The game was scoreless going into the bottom of the fourth, when McCarver reached on an error that scored a run. After Mike Shannon singled McCarver to third, St. Louis manager Johnny Keane called for a double steal. Shannon broke for second, and on Ellie's throw to me there, McCarver took off for home. I cut in front of the bag, fielded Ellie's throw, and fired back to home. The throw wasn't in time to get the sliding McCarver.

The Cards scored one more run in that inning, and we were down 3–0 with Gibson on the mound. An inning later St. Louis handed its ace a 6–0 lead. We had to find a way to put a couple of runs on the board against Gibson and hope he tired late. We could not afford to go into the late innings down by six.

To start the sixth inning, I reached on an infield single, and Maris singled to right. Mantle then hit a three-run homer to left center to cut our deficit in half, making the score 6–3. That was Mickey's third home run of the Series and the eighteenth of his World Series career. He had erased Babe Ruth's record of fifteen.

Ken Boyer hit his second home run of the Series in the bottom of the seventh, and St. Louis was up 7–3. Gibson went on to sit down Mantle, Howard, and Pepitone in order in the eighth. It was going to take a ninth-inning rally against Gibson for us to have a chance to win.

We almost got that rally. Clete Boyer and Linz hit solo home runs to make the score 7–5. With two outs, I came to the plate. I knew all I needed to do was get on base and then a tiring Gibson—if he was left in the game—would be looking at Maris at the plate and Mantle on deck. But I made the final out, hitting a pop fly to Dal Maxvill at second base. If I could have just gotten on base, Maris and maybe Mantle would have had a chance. Instead, we ended up losing both the game and the Series.

I don't think enough can be said about Bob Gibson's performance in that Series. On limited rest he made three starts, threw twenty-seven innings, allowed twenty-three hits, and struck out thirty-one batters. He well deserved his MVP award.

Gibson was a great athlete—he also played basketball for the Harlem Globetrotters—and a real competitor. I've always considered him a right-handed Koufax, with one key difference: Gibson was mean on the mound. He pitched throughout his career with a well-earned reputation for knocking down batters. He loosened me up in the batter's box on two occasions—and both were in Old Timers' Games!

The first time came after José Cardenal had homered off Gibson. I was the next batter. "I wouldn't go up there if I were you," Cardenal joked.

"Surely," I said, "he wouldn't hit a sixty-year-old guy who hasn't picked up a bat in all these years."

When the first pitch sailed behind my head, everyone in the game, including Gibson, started laughing. Even though Gibson was playing around, I did *not* think that would be a good time to remind Bob that I had gotten seven hits off him in the '64 Series.

Chapter 14

HEADED FOR HOME

THE DISAPPOINTMENT of losing the 1964 World Series was similar to what we felt after losing to Pittsburgh in '60—and to me it felt very personal. Any seven-game Series has opportunities to go either way, but I felt like my error in Game 4 had been the hinge moment. My batting average for that Series was my highest yet—.406, with at least one hit in all seven games—but what I remember best all these years later is that bobbled grounder that should have been a double play.

When my season-ending pop-up had been secured and I veered right from the first base line toward our dugout, I could not have imagined that my at bat would be the last for any Yankee in a World Series for twelve years. The 1964 season is now marked as the end of that Yankees dynasty. The slide was unexpected and unbelievably rapid. The changes began almost immediately after the Series.

On the charter plane returning to New York, Betsy and I sat with Yogi.

"I'm meeting with the Yankees tomorrow," Yogi said. "Do you think I should ask for a two-year contract?" (At that time managers worked on one-year contracts.)

"Absolutely!" Betsy said. "If it hadn't been for Robert making that error, we'd have won the World Series."

Yogi offered a small chuckle while I squirmed in my seat. Betsy still claims she wasn't trying to say anything negative about me, just trying to encourage Yogi. *ThAnKs!*

The day after the team arrived in New York, Betsy and I started home for South Carolina. As we drove, we heard on the radio that Yogi had been fired as manager. We both were stunned, and the impact of my Game 4 error suddenly stung me even more. I might have cost our team the World Series. Could I also have cost my friend Yogi his job?

I don't have an answer for that because I still don't understand why Yogi was fired. Neither do the teammates I've discussed this with.

Yogi was a good manager. That was a difficult season, and there were several points in the regular season where things could have fallen apart, but Yogi got us through them. Even though he had been our teammate just the year before, we always understood that he was our manager now. He was never buddy-buddy with the players, even though we laughed and had a lot of fun together. And we were always clear where we stood with him. Even on that first day in spring training, when Mickey threw down his bat and walked out of the meeting, Yogi knew he didn't mean it, and everyone there that day knew Yogi had Mickey's full support.

We played hard for him. Yogi wouldn't stand for anything less. If a player needed a little motivation, Yogi never hesitated to provide some for him. Often he did so in an animated, colorful

manner, but we didn't mind. He was just passionate about baseball being respected and played the proper way.

I wasn't a pitcher, but I thought Yogi did a fine job of handling
our pitching staff too. As a catcher, he had a good instinct about
when to leave a pitcher in and when to take one out. I can't remember a time during that season when I looked back and wondered why
Yogi had made a particular move. That's why his firing is still a mys-
tery to me.

Shortly after Yogi was let go, Johnny Keane was introduced
as our manager—the same Johnny Keane whose Cardinals had
just defeated us in the World Series. It was later reported that the
Yankees' decision to fire Yogi had actually been made during the
summer, over concerns that he had lost control of the team. (He
hadn't.) But I don't think the Yankees would have been able to fire
Yogi if we had won the World Series, and if I hadn't bobbled that
grounder in Game 4, we probably would have.

Other factors were clearly at play, of course, including a
change in ownership. In early November, CBS had purchased
80 percent of the Yankees franchise from the ownership team
of Dan Topping and Del Webb. Although the transaction date
occurred after the World Series, the process would have required
several months, and I wondered how it affected Yogi's firing.
(CBS would later obtain the remaining 20 percent and maintain
ownership until 1973, when a group led by George Steinbrenner
bought the club. The Yankees would never make the playoffs
under CBS's ownership.)

Public relations may have played a role in Yogi's firing as well.
The New York Mets had joined the National League in 1962 and
hired Casey Stengel as their first manager. Although Casey's early
teams suffered through the poor seasons expected of a start-up
club, Casey's popularity among the New York media had created
an immediate competition for fans. The criticisms of Yogi as a

manager—especially exaggerated reports about the harmonica incident in Chicago—were public relations losses for the Yankees.

Whatever the reasons for Yogi's firing, the changes that followed it were dramatic and came in a flurry. They came at a time when I was considering a dramatic change myself: retiring from baseball.

I had accepted the traveling schedule of a major leaguer as part of the lifestyle, but during the '64 season I'd begun to regret how much time I was spending on the road. We had four kids, and that was a big load for Betsy when I was on road trips. Plus, our two oldest, Robby and Ronnie, had turned seven and six, respectively, during the summer. At their ages they were well into the school routine, and for our family that meant a very complicated school routine.

In the spring we'd take them out of school in Sumter and send them down to Florida, where they would spend the seven weeks of spring training in a private school that could accommodate them for that short time. Then they would return to Sumter while I headed north for the regular season. When school ended, Betsy and the kids would join me at the home we rented in New Jersey. Then when it was time for school to start back up, they would return to Sumter, and I would rejoin them there as soon as our season ended.

All that moving required a lot of work—mostly for Betsy—but we wanted to spend as much time together as a family as we could, and not just during the off-seasons. Some players didn't do that for various reasons. Mickey's and Roger's families, for example, did not move to New York for the season. Betsy and I believed our togetherness was worth the effort, but as the kids grew, it was getting harder and harder. Besides, Robby and Ronnie were at the ages where they could begin playing sports in leagues, and it absolutely ate at my insides to be missing their games.

Late in the season, as I had done once before, I went to Ralph Houk and told him I thought it was time for me to retire. Again Ralph advised me otherwise. He understood my situation, but he stood firm in his belief that the spiritual impact I wanted from my life could best be made as a member of the Yankees.

During the off-season I told Ralph that I would return to New York for another year. Before we began spring training, a reporter learned that I had intended not to return and then changed my mind. The reporter put two and two together and came up with five. The result was an article that said I had decided to retire if Yogi returned as manager but then decided to come back after he was fired.

I had a good relationship with the media that covered us and had friends among the press corps. They treated me kindly throughout my career. However, it seemed there was always one sportswriter in the group who jumped to conclusions in his reporting, and that article demonstrated the harm even one article could cause.

The newspaper printed a large retraction of the story, but not even the retraction could undo all the damage. I cleared things up with Yogi, telling him the story was not true. He knew I had been a big supporter of his, so there was no problem there. But after the article came out, I began receiving hate mail from Yankees fans who supported Yogi. Betsy quit reading my mail for a while because of that. I wish we could have brought that sportswriter in to help answer the fans' letters!

The Decline Begins

The 1965 season turned out to be a tough one for the Yankees. We had missed the playoffs back in '59, but that year felt like an anomaly. That had been a season in which we battled injuries and things just never seemed to get going, and the feeling was frustration more than anything else. In '65, the predominant feeling was hopelessness.

I think the effects of the Yankees' sale began to become evident during that season. We didn't know what all had taken place to prepare the franchise for sale, but it was widely speculated that some cost-cutting in the farm system had been part of the process. Whatever the reason, our minor leagues had thinned out talentwise.

In the past, it seemed like every season we'd hear names of up-and-coming players who were being developed to fill positions with the parent club. That depth allowed us to trade off name players, who were beginning to start the descent in their careers, for young talent that could either step in and play for us right away or be sent down to develop while a primed youngster from Triple-A came up and joined us. But with our farm system producing fewer of those prospects, we became one of the teams trading young talent for veteran players who, it was hoped, could help us win that season.

In '65, we were hit with the combination of injuries (again) and veteran players who were beginning to show their age.

Catcher Elston Howard had elbow surgery and played 110 games. Shortstop Tony Kubek's back pained him so badly that at times he had difficulty simply bending over, and he played 109 games. Mickey Mantle moved from center field to left to remove some of the burden on his aching knees, and he played hurt most of the season while appearing in 122 games. Right fielder Roger Maris suffered a hand injury and played 46 games.

Our numbers told the story that year. Mickey hit .255 with only nineteen home runs. Tom Tresh, who moved to center field, led us in home runs (twenty-six), runs batted in (seventy-four), and batting average (.279). Those weren't anywhere near typical team-leading statistics for us. My numbers were down too. My batting average slipped twenty points, from .267 to .247. My runs scored dropped from ninety to seventy-six.

Among the pitchers, Whitey Ford's arm soreness worsened. There were days when Whitey had trouble even lifting his arm above his head, but he was a gamer and was going to take the ball every time he was scheduled to start. Whitey won sixteen games that season, but he also lost thirteen—the most in his long career.

In his second year, Mel Stottlemyre was our best pitcher and won twenty games. But Al Downing finished 12–14, and Jim Bouton dropped from 18–13 the year before to 4–15.

Despite a three-game winning streak during the first week of the season, we got off to a 3–6 start. We didn't spend a single day in first place and ended up with a 77–85 record, putting us in sixth place in the ten-team league and twenty-five games behind the first-place Minnesota Twins.

On road trips that season Tony and I sometimes sat around in our hotel rooms and discussed our futures. For a variety of reasons, neither of us planned on sticking around for 1966.

More than ever I yearned to be home to take my kids to school, help them with their homework in the afternoons, and watch their games or help coach their teams. Tony shared my yearnings for a normal family life, and his feelings were multiplied by his persistent back problems.

On top of that, it seemed our team was falling apart. The players who had been most responsible for our success finally seemed to be reaching the downside of their careers in '65. There wasn't enough help coming from the top end of our minor league system. And the lower levels had become so depleted that there wasn't enough there, either, to use in a trade for a veteran or two who could lift us back into pennant contention.

Some of the younger players who did come up didn't seem to understand the Yankee way of doing things. There was more interest in individual achievements than team accomplishments. I had noticed signs of that after the '63 and '64 World Series, when it came time for us to decide how to split our postseason earnings.

When I came up, the veteran players had been generous in including younger players who hadn't played much (such as me). Later, when I had earned a few stripes, I'd been part of the group that wanted to make sure we continued that practice. For instance, we had voted to give batboys a full share. We were making good salaries, and that bonus money meant a great deal to the young players and the batboys.

But in '63 and '64, some of the newer players had been out-spoken in saying the players who had played less "deserved" less. *Deserved* wasn't a good word to me because I had never under-stood why baseball players "deserved" better salaries than, say, schoolteachers.

The "me first" attitude I saw developing was yet another reason I thought it was time to retire. So I played practically all of the '64 season thinking that my double play partner and I would go out together after that year.

Knowing that Kubek and I planned to make '65 our final sea-son, the Yankees asked whether one of us would stay through '66 to help tutor our infield replacements. Tony agreed to stay. But as the '65 season wore on, the condition of Tony's back made it obvious he would not be able to play beyond that season. So the Yankees asked if I would reconsider and stay through 1966.

Houk wanted to talk about a possible contract with me. I wasn't the best negotiator, and in that era of baseball, players were not represented by agents. When I was with the Yankees—and I assume this was true with many other teams—a player could not bring along anyone else to help him with his contract. After the '61 season, Maris's brother, who was a sharp businessman, had asked to accompany Roger when it came time to discuss his next season's contract. He'd been kicked out of the office. "We'll only talk with Roger," he was told.

After the '62 season, when I had led the American League in hits, I had gone in to discuss my contract for '63. Roy Hamey was the general manager at the time, but only Mickey and perhaps Whitey and Yogi talked directly to the GM about contracts. The rest of us went to the assistant general manager.

"Well, you had a pretty good year," the assistant GM told me. "I was thinking in terms of a five-thousand-dollar raise."

"Five?" I asked. "I was thinking about fifteen."

"Okay, okay," he said. "We'll settle at ten."

"Okay," I said, and that was the extent of the "negotiations."

When I met with Ralph to talk about my final contract with the Yankees, he said, "We'll offer you sixty thousand dollars to play one more season."

"I'm not worth sixty thousand," I said. I had made forty thousand the previous season and didn't feel I warranted a twenty-thousand-dollar raise. (There's probably a reason that players today aren't clamoring to have me as their agent.)

"How about you pay me forty-five thousand and give fifteen thousand to charity?"

The Yankees wrote out three five-thousand-dollar checks to give to charities of my choice. Also, in appreciation of my returning to help them out for the '66 season, they added four years to my contract at fifteen thousand per year to be their "special assignment scout." Or, as Ralph explained, "You don't have to do anything."

The Season That Wouldn't End

The 1966 season turned out to be a long one. Only seventeen games in, we were already ten games out of first place. With our record at 4–16 on May 7, Johnny Keane was fired, and Ralph came back down from the front office to manage.

Keane wasn't a good hire for our team. He was a wonderful man, and Betsy and I once had an enjoyable visit with him and his family in Texas. However, he had a National League managerial style, and though it had won a world championship with St. Louis, it just wasn't a good fit for us.

For instance, he would relieve Whitey Ford in the final innings of close games even though Whitey was pitching well. When Whitey was on, the best thing to do was to leave him in because we would eventually score a run for him.

In his season-plus with us, Keane never could develop a rapport with the players, and we just went down, down, down until he was fired.

Even with the managerial change and 140 games remaining, it was clear that we weren't going to work our way back into contention for the pennant in 1966. So it became a long, long season for us. The games didn't just *seem* to take longer; they actually were longer because we were giving up a lot more runs. The road trips become longer too, when you're losing the way we were.

Yankees fans were really down on Roger Maris that season. He was still bothered by the hand injury from the year before and slumped to a .233 average, with only thirteen home runs and forty-three RBIs. He knew I would be retiring and told me during the season that he wanted to retire too, even asking what paperwork I had completed.

"I put my name on the voluntarily retiring list," I said. "That means I'm saying I won't be back next year, but I can change my mind. If I do, I'll have to wait a certain amount of time in April before I can come back and play."

Roger indicated he might do that too.

"You don't need to do that," I told him. "The most they'd cut your salary for your next contract is 20 percent. You ought to wait until you get your contract offer. See what it says, and then make a decision."

"I'll do that," he said.

As it turned out, he never needed to. After the close of that season the Yankees traded him to St. Louis for Charley Smith, an infielder from Charleston, South Carolina.

Roger played two years with the Cardinals, whose fans properly appreciated him.

Saying Farewell

We trudged our way through the 1966 season, finishing 70–89 and in last place, twenty-six and a half games back. I ended the season with a .251 average, seventy-one runs scored, seven home runs—seven!—and six stolen bases. I made the All-Star team for the seventh time, but my Gold Glove award streak was ended after five seasons in a row by Bobby Knoop of the recently renamed California Angels.

Ralph started me regularly at second base, with prospect Horace Clarke playing shortstop most of the second half of the season. With about two weeks to play, Ralph pulled me aside and asked if I would mind sitting out some games so he could move Clarke to second and give another prospect—Bobby Murcer—a look at shortstop. (Murcer was the one who would wear jersey number 1 after I retired.) I agreed to cut back my playing time, and Ralph gave me the opportunity to make a trip home to Sumter to see my family after the kids had settled in to school there.

Saturday, September 17, was set up as Bobby Richardson Day at Yankee Stadium—part of the final home stand of the season. I was the tenth Yankee to be honored with an on-field ceremony. With us so far out of the pennant race, attendance had dwindled to the point that we weren't even drawing ten thousand fans for our final home games. So I was honored and humbled to learn that more than twenty-one thousand came out for Bobby Richardson Day.

Betsy and the kids drove in for the special day. My mother and Betsy's mother came too, as did several of our friends. The mayor of Sumter also was in attendance, along with a large group from back home. Betsy and I were busy coming up with places for our friends to stay.

I had asked that George Beverly Shea, a dear friend from the Billy Graham Crusades, sing "How Great Thou Art" as part of the ceremony. Bob Fishel, the Yankees' public relations director, had expressed reservations about granting that request. But once Bob found out how ticket sales for that game were going as compared to sales for our other games, he said, "Go ahead. He can sing anything he wants to."

George actually got into a bit of trouble with his sister when she found out that Ballantine Beer sponsored Yankees' broadcasts. "I can't believe you're singing on television for Ballantine Beer," she scolded him. Betsy and I saw George in 2011 in North Carolina, and he was still telling that story.

Our entire family went out on the field for the ceremony. Robby and Ron looked grown-up in their dark suits, and Christie and Jeannie looked so cute in their red dresses and white gloves. Christie, with her sweet and gentle personality, stayed by Mom's side. Jeannie, two at the time, was a daddy's girl. When we walked out on the field, Jeannie pleaded that I carry her, so I held her in one arm during most of the ceremony.

Steve Hamilton, my roommate that season, gave me a beautiful oak gun case on behalf of the players. I was also presented with a brand-new Dodge Monaco station wagon.

When my turn came to speak, little Jeannie still didn't want me to leave her, so we walked to the microphone hand in hand. When I began to speak, I could hear an echo reverberating throughout Yankee Stadium. It was then—not the first time I visited Yankee Stadium as a seventeen-year-old or when I played my first game in the House That Ruth Built—that I had my first "Wow, this is Yankee Stadium!" moment. The echo of my voice reminded me of when I'd heard Lou Gehrig's gripping farewell speech on this same field in *The Pride of the Yankees*.

Using the words Gehrig had used and Mickey had echoed in

a similar Yankee Stadium speech, I concluded by telling the fans, "How lucky it has been for me to have been a Yankee."

Then I added, "To God be the glory."

Later Betsy's mother good-naturedly corrected me for saying "lucky." "We're not lucky," she said. "We're *blessed*!"

Even though I was spending more time out of the lineup by that point, Ralph had told me he wanted me to play the final game at Yankee Stadium and the final game of the season in Chicago.

On Sunday, September 25, I said farewell to the old Stadium in a 3–1 win over Boston by going 1 for 4. I cleanly fielded two grounders in the last inning, both times flipping to the shortstop for a force-out at second. Why couldn't that have happened in the '64 Series?

Then on Sunday, October 2, I said farewell to the majors in a 2–0 win over the White Sox by again going 1 for 4.

My last game was not an emotional day for me. By that point, I was so ready to go home to my family that I wasn't really thinking about anything else—or the fact that this would be the final game of my career. It is sad to say now, but I felt more relief than anything. The season I thought would never end had finally ended.

When I look back on that last day in Chicago, what stands out most to me is something that happened off the field. A couple of weeks earlier, when Ralph Houk had said he wanted to play me in the final game, he also invited me to do something else on my last day as a Yankee. I hope it was an indication of what type of impact player I had been for all my career.

Ralph looked at the schedule and saw the game was on a Sunday. "Let's have a team devotion," he said. "And you be in charge of that devotion."

Chapter 15

NO REGRETS

I FEEL BLESSED TO HAVE walked away from my career with the Yankees still loving the game of baseball. The major league lifestyle—mostly the road trips—had become a sacrifice I was no longer willing to make, and the many losses in '66 had us all looking to the calendar to see when that miserable season would mercifully end. But I left major league baseball with no bitterness toward the game.

Baseball had been great to me. However, I also knew my retirement was coming at the right time. There had been no drop-off in my skills over the previous two or three years. How many more seasons could I have played at that level? I don't know. But I had no regrets about how I left the Yankees, nor did I ever regret retiring.

By giving me four years on my contract beyond my final playing season, the Yankees did me a great service. Although the fifteen thousand dollars per year was a reduction from what I had made as a player, the Yankees basically allowed me four years to decide what I wanted to do with my life.

As a special assignment scout, my job was to visit with the minor league teams to encourage the players and share principles of the Yankees' organization. With no other required duties, I was able to devote the first portion of my retirement years to staying home year-round, doing things around the house and with the kids that I hadn't been able to do before. (I spent some time hunting, too, of course.)

I was pleased to receive plenty of opportunities to speak and share my faith. Being a *former* Yankee did nothing to decrease the number of offers I received. I traveled and spoke quite a bit, in fact. But I was in control of my schedule, and the trips away were short—nothing like the two weeks at a time I'd been away in the majors.

I also took advantage of my free time to play in Old Timers' Games, even though at age thirty-one I made for a young old-timer. It was a special treat to play in the exhibition games with legendary players I had grown up watching. Those games allowed me the opportunity to get to know the likes of Stan Musial, Warren Spahn, Bob Feller, and Allie Reynolds, to name just a few of the friends I made.

There was a pecking order for how players were introduced before Old Timers' Games, and I still remember how the fans' cheers would increase as the announcer worked his way to the biggest names in baseball. There was nothing quite as thrilling as being in Yankee Stadium when the end of the list was reached and it was Joe DiMaggio's time to be introduced. The announcer would begin, "The greatest living Yankee . . ." and the cheering would become so thunderous that we could not hear the announcer say DiMaggio's name.

When I was thirty-three, I played shortstop at an Old Timers'

Game in Atlanta, and the Braves asked if I would consider coming out of retirement to play for them. Even though it would have been fun to play close to home, I told the Braves, "No, if I were going to play again, I'd play for the Yankees."

But, truly, I never had any desire to return. I've never said, "I wish I had played four or five more years."

A New Challenge

Paul Dietzel, the athletic director/football coach at the University of South Carolina in Columbia, had asked me right after I retired whether I would be interested in coaching his school's baseball team. I told him no.

"I've got four years left on my contract," I said. "So I'm not ready to do anything like that yet."

When I later spoke at an athletic banquet at the school, Dietzel made the same offer. Again I declined.

Some time after that, he asked for a third time. "I'm not going to bother you anymore, but I'd really like you to be the baseball coach."

The third time was the charm.

"Well," I said, "I'm ready to try it."

Then Coach Dietzel told me what my salary would be.

"I can't live on that," I told him.

Dietzel upped the offer.

"Okay," I said, "I'll come and try it."

That was in 1969, and I was still under contract to the Yankees. NCAA rules would not allow me to coach if I had a contract with a professional team. So before I could sign my contract with USC, I had to talk to the Yankees about getting out of my contract with them.

I called Lee MacPhail. Lee had worked in the Yankees' front office when I joined the franchise and had gone on to be general manager and club president of the Baltimore Orioles during part of my playing days. His younger sister, Jeannie, was a close friend to Betsy and me who often visited our home in Sumter. Now Lee was back with the Yankees as the GM.

"Now wait a minute," Lee told me. "If you want to come back, you can be our Triple-A manager, or you can be a broadcaster, or you can be one of our major league coaches."

"No," I told my old friend, "the reason I got out was the travel involved."

Lee said the team would be happy to pay off what remained of my contract so I could coach at South Carolina. "When you get settled," he closed, "give us a call, and we'll bring the Yankees down to play your ball club."

My first season at USC was 1970. I was the school's first full-time baseball coach, and my assignment was "to put Gamecock baseball on the map." One of my first moves was to add pinstripes to the uniforms.

I continued to live in Sumter and commuted the forty-five miles to Columbia. In my first year at USC, Betsy and I had the whole team out to our house for a meal. I wanted to pull off a practical joke on my players. So I arranged with a friend who was a highway patrolman to pull over the team on its way out of Columbia. I had tipped off one of the players—Eddie Ford, Whitey's son—and told him that the patrolman would give the players a hard time and might even handcuff a player or two.

Eddie was a lot like his father when it came to jokes and pranks, so I knew he would play along perfectly. Sure enough, when the guys were stopped, Eddie started mouthing off to the patrolman. Some of his teammates began to panic. They kept trying to calm him down and get him to be quiet, but he continued to play along with the patrolman. "What are you doing?" the players asked Eddie. "He's going to put us *under* the jail if you don't stop."

Finally, the patrolman started laughing, and Eddie couldn't hold back his laughter any longer either. The patrolman let the boys off the hook, but they sure had a good story to tell when they arrived at our house.

Our USC team wasn't very good that first season, finishing 14–20. We were better the next year, with a 19-13 record. We steadily improved, until in 1974 we compiled a 48–8 record. That season ended with a 2–1 loss to the Miami Hurricanes in the NCAA regional tournament.

Before the next season, with a strong team coming back, I called Lee MacPhail.

"I'm ready for the Yankees to come play us," I informed him.

"I have a little problem," Lee told me. "We're traveling north with the Mets out of spring training. Would it be all right if the Yankees *and* the Mets come and play your club in Columbia?"

It didn't take me long to assure Lee that would be okay. And once the teams arrived, I made sure they received first-class treatment— except for the bus ride, that is. I picked up both teams at the airport in a red-and-white school bus, and I was driving the bus.

Our USC team chartered Greyhounds for our road trips, but it seemed like a waste of money to arrange charter buses just for a short ride from the airport. At least I knew the Yankees and Mets would have a friendly bus driver with me behind the wheel.

I had obtained a license to drive buses before we began chartering the Greyhounds. Up to that point, we often had a driver from the motor pool who would hop into the driver's seat with a cigarette dangling from his lips and pretty much staple the accelerator to the floor. I'd been so uncomfortable with that driver that I decided to get a license and drive the team myself.

The Yankees and Mets might not have had the fanciest mode of transportation, but we did treat them to a wonderful steak dinner—and a packed stadium. As if hosting both major league teams wasn't attractive enough to our fans, we had the added benefit of Yogi Berra, who was serving as the Mets' manager at the time. We filled every seat, and there were people standing anywhere there was a space.

We played three innings against the Yankees and three against the Mets, and then the Mets and Yankees played against each other under our stadium lights. To level the playing field, Yogi pitched against our team. It was a fantastic night for our players, our fans, and our program.

The big leaguers seemed to enjoy the exhibition too. Before the teams left, Mets pitcher Tom Seaver, who had played collegiate ball at the University of Southern California, said he had never seen a facility as nice as ours. That almost made me pop a few buttons on the chest of my jersey—I was so proud of what we were building at South Carolina.

In '75, we swept a late-season doubleheader against Georgia Southern, with whom we had built up a pretty good rivalry. Ron Polk, Georgia Southern's coach, resigned after that doubleheader. Because Ron left, fans of his team began hanging me in effigy. I asked myself, *What have I gotten myself into? Is it worth all of this?*

I tried to hire Ron as an assistant coach, but he became head coach at Mississippi State, where he would become known as the Father of Southeastern Conference Baseball. Ron retired in 2008 as one of college baseball's all-time winningest coaches, with a 1,373–702 record.

We finished the '75 season with a 51–6–1 record and reached the College World Series in Omaha, Nebraska, for the first time in school history. We advanced to the championship game but then lost 5–1 to the University of Texas team under coach Cliff Gustafson.

The following year would be my last at South Carolina. We

again reached the postseason, but Furman eliminated us. We ended the '76 season with a 38–14 record. That was the end of my run with the Gamecocks.

Teaching Baseball

I enjoyed teaching baseball to younger players, and I coached some fine young players at South Carolina. One special ballplayer was the son of my former teammate Whitey Ford. When I became coach at USC, I needed a shortstop, and Eddie Ford was the first player I recruited for that spot. I had watched Eddie work out occasionally at Yankee Stadium and knew he was a good fielder. Plus, he was a switch-hitter. Whitey and Eddie came in for a visit, and Eddie decided to join our program.

Whitey would visit to watch his son play, and if my team was in a little slump when he came in, Whitey would joke with me, "Let me take them out this weekend, and I'll get 'em loose for you."

"Aw, no, Whitey," I'd tell him. "You can't do that!"

That was Whitey—always cracking a joke.

Eddie once tried to pull off a hidden-ball trick that I actually foiled myself. I didn't like hidden-ball tricks, partly because of the one Puddin' Head Jones pulled on me during that exhibition game in 1956. I just didn't think trickery was the right way to defeat an opponent.

We were playing Clemson, an in-state rival. I also had a fun little coaching rivalry going on at the time with Clemson coach Bill Wilhelm.

A Clemson player doubled, and Eddie took the throw back into the infield and walked toward the mound. When he got to the back of the mound, he picked up the resin bag and handed it to our pitcher instead of the ball. Then, with the ball hidden in his glove, he started walking casually toward second base, where the base runner was standing away from the bag.

I recognized what Eddie was up to. "The shortstop's got the ball!" I shouted. "The shortstop's got the ball!"

The Clemson runner heard me and stepped back onto the bag before Eddie could tag him out. Eddie threw out his hands to ask what I was doing. Bill Wilhelm, who was in the third base coach's box in front of our dugout, turned and looked at me as though I were crazy. Perhaps I was crazy, but I hated that trick play so much that I wasn't going to allow even one of my players to pull it off.

I saw Eddie recently in New York City, and he brought up that play. He told me what he'd said when he learned that my son Rich and three of my grandchildren had graduated from Clemson: "I knew it! He was a double agent for Clemson." I'm still loyal to the USC Gamecocks, but I need a divided license plate to support both universities! Clemson is a fine school and an asset to our state.

Eddie became as good a defensive shortstop as there was in college baseball. He could drag-bunt as well as anyone I had seen since Mickey Mantle. Eddie had been our batboy, so he probably learned how to bunt like that from watching Mickey.

In 1974 Eddie was drafted in the first round by the Boston Red Sox and advanced up to the Triple-A Pawtucket team. The Red Sox wanted to send an infielder down to Pawtucket, and that would have temporarily bumped Eddie back down to Double-A. But he didn't want to go down, so he left baseball to work in a business that Whitey set up for him. Even if Eddie had gone to Double-A, I am convinced he would have quickly moved back up and played eight to ten years in the majors.

Eddie definitely stands out in my memory from those days at South Carolina. My favorite player of that era, though, was a right fielder named Robby who was there only one semester. His last name was Richardson, and he liked to call me Dad.

Robby started out at USC in the fall of '75, and it looked like he was going to be our fourth outfielder. We also knew by then that I would be leaving the next year, so Robby decided to go ahead and transfer out after one semester. As a transfer, he would have to sit out a season at his next school, and he wisely thought it would be best to do that as a freshman so he could still have three consecutive years to play. Robby transferred to Taylor University in Indiana and played there. He was a great player and a captain of his team.

I never got to coach my second son, Ron, who played at Wheaton College in Illinois. Like his brother, Ron was a great player and a team captain. He was also an Academic All-American. Robby teases Ron by saying that he made Academic All-American because his school gave him a better public relations push than Robby's school did. I was (and am) tremendously proud of them both. I was happy that they were able to earn what I never had: a college education.

During recruiting, I always emphasized the importance of that college education. When I came out of high school, there were no college scholarships for baseball, and back then, going to college did not really prepare a player for professional baseball. By the time I was a college coach, the level of play among the large college programs had improved so dramatically that they served as great preparation for professional baseball while allowing student athletes to receive free schooling.

I told recruits that if they came to South Carolina, they would play a sixty-game schedule against competition comparable to any minor league they could play in at their age, and after three years they would be eligible to be drafted by a major league franchise. I encouraged them to go to college, play in a great program, and receive an education that would open doors for them. Then if the opportunity presented itself to sign into professional baseball, that would be a great life. I still encourage young players to do the same today.

Not all my potential recruits followed my advice, though. Wade Boggs, for instance, opted to go straight to the minors out of high school. He spent eighteen seasons in the majors, had a .328 lifetime batting average, and was voted into the Hall of Fame the first year he was eligible.

I shared a table with Wade at a banquet in the early '90s, after he had left the Red Sox and signed a three-year contract with the Yankees.

"Do you really think you made the right decision about not playing for me?" I asked him.

Wade laughed. "Let me think for a minute. I just signed an eleven-million-dollar contract. Yeah, I think I did."

As good as those South Carolina teams were, I can't help but think of the players who could have made them even better. Among the recruits I was unable to convince to come to South Carolina were future major leaguers Willie Mays Aikens and Tino Martinez. To me, Tino looked the way I always pictured Lou Gehrig would have looked in person.

One of the best I did recruit wasn't a player. I was able to bring in Johnny Hunton as an assistant coach. Johnny was the older, more mature player who had taken me under his wing with the Binghamton Triplets in 1954 and had set the example for me of how to live a genuine Christian life in baseball.

I thoroughly enjoyed being back in a dugout with Johnny. He was one of the many people I would miss when I left coaching at South Carolina for, of all reasons, a chance to enter the crazy world of politics.

Chapter 16

A DIFFERENT TYPE OF RUN

HOW COULD I TELL the president of the United States, "No thanks, I'll pass"?

Even though I had no political experience or aspirations, President Gerald Ford asked me to run for the United States House of Representatives in 1976.

I had met my share of politicians through the years and had even been invited by President Richard Nixon to speak at a Sunday morning service in the White House. My sister Ann's husband, Art Beckstrom, who had flown over the Bay of Pigs, was commended for his service posthumously during our White House visit. We were able to take longtime friends Buck and Jenny Jackson with us on our trip to Washington. (Buck was the friend who had driven my family from Sumter to New Jersey each season after school let out.) At that time, of course, we had no idea that the president was in the middle of a scandal that would soon go public and become known as Watergate.

Despite my opportunities to meet with politicians, I had never given much thought to becoming one until President Ford asked me to run for office.

I knew President Ford through Billy Zeoli, a friend of his who also served as a kind of information spiritual adviser at the White House. Billy was a close friend of mine, too, and my son Robby would work for a number of years with him at Gospel Films. Billy had introduced me to President Ford, and I'd visited him several times in his home city of Grand Rapids, Michigan, and at the White House.

The president encouraged me to run for the House of Representatives seat from the Fifth Congressional District, but Harry S. Dent played the largest role in convincing me to make that move. Dent was a political strategist from South Carolina who had been a top advisor to President Nixon and had helped him win over traditionally Democratic voters in the South when Nixon defeated Hubert Humphrey in the 1968 presidential election. More recently he had become a Christian. Dent told me that Congress needed more conservatives and that he thought I could help my state and the nation in Washington, DC. I prayed and felt that I should make a bid for Congress.

Betsy wasn't as excited about my decision to run, but that changed when we received a letter from Walt and Lois Zigrang. They were missionaries in Africa whom we had met in a young couples' Sunday school class, starting a special friendship of more than fifty-five years. The Zigrangs did not know of my political plans. Their letter included a reference to Psalm 71:16: "I will go in the strength of the Lord GOD: I will make mention of thy righteousness, even of thine only." When Betsy read that verse, she suddenly felt peace about my running for office because she believed it would provide me with more opportunities to share my faith.

I ran against Democratic incumbent Ken Holland. Our part of South Carolina leaned so heavily toward Democrats at the time that there were longtime friends who told me, "I love you like a brother, but I've gotta vote straight Democrat all the way through." One lady in the lobby of a bank told me, "I'd die before I'd vote for a Republican."

It was shaping up to be a close race, and I was leading in the polls until right before Election Day, when presidential candidate Jimmy Carter made a swing through South Carolina in support of Democratic candidates. Still, I thought I would win up until the night of the election, when television broadcasts began projecting my opponent as the winner.

I lost the election by 3.2 percent—4,007 votes.

I have to tell you, that loss stung. I'm a competitor, whether I am in a pennant race, a political race, or a round of miniature golf with Betsy. And I really don't like to lose. In the long run, though, losing that election was probably one of the best things that ever happened to me.

Now I am thrilled that I did not win. I think my life would have turned out pretty awful if I had gone to Washington, DC. On one visit there, Betsy and I had been given tickets to a State of the Union address. The traffic was terrible, and I wound up giving away our tickets so I could stay at the hotel and watch the championship game of a big college basketball tournament. Sports was more for me than politics was.

Since that lost election, I haven't given serious thought to running for any other office. I did head up a South Carolina effort to vote in Ronald Reagan as president. I was able to meet Mr. Reagan, and we discussed his years in radio when he broadcast Chicago

Cubs games using telegraph accounts of their games as they happened. I felt like a kid again that day as we talked.

After Reagan won the election, he wrote me a letter expressing his appreciation for my help, and he later asked me to speak at National Day of Prayer events.

I still keep up with politics and speak at political prayer breakfasts because I am concerned about the direction our nation is headed. I'm dismayed that we have taken prayer and the Ten Commandments out of our public schools. When I speak in political settings, I like to remind the listeners of 2 Chronicles 7:14: "If my people, which are called by my name, shall humble themselves, and pray, and seek my face, and turn from their wicked ways; then will I hear from heaven, and will forgive their sin, and will heal their land."

So I stay active in politics, but don't expect to see my name in any elections. I almost moved to Washington, DC, once, and I don't think I could have lasted up there.

After my political loss, one habit from my baseball days helped me move on quickly. In baseball, players can't afford to dwell on losses. We played just about every day during the season, so losses had to be put behind us right away.

Every night I would go home or back to my hotel room and review that day's game. I would replay it in my head: *In the third inning I did such-and-such.* I could recall every moment. But after replaying that game in my mind, I knew it was time to move on to the next day's game. *So-and-so is pitching against us tomorrow, and we'll pick it up there and see how we go.* Or, *We're two games out of first, and we need to make sure we win three out of four in this series.*

That's basically what I did after the election. I put the election loss behind me and set my sights on what was next. That same week I drove down to Florida for a *Superstars* competition.

No Superstar

Young readers might not know much about the *Superstars* shows on television that year. (I don't use computers, but my children have introduced me to this *Google* word that lets people learn about things on the Internet. If you're not familiar with the *Superstars*, you can "Google it," as my kids say.) ABC televised these shows, in which athletes and celebrities competed against each other in a variety of athletic events.

Whatever humiliation I felt after the election was nothing compared to what I felt after my performance on *Superstars*. Robby went with me to Florida, where the show was being filmed, and chose the events he thought I'd have the best chance to do well in. I hate to think what would have happened if I'd taken part in the events he *didn't* think I'd do well in.

Robby had joked about signing me up for bowling and tennis because he didn't think I'd hurt myself in those competitions, and he was right. But he also entered me in cycling, and when I got off the bike, my legs were so sore I could barely walk.

In weight lifting I went up against Floyd Little, the great Denver Broncos' running back who had retired only the year before. Unlike today, when I was playing baseball, we were discouraged from lifting weights because it was thought that adding muscle would make us too tight and rob us of flexibility. So I had never lifted weights in my life. I started the competition lifting 150 pounds. Little—and his last name didn't fit him—started at 250 pounds. I was beaten before I had even grasped the bar.

In the hundred-yard dash, I competed against Jim Ryun, who had held the world record in the mile run. No contest there, either.

The only event I won was tennis, against former Boston Celtics star K. C. Jones.

The final event of each *Superstars* episode was the obstacle course, which included challenges such as a wall climb, a horizontal water jump, a high bar, a tube to run through, and a blocking sled. At the high bar, I jumped and hit the bar, knocked it off its base, and tumbled onto the padded mat. That brought me a penalty of ten extra seconds added to my time—as if my time weren't slow enough already!

That was one of the most embarrassing times in my life. I think I was even more humbled by the *Superstars* competition than by the Congressional election.

Back to School

Because my bid for Congress had been such a public loss, it was known that I had free time on my hands. So the headmaster of Ben Lippen School in Asheville, North Carolina (now in Columbia, South Carolina), mailed me a letter saying that the school had been praying to find the right person to fill an ambassador-type role, that he knew I had lost the election (thanks!), and that he wanted me to consider working with them.

Robby and Ron had both attended Ben Lippen—Robby and our daughter Christie wound up graduating from there—so I had an experiential knowledge of the school's mission and principles. I knew it would be an easy and rewarding assignment to share the school's virtues with others, so I said yes to the offer.

I worked with the school for two years. As a bonus to a role I thoroughly enjoyed, I was able to coach both my daughters on the school's basketball team and help out the baseball coach by pitching to the players during batting practice. Betsy was able to take on a kind of substitute-mother role with missionaries' children who boarded there.

Ben Lippen School had been founded by Columbia Bible College (now Columbia International University). The college did not actively seek donations, though it certainly accepted them. But my job as the school's representative, much to my relief, did not mean going out on the road to make sales pitches.

One of my visits on behalf of the school was with Anthony Rossi, the founder of Tropicana Products. Mr. Rossi was a wonderful and charitable Christian man who had supported the school and supplied orange juice to Ben Lippen and Columbia Bible College.

I was sitting in Mr. Rossi's office in Florida, updating him on what had been taking place at the school and college, when he said, "Tell me about the needs of the school."

I ran through the list of current pressing needs.

"What does that come to?" he asked.

I gave him a six-figure total.

"Well," Mr. Rossi said, "let me write you a check."

"No, no, no!" I said. "I didn't come down here for money. I just wanted to tell you what's happening at the school. Certainly you can pray about whether you want to be a part of it, but I'm not here to get a check from you."

"Okay," he said. I left his office that day without a check that would have covered all the needs on our list.

After about a week, however, a check for that full amount arrived from Mr. Rossi.

Mr. Rossi later asked me to move to Florida and be a part of his Aurora Foundation, which he had created to help fund Christian schools and missions. So Betsy and I lived in Bradenton for a while and then were able to move back to Sumter while I continued working for the foundation.

Although I very much appreciated the opportunity to be involved with the foundation, I had the sense that my calling was still in sports.

Gene Anderson was a good friend who owned one of my favorite restaurants, Aunt Maude's Country Kitchen in Myrtle

Beach. Gene had been a professor at Coastal Carolina University, and he called and asked if I would be interested in coaching the school's baseball team. I visited with the chancellor and accepted his offer to become baseball coach and athletic director.

We had good teams at Coastal Carolina, but my stay with the Chanticleers didn't last long. Wearing pin-striped uniforms, our 1985 team finished 30–19, and the '86 team went 31–19 and won the conference championship. Despite our success in those two seasons, I wasn't a good fit with the school. There was a problem with drugs and alcohol on campus, and I never had the school's support in addressing those concerns and handling discipline matters with athletes.

During my second year at Coastal Carolina, I had lunch with Jerry Falwell, who was visiting our area. Dr. Falwell was the founder and chancellor of Liberty University in Lynchburg, Virginia. When I expressed my frustrations with my job, he said, "Come up to my school. You won't have that problem."

I did, taking the head baseball coach's position at Liberty. In a sense, I replaced Al Worthington, who had started Liberty's baseball program in 1974. Al had planned all along to get the program going, then become athletic director only. That's what he did when the job was offered to me. But Al remained with the program by working with me as the Flames' pitching coach.

Al had pitched in the majors at the same time I played, and his son, Little Al, had played second base for me at South Carolina. Back when Al and I were playing ball, most Christian players did not go public with their faith. Al was one who did. I had always admired him for that, and it was a true joy to work alongside him at Liberty and to get to know him and his wife, Shirley, well. They'd been among the dedicated staff that had helped establish Liberty and make it successful—and not just in baseball.

Good-Bye to a Friend

Early in my first season at Liberty, 1987, I received a phone call
from Dick Howser. I had played against Dick when he was with
Kansas City and Cleveland, and he had played for the Yankees
after I retired. After his playing days, he had been a coach and
a manager for the Yankees, and I had gotten to know Dick when
I returned to New York to take part in Old Timers' Games.

After Dick left the Yankees, he moved over to the Kansas City
Royals and led them to a World Series championship. He managed
the American League team in the 1986 All-Star Game, but during
the game he had trouble giving proper signals to the field. After the
game he admitted that he'd felt ill. Doctors diagnosed him with a
brain tumor.

That was the last game Dick managed before he began treatment. He tried to make a comeback during spring training
of '87, but he just wasn't in the condition to do so. I had followed Dick's situation in the newspapers, so when he called
me that spring, I was aware that he'd been given only a few
months to live.

"I'm really discouraged," Dick told me over the phone that day.
"Can you encourage me from the Scriptures?"

Philippians 4:4-7 from the Phillips translation immediately
came to mind, so I read it to him:

> Delight yourselves in God, yes, find your joy in him at all
> times. Have a reputation for gentleness, and never forget the
> nearness of your Lord. Don't worry over anything whatever;
> tell God every detail of your needs in earnest and thankful
> prayer, and the peace of God which transcends human
> understanding, will keep constant guard over your hearts
> and minds as they rest in Christ Jesus.

"That's just what I needed," Dick said, sounding as though he were ending the conversation.

"Wait. Don't hang up."

I told Dick about a friend of mine named Harold Morris who had been through a battle with cancer and had written a book called *Beyond the Barriers: Overcoming Hard Times Through Tough Faith.*

"Can I send you a copy?" I asked Dick.

After Dick read the book, he didn't call me—he called Harold Morris directly to thank him. That's just the kind of guy Dick was. He was also a radiant Christian who had shared his testimony on national television through ESPN and had spoken at a Billy Graham Crusade even after his diagnosis.

When Dick passed away that June, his wife, Nancy, called. "Dick has written out everything he wants for his memorial service," she told me. "So many of his friends don't know Christ. He wants you to come and present the gospel in clarity."

Dick's memorial service in Tallahassee, Florida, drew about four hundred people, including many, many friends from his lifetime in baseball. It was my honor to stand before those friends and not only talk about the quality of life Dick had led but, at his request, share with them the gospel message that he had embraced and lived out.

Home for Good

The late 1980s was a down period in the Liberty program, and in my four seasons as coach, we recorded only one winning season. However, we did have three players drafted off our 1989 team, and at the time that was the most ever selected from one Liberty team.

When Al Worthington stepped down as athletic director in December 1989, I moved up to that job and coached one more season before handing over the program to my assistant coach, Johnny

Hunton. When I left South Carolina, Johnny had remained there as an assistant coach, but I'd been able to persuade him to join me at Liberty before what turned out to be my final season. Johnny would be named the top Division I coach in Virginia after his first season as head coach and would serve in that capacity for seven seasons before becoming the assistant athletic director for spiritual life and an assistant to the chancellor.

My five years at Liberty were a wonderful experience. The atmosphere around the school was positive and productive, and its broad appeal helped me recruit Christian ballplayers from all over the country. There were boys who came across the country from California to play at Liberty. Even though our record wasn't what we wanted, I thought we had a pretty good program building, and I was excited about the direction of the team.

A big plus to me at Liberty was the Christian focus on campus. I enjoyed the chapel messages and Sunday sermons and had occasional opportunities to speak in chapel services. Dr. Falwell also allowed me to accompany him on various trips for his speaking engagements.

For me, Liberty's biggest drawback was that it wasn't in Sumter. Betsy and I had kept our home in Sumter throughout the time I was working at Ben Lippen School, then in Florida for the Aurora Foundation, at Coastal Carolina, and at Liberty. Even when we weren't living there, Sumter was home, and we knew it always would be.

I was feeling the tug to go home. In 1990, after much prayer, Betsy and I felt it was time to return home to Sumter and basically retire to a life of hunting and traveling around the country to share my faith and my Yankees stories.

Chapter 17

FAMILY, FAITH, AND FUN

WHEN I TELL PEOPLE I feel blessed to have the opportunity to travel and speak, I do mean both words: *blessed* and *opportunity*.

I've always viewed my speaking engagements as opportunities to give my testimony and share how my faith has sustained me. They also offer me the chance to share my experience of big league base-ball. I find both deeply fulfilling—true blessings in my life.

When I meet baseball fans, the most common topic of conversation is my catch of Willie McCovey's line drive in Game 7 of the 1962 Series. But the most asked-about season is 1961, with the M&M boys' home run chase. I'm afraid I've disappointed my fair share of fans when asked for details about certain games or moments, though. I played in 1,412 major league games, and my recollection of many of them has faded through the years. The memories that have stuck the best are those involving my teammates, because as much as I loved the game of baseball when I was playing it, I loved even more the relationships I built through the sport.

Supporting One Another

The Yankees teams I played on were tightly knit. We were a varied group of individuals from varied backgrounds and with varied off-field interests, and we couldn't all be best friends. Perhaps in a different setting, some of us wouldn't have become friends at all. But we were teammates, and in that era of baseball, being a teammate meant you shared a special bond.

Because of my conservative lifestyle, I guess I could be considered one of the most "different" players on those teams, but I always had a good rapport with my teammates. And I never doubted that they had my back.

I've shared that Frank Robinson was the only player ever to spike me at second base, and he did it twice. When he got me during the '61 World Series, some of my teammates got angry. They talked about that play on our bench during the game, and in the spike-for-a-spike justice system of major league baseball, they thought Frank had one coming for bloodying my ankle. I told the guys that the spike was my fault, that I hadn't moved my foot after fielding the low throw, and that Frank's slide was good and the play clean. But it still felt good to have teammates ready to come to my defense.

In 1962 I experienced that solidarity again when Eli Grba of the Los Angeles Angels hit me with a pitch. Eli had pitched for us in '59 and '60, before being selected off our team in the expansion draft. But he hadn't pitched at all in the '60 World Series, outside of being assigned by Casey Stengel to throw batting practice to us, and it was common knowledge that he wasn't thrilled with being left out. So when Eli hit me with a pitch, my immediate thought was that he'd done it on purpose, out of a grudge against the Yankees.

I was hit by a pitch only seven times in my twelve seasons. It was never fun. Plus, Eli was a big guy, so this one really hurt, and it made me mad to think he'd nailed me deliberately. I started down the first base line, then took one step toward him on the mound. "I ought to punch you in the nose!" I shouted at him.

The umpire sided with me, adding, "His nose is big enough for the two of us. I should punch him too."

I saw fear on Eli's face, and that baffled me. If he'd been afraid I'd make a visit to the mound to punch him, why would he hit me in the first place?

Then I noticed that Eli wasn't actually looking at me. He was looking *past* me. I turned around to see Elston Howard, Mickey Mantle, and Clete Boyer outside the dugout and on their way toward the mound too. If I was going after Eli, they were coming with me.

It turned out that nobody actually punched anybody, and I took my place at first base without incident. But as I reached the bag, Eli turned to me, laughing. "Richardson," he said, "I wasn't trying to hit you."

I believed him. The ninety-foot walk to first base had provided the time I needed to settle down. I could tell from Eli's words and the way he said them that he had not hit me on purpose. The pitch had simply gotten away from him. In the years since then, Eli and I have joked about him plunking me. It's funny now, but I did appreciate knowing at the time that my teammates were eager to stick up for me.

The Yankee way of showing support for one another helped lead to a change in baseball. It happened in 1954, a year before I started playing with the Yankees, and it involved the player who had been my favorite Yankee when I was a teenager: shortstop Phil "Scooter" Rizzuto.

Before 1954, players used to leave their gloves on the field during games. That practice went back to the early days of baseball, when players from opposing teams shared their mitts with one another. When one team left the field to bat, the players would leave their gloves at their positions, and the opposing players would pick up the gloves and use them.

When I was coming up in baseball, players still maintained that tradition, even though players no longer shared gloves. After the third out of an inning was made, the second baseman and shortstop would pitch their gloves onto the outfield grass behind their positions; the first baseman and third baseman would toss their gloves into foul territory; and the outfielders would drop their gloves where they were standing. Only the pitcher and catcher would take their gloves to the dugout.

The interesting thing is that I can't remember one time when I tripped over the other second baseman's glove or a batted ball struck a glove on the ground, although I did always make mental note of where the glove sat for when I had to backpedal onto the outfield grass for a pop-up. Anyway, I never had to worry about that once I started in pro ball—thanks to Phil Rizzuto.

Phil, you see, was deathly afraid of insects, and his fear was well known throughout the league. When he left his glove behind shortstop, there were opponents who would put a worm or a bug in the glove, right where he needed to slide in his hand, in order to scare him and break his concentration. To combat that, he started bringing his glove off the field with him to the dugout. As a show of support, the rest of the Yankees players brought in their gloves as well. Eventually a rule was invoked that prohibited fielders from leaving their gloves on the field during a game.

Phil Rizzuto was released from the Yankees in 1956, so I got to play only parts of two seasons with him, and the change in the glove tradition happened before I played with the Yankees. But that story is still a favorite of mine, because it illustrates the Yankee way I was brought up under.

When I was coaching at South Carolina, by the way, I got a firsthand look at just how seriously afraid of insects Phil was. It happened during the time that his son, Phil Jr., was playing for me. Phil and I had planned an overnight golfing trip to Hilton Head on the Carolina coast. During the night he spotted a cockroach in his hotel room, grabbed a drinking glass from next to the sink, and put the glass over the roach.

The next morning Phil called me and asked me to come to his room. I walked in, looked to the floor, and saw the roach trapped in its cage.

"Can you get rid of that for me?" Phil asked. "I didn't sleep a wink all night because I was afraid that cockroach would turn that glass over and get loose."

Family Friendly

My oldest two children, Robby and Ronnie, practically grew up at the Yankees' clubhouse. Elston Howard's son, Elston Jr., spent a lot of time there too. And we always felt the boys were welcome there. The managers and other players seemed to understand the importance of family for those of us who had wives and kids living with us during the season, and they wanted us to enjoy time together.

The boys knew to follow the unwritten rules of the clubhouse—never mess with anything in a player's locker, don't ask for autographs, never set foot in the trainer's room, and only go into the players' lounge when invited—so they were welcome to hang out. And anytime they were in the locker room, the players treated them great. They always seemed to have someone from the team joking around with them, pulling a prank on them, or even roughhousing a little in Big Pete's clubhouse.

I wish people could have been in there during the 1961 season, when Roger Maris was chasing Babe Ruth's home run record. To avoid reporters, Roger often hid in the players' lounge during that stressful season, and sometimes he came across in the press as arrogant and unfriendly. But he was never like that with Robby and Ronnie. Instead, he often joked around and played with my boys. That was such a different Roger from the one that has been commonly portrayed in the media.

Roger—like Mickey—had sons my boys' ages who did not live with him during the season. During the intense pressure of the home run race, I think Roger enjoyed having my boys as stand-ins, in a way, for his own sons. I know my boys still have fond memories of the attention Roger gave them during the last part of that season.

My older son, Robby, especially, was a locker-room rat who couldn't be in there enough as far as he was concerned. Ronnie had a good time around the guys too, but if Betsy wanted to ask one of the boys to go to the game later with her instead of going early with me, or to just stay home, Ronnie was the one to ask. If she asked Robby, he'd say, "Please not today, Mom. I really want to see today's game." Then Robby would tell her who we were playing and who was pitching against us and which players on the other team he wanted to see and why that day was the day he absolutely did not want to miss. The next day, of course, he would go through the same routine. He didn't want to miss *any* game.

Robby spent so much time in our clubhouse, in fact, that he picked up a nickname from Big Pete: Butterball. Years later, in 1987, a grown-up Robby returned to Yankee Stadium to speak at a chapel service. It was the last game of the regular season, so the cold weather had arrived in New York City. Robby had been given a credential for access to the clubhouse, but his credential was covered by his overcoat, so he started unbuttoning the coat as he approached the security guard.

"You don't need to do that—I know who you are," the security guard said. "I've been here thirty years. You're a little bigger than when I used to let you in back then, but you look the same. You're still Butterball."

Robby still jokes that he never saw the ninth inning of any of our games. For most home games I would carpool to the Stadium, sometimes taking one of the boys with me, and Betsy would drive in later for the game and park in the players' parking lot. We wanted to get home as soon as possible after a game, so we had a routine worked out. Because we won so often at home, we frequently didn't bat in the bottom of the ninth. So when we made our final out of the eighth inning, Betsy and the kids knew to head to the family lounge near the clubhouse.

After the game I would take a quick shower. Because our team had so many stars, there usually wasn't anyone from the press waiting at my locker to talk to me. So I would dress, pick up Betsy and the kids at their lounge, and hurry to our car. Because the players' parking lot was close, we could pull out of the Stadium and head across the George Washington Bridge, beating the after-game traffic.

Yet another favorite memory for our boys concerns Frank Crosetti—and Bazooka bubble gum. In those days, a seemingly endless supply of Bazooka bubble gum was kept near the clubhouse door so the players could grab a handful for a game. Before Robby and Ron left the locker room to go up into the stands to watch the game with their mother, they would load up their jeans pockets with pieces of gum. But then they had to pass Crosetti, whose locker was closest to the door.

Crosetti was in charge of the baseballs, and he guarded them almost militantly to keep them from disappearing. So when he saw Robby or Ronnie walking by with that round pocket bulge, he'd get suspicious. "Uh-uh-uh, Little Rich. Come over here. I see that baseball in your pocket." Robby or Ronnie would then have to prove to Crosetti that he was smuggling gum, not one of Crosetti's precious baseballs.

There was only one instance in all my years with the Yankees that I had to step in and chastise a teammate for his behavior around my kids. When Robby was little, Hank Bauer called him over.

"Hey, Rich—Little Rich!"

Robby walked over to Hank.

"Why don't you have one of these beers here?" Hank asked him. "It'll make you big like me and not little like your dad!"

Hank handed Robby a can of beer, and I just about came unglued. That was one of the few times my teammates ever saw me openly angry.

Hank quickly backtracked. "I'm sorry. I didn't mean it."

I know that was true, that Hank was just joking. But what he did was inappropriate, and I had to show my disapproval.

About a year or two before Hank passed away, Robby saw him at the Fort Lauderdale airport and went over to talk to him. Hank pulled Robby over to where the two of them were alone and asked, "Are you the one I gave the beer to?"

"Yes, sir, I was," Robby answered.

"I'm sorry," Hank said. "I didn't mean anything by it."

"Don't worry about it, Mr. Bauer," Robby told him. "It's okay."

That was almost fifty years later, and Hank still felt bad about what he had done.

Faith and Friendship

I played baseball in a different era—not only in terms of the game, but also when it came to Christian witness. A Christian athlete was more alone in those days, and public displays of faith were rare.

Nowadays it's common to see an elite athlete such as Mariano Rivera or Tim Tebow speak publicly about his faith. Football players from both teams gather at midfield after a game to pray together. A baseball player will point heavenward when he crosses home plate after hitting a home run, or a football player will take a knee and pray in the end zone after scoring a touchdown.

As someone who played when that sort of thing was just not done, I am happy that athletes now feel the freedom to give God credit from the platform He has provided for them—although I must add that when a football player catches a touchdown pass, does a dance in the end zone, throws the ball to the ground, and *then* gives credit to God, I'm not impressed with the order of his priorities.

Athletes have such a tremendous platform, and when they use it to make a genuine expression of their faith, God can be glorified in a spectacular way. I still recall when Orel Hershiser appeared on *The Tonight Show* with Johnny Carson after the 1988 World Series and sang the Doxology. That was a powerful moment because it was evident that Hershiser's faith was real.

When I played, though, most Christian athletes didn't feel that freedom of expression. I'm not sure why. I know that we in that generation were less expressive with just about everything. We also didn't have the kind of organizational support that players today have. The Fellowship of Christian Athletes was a very new program back then, and Baseball Chapel wasn't around yet.

Whatever the reasons, not many baseball players in my day seemed willing to take a stand concerning their testimonies. There was maybe one such player on each team. Al Worthington, Carl Erskine, Jerry Kindall, and Don Demeter stood out to me as baseball players who were most vocal about their faith. And because of my public speaking, particularly with Billy Graham, I became known as "the Christian on the Yankees."

I do think that my being a Yankee amped up this reputation. If I had played in Cleveland or Kansas City, for example, I don't think my Christianity would have been noticed quite as much.

Also contributing was the fact that I grew up in the Baptist church, an evangelical denomination that emphasizes the importance of sharing your faith with others.

While the attention that went with playing in New York opened many doors that otherwise would not have been opened, it also put me in a position to be criticized. For instance, I received many, many letters from fans either questioning my faith or judging me as being out of God's will because I played on Sundays.

Coming up through baseball, I recognized that if I played in the majors, I would have to play on Sundays. Sundays were important days in our era of baseball because we played Sunday afternoon doubleheaders. I felt that the Lord had created an opportunity for me to be involved in baseball, and playing on Sundays was a part of the sport. I did go to church on Sundays whenever I could, even on road trips, and I often spoke in churches as well. I would go to church in the morning, then play in the afternoon. When Ralph Houk was our manager, he graciously allowed me to arrive late for batting practice on Sundays when I was speaking at or attending a church. Later we began holding Sunday team chapels, so there were opportunities throughout my baseball career for fellowship with other believers on Sundays.

I never encountered any problems with my teammates because I was a Christian. They all knew my beliefs and accepted them. Sure, there were occasional jokes thrown my way about my clean living, but they were good-natured, and I laughed along with the guys. My teammates were respectful of my faith and, if anything, went out of their way to honor my beliefs.

Whenever you get twenty-five major leaguers on, for example, a bus, there will be crude jokes told. But the guys around me would make an effort not to say something I would consider inappropriate, or they would warn me, "All right, Rich, this would be a good time for you to go to the front of the bus." I would simply heed their warning and look for a different place to sit. I never minded because I knew the guys' intentions and believed that their warning was their way of looking out for me.

It was always a given that I wouldn't go out drinking after a game. We would all joke around and cut up in the locker room after a game, and then we would go out in our separate groups. There was a group that went out drinking and a group that didn't drink—usually including Tony Kubek, Bob Turley, and me. But there were no tensions or conflicts between the two groups. I never felt that the ones in my social group were my friends and the guys in the other group were just my teammates. It was more as if I had two types of friends on the team, and my rapport with both groups was great.

In the off-season, and even after I retired, I never lacked for teammates who came to visit me in Sumter to go hunting, and that included guys from the "drinking" group. Clete Boyer is a good example. We were very close friends when we were Yankees and remained that way long after our playing days.

When we began flying instead of taking trains, a few of the guys were nervous about being on an airplane, and they handled their fears by drinking more. I remember Johnny Blanchard would feel the need to explain, "Now Bobby, I'm going to have a couple of drinks, but I want you to know that it's because I'm flying."

There was one chartered flight when I was the only player not on board, because I had received permission to make a quick trip home on an off-day before rejoining the team. The pilots encountered problems getting the landing gear to go down. When word circulated in the cabin, Blanchard said, "Oh my goodness! We're in trouble—Richardson's not here!"

I wish there were an easy formula for how to live an exemplary Christian life among non-Christians. I think the key for me was not to try too hard to be a certain kind of person. I didn't try to be Bobby the Christian and also Bobby the teammate; those two couldn't have been separated anyway. All I tried to be was who I was—a sinner grateful to be saved by grace. Anything else I might have tried to be wouldn't have been sincere.

Although I spoke about my faith a lot, I wasn't always pushing my faith on my teammates. That's not my personality type. With practice, I became comfortable speaking in front of large crowds, but I was more reserved in one-on-one conversations. I just hope my fellow Yankees thought of me the way Joe DiMaggio apparently did.

Though Joe was retired from playing by the time I became a Yankee, he served as our hitting coach for a short period, and I was able to become good friends with him. Betsy and I went out to dinner with Joe a few times, and Joe came to South Carolina—at his own expense, by the way—to endorse my bid for Congress. I had always looked for opportunities to witness to Joe, and on his trip to South Carolina, I handed him a copy of Chuck Colson's book *Born Again*.

Joe had two brothers who also played in the majors, Vince and Dom. One day I read an article in *Decision* magazine that said Vince had been born again. He even referenced the Chuck Colson book. I clipped out the article and mailed it to Joe. The next time I saw Joe, he said, "I got your letter." That's all he said, because Joe was a man of few words.

After Joe passed away, a sportswriter called me and said he had interviewed Joe a few weeks before he died. Apparently Joe had talked a lot about me, and the interviewer wanted to send me some of his notes. When they arrived in the mail, I read through them with interest.

What Joe had told the writer was that I didn't wear my religion on my sleeve in an obtrusive way. He said that I just shared my faith with him in simplicity as a friend.

I don't know if Joe asked Christ to be his Savior or not before he died. And naturally I've wondered whether I could have or should have done more in communicating my faith with him. But I haven't forgotten what Joe told that sportswriter about my sharing with him as a friend. That touched me deeply.

I don't know many words more meaningful than *friend*. That's what each of my teammates was to me. And I hope I was that to them as well—because that's the best kind of Christian witness I know.

Chapter 18

TEAMMATES AND LIFELONG FRIENDS

IT MAY HAVE BEEN the best infield in baseball in its day. I certainly believe it was the most tightly knit.

I'm referring to the Yankees' infield consisting of Moose Skowron at first, me at second, Tony Kubek at shortstop, and Clete Boyer at third. The four of us made up the Yankees' infield for three full seasons, from 1960 through '62.

Because that was probably the peak of that Yankees dynasty, we were often asked to make appearances in the New York City area and autograph different types of memorabilia. I don't know how many photographs we signed of the four of us posing together. But there was one particular pose of us taken on the steps of our dugout that became quite valuable if it bore all our signatures. I once saw one of those autographed pictures advertised in the *New York Times* for around four hundred dollars.

That photo was so heavily requested that we decided we should sign a bunch so we could always have a supply on hand when a fan asked for one. I must have given away hundreds of those through the years and never sold one, although I did give one to a plumber who then gave me a discount on his services in return. I liked to place the photos in frames and give them to charities so they could auction them off in fund-raisers.

As far as I know, Kubek never sold one of those autographed pictures either. But Tony and I knew that Moose and Clete were selling them.

For a picture to have its highest value, it had to be signed by all four of us. One of us would sign a stack of photos, then send it on to the next, and so on until all four of us had signed them. Because Tony and I wanted to be able to have our own that we could give away, we worked out the signing rotation so that Tony was always the last one to sign. Thus, the photos would end up with him to distribute among the four of us.

When Moose was running the Yankees fantasy camp, my son Robby liked to take part. Moose would tell him, "Okay, Richardson, everybody else paid five thousand dollars. You don't have to pay, but tell your dad to give me fifty of those signed pictures!" Instead of paying for Robby to attend, I gave Moose fifty photos and let him sell them.

Moose Skowron: Funny Guy

Moose was always the comedian of the bunch. With Mickey, Whitey, Yogi, and Roger, the reporters had an ample supply of superstars to quote, but when the topic was humorous, Moose was the press's go-to guy. But Moose didn't just make reporters laugh. He cracked us up too.

Moose wasn't as big as his nickname might make you think. He was five feet eleven and weighed a little less than two hundred pounds. His nickname had nothing to do with his size, in fact.

When Moose was a kid, his grandfather gave him a bad haircut that reminded family friends of the hairstyle of the Italian dictator Mussolini. They began calling Bill, "Mussolini," and that got shortened to "Moose" and stuck permanently.

When he played with us, Moose had a distinctive crew cut, and he would offer to buy my sons and other kids in the clubhouse a hamburger if they would get a haircut like his. Nobody took him up on his offer.

Moose was a fine all-around athlete who had played football, basketball, and baseball at Purdue University. He went on to a pro baseball career while his baseball coach at Purdue, Hank Stram, became known more for his football coaching abilities, eventually being elected into the Pro Football Hall of Fame. Moose also made it into a hall of fame: the National Polish-American Sports Hall of Fame. (Years later, after I had conducted several teammates' funerals, Moose told me I couldn't do his because I don't speak Polish.)

When he struck out, Moose tended to cuss. He'd come back to the dugout and walk the length of the bench uttering profanities. When he would come to me, he'd stop cussing long enough to say, "Excuse me, Bobby." Then, once he got past me, he'd resume his profanities.

Language aside, Moose had a lovable personality and was about as generous a person as anyone could hope to know. He was the type of guy that the phrase "He'd give you the shirt off his back" was created to describe.

When Moose was traded to Los Angeles after the 1962 season, we lost a great guy, a good friend, and a big dose of fun in our infield. Moose hated that trade as much as we did. He had produced great seasons in New York and thought he had more in him.

In the 1980s, when Mickey Mantle and Whitey Ford started holding Yankees fantasy camps for Yankees fans to play baseball with some of the franchise's legendary players, they brought

Moose in to take part. He provided the laughs at all the camps. The campers, especially the older ones, loved being around Moose. Eventually, he took over running those camps from Mickey and Whitey. And even though Moose had played for the Dodgers, Senators, White Sox, and Angels after he left our team, there was something that just felt right about seeing Moose back in Yankees pinstripes at those fantasy camps.

Clete Boyer: Shy Guy

Clete Boyer was the only one of us four who didn't come up through the Yankees' system. I remember seeing Clete for the first time in 1955, as he was preparing to sign his first contract. Clete was from Missouri and came to work out with us on one of our trips into Kansas City. He was seventeen years old. I remember saying to myself, *Man, what a good arm—and he's a great fielder.*

The Yankees wound up not signing Clete at that time because of the number of "bonus baby" players to whom major league roster spots had already been committed for the next two years. Instead he signed with the Kansas City Athletics for more than four thousand dollars. The Yankees acquired him from the A's during the '57 season as the "player to be named later" from an earlier trade between the teams.

Clete was eligible to go to the minor leagues by that point, and the Yankees sent him down to develop. He got the call back up late in '59, when we had Andy Carey, Héctor López, and Gil McDougald playing third. By early June of the 1960 season, the third base job was Clete's.

I played every day with Clete for eight seasons, and I consider him to have been one of the best third basemen of his time. That's even compared to Brooks Robinson, who had fifteen All-Star seasons and sixteen consecutive Gold Glove awards and is often acknowledged as the best defensive third baseman in major league history.

Brooks was probably a better all-around player than Clete because of his hitting. But Clete was an excellent player who has never seemed to receive the recognition he deserved. Just a highlight reel of Clete's defense during the '61 World Series would be enough to prove my point. And he was no slouch as a hitter, either. As Tony Kubek once pointed out, Clete batted eighth for us, but when he went from New York to Atlanta, the Braves put him in the fifth spot behind Hank Aaron and Joe Torre. After playing for Atlanta, he spent time in Japan as a player and then as a coach, and later he coached for the Oakland A's and the Yankees before retiring.

Clete, a quiet man, was especially close to Roger Maris. I sat next to Clete at Roger's funeral. I was part of the program, and when I returned to my seat, I learned over to Clete and said, "You really ought to say something today."

"Oh no," he said, "not me."

At one point in the service, it was asked if any other teammates of Roger's would like to talk about him.

I stood from my aisle seat, stepped back, and motioned Clete to go forward. I purposefully put him in a position where he had to get up and walk to the front. And Clete did a fantastic job. It was obvious he was speaking from his heart and as a true friend. Clete thanked me several times after that day for putting him on the spot like that.

Even though Clete and I were friends, we lived opposite life-styles. He was known for his hard living and his constant battle with alcohol. I prayed many nights for my good friend. After he retired, Tony and I were so concerned for him that we both came to Atlanta to see what we could do to help.

Clete's family was concerned too, of course. One of his daughters faithfully prayed for him year after year. Her love for her father really touched Clete's heart.

When Clete died of a brain hemorrhage in 2007, that daughter asked me to take part in the memorial service. I shared a story from a year or so earlier, when Clete came to visit Betsy and me for Christmas.

Clete had visited me in Sumter several times and loved for me to take him hunting. Betsy and I still laugh about a night during one of those visits, when a loud noise came from the guest room. The slats holding up the bed had fallen, taking Clete to the floor with them. Clete didn't sleep very well that night.

But I told those gathered at Clete's memorial service about a different night during Clete's most recent visit. While I was out running an errand, Clete and Betsy had a good talk. Betsy showed Clete a special gospel tract and laid it on a table. Noticing that Clete kept looking at that tract, Betsy felt she should leave the room for a few minutes.

"Betsy," Clete told her when she returned to the room, "I want you to know that I prayed that prayer at the end. I received Jesus as my Savior."

As Clete was leaving our house to return home, we gave him a Christmas present: a Bible. Clete accepted it proudly.

Tony Kubek: My Milkshake Twin

Tony Kubek was my best friend on the Yankees. We roomed together while playing for the Bears in Denver and were roommates with the Yankees every season until he retired, except for the year he was called into active military duty.

Tony was the other half of what the press called the "Milkshake Twins" because we had been followed by detectives and caught engaging in nothing shadier than playing Ping-Pong and enjoying some milkshakes. Tony laughed about that incident when it happened. But later he tried to distance himself a little from that label because first, he didn't drink milkshakes that often, and second, he didn't want to be portrayed with such a squeaky-clean image.

Tony's "Milkshake Twin" reputation did win him one significant advantage, though—a brief phone relationship with a very beautiful and famous movie star. Back in the early 1950s, after he retired from playing, Joe DiMaggio had been briefly married to Marilyn Monroe, and they remained in contact after their divorce. During the time that Joe served as our spring training and special hitting instructor, he didn't make the longer road trips with us. Often it would be a last-minute decision as to whether Joe would travel on certain trips. With Marilyn's busy schedule, Joe couldn't always get word to her when he wouldn't be traveling. Because Joe knew the clean-living Milkshake Twins were likely to be in their hotel room during trips, he'd told Marilyn to call us if she couldn't reach him.

Tony wasn't married yet, so I thought it would be more appropriate for him to answer the phone when we knew Marilyn might be calling and let him tell her that Joe had stayed back home. So Tony had several conversations with Marilyn during that period.

Tony was a Christian like me, but the form of our faith differed. He had been raised a Catholic. His wife, Margaret, whom he married after the 1961 World Series, was the daughter of a Lutheran minister, and Tony left Catholicism to join the Lutheran church. He was an avid reader, and I employed a sneaky method of sharing my own kind of faith with Tony. I would leave Christian books around the hotel room, knowing that Tony's curiosity wouldn't be satisfied until he picked up the books to see what they had to say.

There was a church I would speak at in Kansas City, and when I'd ask Tony if he wanted to go, he would say, "No, I'm not interested." Yet he would end up at that church service almost every time.

On a trip to play the Twins, Tony and I planned to visit the church of a pastor friend in Minneapolis, not far from the Twins' stadium. We asked Mickey Mantle if he wanted to go, and he said he would join us. We were playing a doubleheader that day, so the first game would have an early start.

When the cab dropped us off at the church, I told Tony and Mickey, "Listen, we're going to have to leave about ten minutes early to get to the ballpark on time. I've arranged to have a cab waiting for us. As soon as the pastor starts winding up his message, we'll slip out."

Everything was fine as the minister started to bring his sermon in for a landing. But when we got up to leave quietly, we were recognized because of Mickey, and half the congregation got up with us. The pastor ended his message early so he and his son could have a picture taken with Mickey. Mickey didn't like a lot of attention when he was in a hurry. After greeting the people and posing for photos, we missed almost all of batting practice.

I still have the copy of the photo that the pastor sent me. Tony, the pastor, his son, and I are smiling, while Mickey has a we-need-to-get-going look on his face. For years after that, Tony and I enjoyed razzing Mickey about the Sunday he made us miss batting practice.

Mickey was known as a prankster. But Tony was one in his own right, and he didn't mind targeting Mickey, either.

After Mickey's final season, I asked him to come to Sumter to put on a batting exhibition for a YMCA fund-raising campaign I was heading up. I brought Tony in to be a part of it too. We had a capacity crowd all the way around the field. When Mickey came out in his Yankees uniform, the crowd cheered wildly.

Tony had a straight overhand delivery with his throwing motion—perfect for a batting practice pitcher—so I asked if he would feed some fat pitches to Mickey so he could wow the people with long home runs.

Tony agreed. I should have become suspicious when he *readily* agreed.

On his first pitch to Mickey, Tony decided to cross him up and threw a changeup. Mickey was caught off guard, tried to recover with an off-balance swing, and his front leg went out from under him. Mickey stepped back and gathered himself, but it was obvious he had hurt his leg reaching for Tony's changeup. If Mickey could have run on that bad leg, he would have chased Tony.

Mickey got back into the batter's box and took more swings, but his leg was bothering him so much that he didn't have the strength to hit a home run. He hit line drives, but not a single homer. We also had a fun exhibition game scheduled, and Mickey was unable to play because of his leg. Tony and I played, though, and his first time at the plate, Tony hit a home run into the top of the light tower in right field.

To help handle the huge crowd, we had lined a rope around the outfield for the fans to stand behind. In one of my at bats, I hit a fly ball to left that carried just over the rope for a home run. When I rounded third base for home, Tony and Mickey were sprawled out on the ground near the plate, acting as though they had fainted over my power display.

Some folks reading this book will recall Tony as a broadcaster, not a Yankees shortstop. After he retired, Tony became a color commentator on NBC's *Game of the Week* Saturday broadcasts. Tony also worked broadcasts for the Toronto Blue Jays and the New York Yankees.

The funny thing is that back when Tony was a player, he was so shy that he wouldn't take part in any radio or television interviews. Yankees TV broadcaster Red Barber tried to have every player on his show at least once each season, but he couldn't persuade Tony to consent to an interview. Tony would tell him, "Sorry, Red, I just don't do that."

One day Red came up to me and asked, "Do you think you could talk Tony into coming onto my show?"

I pitched the idea to Tony on Red's behalf.

Tony relented, under one condition: "I'll go on it only if you'll get on it with me and be the one who interviews me."

I passed that along to Red, who told me, "Absolutely. You interview him."

We got through that interview fine. And years later, the shy Tony—who practically had to be begged to appear on Red Barber's program—became not only a broadcaster, but an excellent one. In 2009, the National Baseball Hall of Fame presented Tony with its Ford C. Frick Award, given annually to a broadcaster who has made major contributions to baseball.

Tony worked NBC's *Game of the Week* broadcasts until the network lost its television rights for baseball after the 1989 season. Tony had also broadcast Toronto Blue Jays games when he wasn't calling NBC games. From there, Tony moved over to the MSG Network to announce Yankees games.

Even though Tony was making great money in broadcasting, he left the TV booth for good when the players went on strike during the 1994 season. Tony had become fed up with the greed that had become prevalent in baseball and decided that if he was going to watch a baseball game, it would be one of his kids' games. As far as I know, since the '94 strike, Tony has not watched one major league game.

Tony's honesty is what made him a great announcer. To Tony, the truth was the truth, and he harbored no concerns about expressing it, regardless of whose feathers that might ruffle. I know his viewers appreciated that. Tony had no fear of publicly criticizing the way George Steinbrenner ran the Yankees, though it created hard feelings toward Tony from the top of the organization. Even if someone were to disagree with Tony's opinions on a matter, there was no need to search for any hidden meanings or agendas behind Tony's words. Whatever Tony said, he spoke from his heart, with conviction, and for the benefit of others.

I've stated publicly many times that Tony would have made a great commissioner of Major League Baseball. Tony is a smart,

smart man. More important, if he had been commissioner, he would not have been afraid of the owners and would not have taken sides between the owners and the players. As a former player, he certainly would have looked out for the players, but he would have done the same for the owners. All his decisions would have been made with only the best interests of baseball in mind.

Tony put a premium on the word *teammate*. If you were Tony's teammate, he had your back, whether you were a superstar or a rookie just trying to hang on to a roster spot. A good example of how Tony cared for all his teammates is the way his excellent book, *Sixty-One: The Team, the Record, the Men*, came to be written.

A publisher asked Tony to write an insider's look at Maris and Mantle and their pursuits of Babe Ruth's home run record in 1961. Tony said he would write the book, but he wouldn't just focus on Roger and Mickey. It would be about the entire team.

"I have twenty-four teammates," Tony told the publisher, "and I'll be glad to write on all of them. But I won't write only about two individuals like that."

The publisher said it wasn't interested in such a book. Tony said that was too bad. But he didn't change his stance.

The publisher wound up coming back to Tony and saying it would be interested in a book done his way. Tony got in touch with all of us, interviewed us, and produced the first book I recommend to anyone who wants to learn more about our '61 team.

Tony remained a close friend long after our playing days were over and is still a friend today—we talk on the phone about once per month.

Roger Maris: Family Man

My fellow infielders were not my only memorable teammates, of course. During my years as a Yankee, I was blessed to play baseball—

and build indelible friendships—with a number of talented and interesting men.

Roger Maris, for instance, is associated with power hitting because of his home run record, but people forget how good an all-around player he was. He was a great right fielder with a strong and accurate arm. He was faster than most people realize too, and he possessed an aggressive mind-set on the base paths. Those who claim a triple is the most exciting play in baseball would have loved watching Roger leg out a three-bagger. He was as adept at turning a double into a triple or going from first to third on a single as anyone I saw play.

More important, I think, Roger was the most dedicated family man I knew in baseball. He came to us for the 1960 season from the Kansas City Athletics and chose not to bring his family with him to New York. He and his wife, Pat, believed their home near Kansas City provided a better environment for their kids to grow up in. But being away from his family for a big part of the year was clearly difficult for Roger.

When he interacted with my sons in the locker room, it was obvious that he missed having his kids around during the season. It was evident how caring a father he was too. Whenever we did see Roger with his kids, we could see how well he related to them. The Marises had a close family, and our family always enjoyed being with them.

I was tickled to death when we traded for Roger and brought him to New York—and it wasn't just because I wanted a great ballplayer on our team. From my second baseman's perspective, I also didn't want him on an opposing team. Second basemen take note of who's running at first base in a double play situation. When Roger was with the Athletics, I really disliked seeing him standing on first base next to Moose. He was the player I least wanted sliding into my bag when I was turning a double play.

The way I preferred to turn a double play was to straddle the bag, catch the throw, turn toward first, make my throw, and jump over the runner as he slid into second. When Roger was on first, however, I had to take the throw going across the bag so that I was a full step away when I threw. That was slightly slower and not quite as easy as my preferred way, but it would keep me from getting spiked or getting knocked all the way to our left fielder. And Roger would do that. As nice a guy as he was, he had no qualms about taking out a second baseman to protect the batter running to first.

Like Moose, Roger had a football background. He had been a three-sport star—in football, basketball, and track—at his high school in Fargo, North Dakota, and played American Legion baseball like me. Although he'd been offered a football scholarship to the University of Oklahoma, he'd chosen to stick with baseball and had signed with the Cleveland Indians. But football had made its mark on him as a player.

I had to go across the bag when Roger was running at first because if I tried to jump over him, he would come up and throw a rolling block. Bob Allison of the Washington Senators/ Minnesota Twins threw a similar rolling block with his slide, but Roger had slightly more speed than Bob and got to a second baseman a little quicker.

Roger and I hit it off right away when he came over from the A's. Because he was a quiet guy, we had a more reserved friendship than I had with other teammates, but we were close nonetheless.

Roger took a particular interest in my baseball mentor from back home, Harry Stokes. Roger knew how important Harry was to me as a player and as a person, and he went out of his way to make sure Harry was welcomed as a member of the Yankees' extended family when he came to visit me.

Once when Harry had come up to New York to visit and take in a couple of games, Roger said, "Hey, Harry, we're going to Kansas City next. Why don't you come out with us? You can stay at my house and enjoy a couple more games in Kansas City." Because Roger's family lived in Kansas City, he usually flew out ahead of the rest of us so he could spend more time with them. Roger arranged for Harry to fly with him. He stayed at Roger's home and had a great time. I barely even saw Harry on that trip.

On Bobby Richardson Day near the end of my final season, the players presented me with a beautiful gun case as my going-away present. That wasn't enough for Roger, though. He had a watch made for me with my uniform number all the way around the face, so there were twelve 1s. I was touched that he made the effort to present me with an extra gift.

While we were teammates, Roger would sometimes call out of the blue during the off-season and say something like, "I'm going to be playing golf at Pinehurst in North Carolina. Would it be all right if I stopped by to see you?" We enjoyed some delightful visits in our home. He kept on doing that even after we both were out of baseball.

On one visit Roger went with us to watch Robby and Ronnie play an American Legion game in nearby Manning. Ronnie was playing right field, and early in the game a line drive was hit in his direction. Ronnie started in, then stopped when he realized the ball had been hit harder than he thought. The line drive carried over Ronnie's head as he turned to chase it.

"Looks just like me," Roger told me. "Sorry for that influence."

After the game a friend came up to us, looked at Roger, and said, "Boy, you look a lot like Roger Maris."

"Well, thank you," Roger replied with a smile. "I appreciate that."

We didn't tell my friend otherwise, and when he walked away, Roger and I enjoyed a good laugh over that one.

Elston Howard: Man of Dignity

Growing up in the South in the middle of the century, I was quite familiar with segregation, but I was still shocked when I encountered it in the major leagues.

Jackie Robinson had broken the color barrier in major league baseball in 1947 with the Brooklyn Dodgers. Later that season, Larry Doby of the Cleveland Indians had become the first African American player in the American League. I entered professional baseball six years later, and while I saw how the black fans were seated apart from the white fans while I was with the Norfolk Tars, I wasn't an eyewitness to much open segregation on the teams. Of course, there were attitudes that were slow to change throughout the sport, but it really wasn't until I first reported to spring training with the New York Yankees that I saw something that made me doubt whether progress was being made.

During spring training, the players stayed at the Soreno Hotel in St. Petersburg, Florida. Not all the players, though. Elston Howard was not allowed to stay at the team hotel. I couldn't believe that still happened in the big leagues—and not just with the Yankees.

Elston, who had played for Buck O'Neil with the Kansas City Monarchs of the Negro Leagues, was the Yankees' first African American player. The Yankees were among the last integrated teams, with Ellie making his big league debut in 1955—eight years after the color barrier had been broken. I heard that the Yankees could have integrated earlier but had held off because they believed it would require a special person to handle the pressure of being the franchise's first African American player.

Whether that story was true or not, Elston Howard was indeed a special person.

At six feet two and nearly two hundred pounds, Ellie was a gentle giant, big enough that someone would be foolish to pick a fight with him. But Elston certainly wasn't going to start a fight, and I think someone would have had to work hard to provoke him into one.

I'm sure that being the Yankees' first African American was tougher than Ellie let on at the time. I've read interviews from after Ellie's career in which he addressed difficulties he had faced. But he never brought up those issues in the locker room or on our train rides and flights. *Dignity* is a word that comes to mind when I think about how Ellie handled the pressure. Ellie was a true gentleman.

I don't think there was a more respected man on our team than Elston Howard. He also may have been the best liked. However, that didn't exempt him from being the target of good-natured jokes, much as I was because of my faith.

Once when Elston boarded our bus, Mickey Mantle was already sitting in the front, on the left-hand side. When Ellie started to sit next to Mickey, Mickey laughed and said, "Oh, no, no. You go to the back of the bus."

"No," Ellie shot back, "I want to sit by you." Then big ol' Ellie plopped down right next to Mickey in the front. Everybody on the bus broke out in laughter, including Mickey, who knew Ellie had gotten him on that one.

From my nonminority perspective, it seemed that the attitudes concerning race in baseball progressively improved during the time I was a player. I hate that racism was ever a part of our sport, not to mention our society, but I am glad I was able to see a man I admired handle a difficult time with such grace.

In a way, I benefited from my fellow Yankees' respect for Ellie. When I scheduled a chapel service for the team, Elston would be the one going around to the players and saying, "Richardson's having chapel, and we're gonna be here tomorrow. Make sure you're there." Our small services were well attended, and I wondered at times how much of that was because Ellie delivered the invitations and said he would be there.

As a player, Elston's talent was immense, though he remained humble. He made nine consecutive All-Star teams from 1957 to '65. What makes that especially impressive is that for about half of that period, he did not have his own position. Ellie was an outfielder converted to catcher, but Yogi Berra was our starter at catcher. Ellie was his backup and also played left field, right field, and first base. It wasn't until the 1960 and 1961 seasons that Ellie took over the starting catcher spot, with Yogi gradually playing outfield more. In 1963, Elston became the first African American to win the American League Most Valuable Player award, and he finished third the next season behind Brooks Robinson and Mickey Mantle.

The Yankees traded Ellie to the Boston Red Sox during the 1967 season, and his career ended when the Red Sox released him after the '68 season. When he retired, he held the record for the highest fielding percentage ever for a catcher: .993. But numbers cannot reflect how well he called games for our pitching staff. His even-keeled personality had a calming influence on our pitchers. Ellie had a way of making them feel like everything was under control with him behind the plate.

Ellie wasn't happy about being traded from the Yankees. (He told me later how much it had hurt.) But he was able to return to the franchise as an assistant coach—the first African American coach in the American League. He could have been the first black manager in the majors too—Frank Robinson became the first in 1975—and that was a strong desire of his. But for some reason he never was given the chance to manage a team. I know he would have been a great manager.

Ellie left us way too soon. He died in 1980, at age fifty-one, from myocarditis, an inflammation of the heart muscle. His number—32—was retired four years later, and a plaque in his honor was dedicated at Yankee Stadium's Monument Park. I like the way the inscription on that plaque describes him: "A man of great gentleness and dignity." It concludes with these words: "If, indeed, humility is a trademark of many great men—Elston Howard was one of the truly great Yankees."

Whitey Ford: A "Slick" Ace

It should be no secret by now that I believe Whitey Ford was a great pitcher, definitely one of the best. I may be up in years, but I can't go all the way back to the days of Walter Johnson, Cy Young, and Christy Mathewson. During the era in which I played, though, I would put Whitey on top of the list—even over Sandy Koufax, because Whitey's career lasted longer.

The Chairman of the Board was a pleasure to play defense behind. Because he stayed ahead in the count and rarely walked batters, Whitey gifted us with a slew of two-hour games. We also could depend on Whitey pitching deep into games. If he didn't go the full nine, we knew he would at least get us *to* the ninth. Then Luis Arroyo could come in to close out the victory.

When Casey Stengel was manager, he worked the pitching rotation so that Whitey not only pitched against the best teams, but also against the best teams' best pitchers. When Ralph Houk replaced Stengel, he pitched Whitey every fourth day regardless of the opponent to get him extra starts.

It's enough of a testament to Whitey's talent to point out his place in the Hall of Fame. The fact that there were several years during his career when he pitched with a sore throwing arm ups my respect for him. With Whitey on the lineup card, we believed we had the upper hand on our opponent before the first pitch was thrown.

The name *Whitey* was a nickname—his real name was Edward Charles. But he also acquired two more nicknames: Chairman of the Board (because of his quiet confidence under pressure) and

Slick. In a team meeting, Stengel once referred to players who were getting "whiskey slick." We weren't sure what Casey meant by that expression, but there was no doubt that he was talking about Whitey, Mickey, and Billy Martin. After that meeting Whitey and Mickey began calling each other Slick.

Whitey and Mickey knew how to have fun—at least their brand of fun—and they certainly made playing for the Yankees fun for the rest of us. They were always coming up with one outlandish scheme after another.

Whitey liked to complain that Yogi Berra's short, stubby fingers made it difficult to see the signals he flashed to the mound. Yogi put white paint on his fingers to try to help, but Whitey still had trouble reading his signs.

One day when Whitey was complaining, Mantle said, "You don't need Yogi! Why don't you call your own game?"

Whitey did, using wipes of his glove and other signals with his hand and body movements to let Yogi and us infielders know what he was throwing. Whitey won that game.

Then Whitey decided to take pitch selection one more step.

"Why don't you call a game?" Whitey asked Mickey.

So Mickey did—from center field. He would give a signal to Yogi for the pitch he thought Whitey should throw, then Yogi relayed Mickey's selection to Whitey. Whitey won that game too.

Whitey and Mickey used to boast about how good they were at basketball. Whitey even claimed that basketball, not baseball, was his best sport. One year Whitey and Mickey decided to organize a basketball game. Whitey put together a team of pitchers and catchers, and Mickey assembled a team from among the outfielders and infielders. They set a date to play at West Point when we were there for an exhibition game.

"Somebody's gonna get hurt," Yogi said. "I don't think we should do that." But Whitey and Mickey were not to be deterred.

After all the regulars had been replaced during the exhibition, we left the ballpark for the gym. It was only about a two-block walk, but as we started our trek, Mickey whistled. A limousine pulled up.

"All right," Mickey said, "my guys in here!" We piled in, but Whitey's team had to walk.

Mickey also had arranged for Rawlings to outfit his team with uniforms and basketball shoes. Whitey's team had only regular tennis shoes and the baseball clothes they had been wearing under their uniforms.

Sure enough, it was a humdinger of a game, going down to the very end. Tommy Tresh scored the game-winning basket to give the outfielders/infielders a one-point win, earning him the coveted Most Valuable Player award.

As Yogi had feared, however, there was an injury. Pitcher Steve Hamilton turned an ankle and missed several days. He was the only player who got hurt in that game—and also the only one who had played in the NBA.

I sometimes wondered how Whitey, Mickey, and Yogi were able to dream up the stunts they came up with. I also wondered how many of them they got away with—all of them, probably—only because of what good ballplayers they were.

Yogi Berra: "Those Ducks Don't Really Talk"

In addition to being one of the best catchers ever, Yogi was the best clutch hitter I ever played with. People assume that Mantle would be the teammate I'd want at the plate in a clutch situation, but Yogi would have to be my choice. Mickey was a great hitter and a great pressure player, but Yogi struck out less than Mickey. Yogi was like DiMaggio with his ability to make contact and keep his strikeouts down.

Yogi was a noted bad-pitch hitter—although, as he once said, if he could hit it, it wasn't a bad pitch. It didn't matter where the pitch was in relation to the strike zone. If Yogi's bat could reach it, he could hit it with authority. Looking back, it might have been best for opposing teams late in close games if they had pitched Yogi right down the middle of the plate.

I don't understand how anyone could be around Yogi and not like him. He endeared himself to Yankees fans with his hard-nosed style of play and the air of simplicity he carried about him. I don't mean "simplicity" in a negative sense. Yogi left school after eighth grade so he could work to help his family financially, but he was a very, very smart man—and that's something for which Yogi has not received enough credit. Yogi was simple in the manner that he wasn't showy or full of pretense. Yogi was just Yogi. What you saw was what he was, and I know fans appreciated that about him.

Yogi, of course, is known for his malapropisms. I would be curious to learn who is quoted more: Yogi or Shakespeare. I'm not sure Shakespeare would want to know, though.

Yogi provided us with such classic pronouncements as:

"It ain't over 'til it's over."

"You can observe a lot by watching."

"It's déjà vu all over again."

"When you come to a fork in the road, take it." (In Yogi's defense, he was giving directions to a place where the road split into a circle, and both directions led to the destination.)

"The future ain't what it used to be."

And fittingly, considering how many Yogi-isms have been falsely attributed to him: "I really didn't say everything I said."

I do have a couple of my own personal Yogi-isms to share, and I promise you they're authentic. Once he and I were seated together on a plane trip. We happened to be in an exit row. As we began our descent to the airport, Yogi told me with a completely serious look on his face that he had figured out what he would do if our plane was going to crash: "Just before the plane hits the ground, I'm gonna open this door, and I'm gonna jump out, and I'll land on my feet and be able to walk away."

Years later, Yogi appeared in one of the popular Aflac commercials that featured talking ducks. "You know," Yogi told me, "those ducks don't really talk." What he meant was that the sounds the ducks made in the commercials were dubbed in. But Yogi had a knack for giving his words a completely different spin from what they would ordinarily mean.

Yogi carried a lot of cash on our road trips. We received meal money for each of our trips, and Mantle typically ran through his before the trips ended. He knew Yogi never spent all his money, so he would go to Yogi and say, "Lend me two thousand dollars, and I'll pay you back when I get home." Yogi would say, "Okay, but you'll have to pay me back three thousand." Mickey would begrudgingly agree to the terms.

"That's a lot of interest, isn't it?" I would ask Yogi, but as long as Mickey kept going to the First Yogi Bank, he had no reason to reduce interest on his loans.

We drew a lot of laughs from Yogi. Now whenever Betsy and I return to New York for a Yankee-related event, we almost always end up going to dinner with Whitey and Yogi—and we spend most of those dinners laughing.

Chapter 19
MICKEY

MICKEY MANTLE was a special teammate, the one fans associate me with the most. On my first visit to Yankee Stadium in 1953, when Mickey came over to me at the batting cage, placed his arm over my shoulder, and told me to step into the batter's box for the first time, I had no idea we were beginning a friendship like no other I would ever have.

As accepted as I felt that day, I learned in my years with Mickey that he'd treated me no differently than he did any other rookie who came up with the Yankees. I think Mickey reached out to rookies because he was always for the underdog, and every rookie is an underdog in the sense of trying to make it among the pros. Mickey never forgot what it was like to be a rookie, since he came up under the enormous pressure of being hailed as the next Joe DiMaggio—while DiMaggio was still in the lineup.

In 1951, after playing one season in Class D and one in

Class C, Mickey started up with the Yankees but was sent down to the Triple-A Kansas City Blues midseason. When he went into a slump in the minors, the nineteen-year-old Mickey called his father, Mutt, and told him he wanted to quit baseball. Mutt, a coal miner, drove up from Oklahoma to Kansas City and began packing his son's clothes. "I thought I raised a man," Mickey's dad said. "I see I raised a coward instead. You can come back to Oklahoma and work the mines with me."

Mickey stayed in baseball, started ripping the cover off the ball for the Blues, and returned to the Yankees in late August. Seventeen years later, he retired as one of the greatest ever to play the game. But he never forgot how lonely and discouraged he'd felt in those early years. And he never neglected an opportunity to befriend a rookie and help him feel accepted in the clubhouse.

That didn't mean, however, that rookies were exempt from Mickey's pranks.

One of his favorite stunts was to arrange for everyone in the starting lineup to charge out of the dugout to begin the first inning. After about ten steps, Mickey and the other veterans would stop and retreat to the dugout, while the rookie continued on toward his position, unaware he suddenly was sprinting by himself.

Yes, Mickey got me with that one. It's a lonely feeling to realize you are the only player on the field, then look back toward the dugout and see your new teammates laughing at you—not to mention the sixty thousand or so people enjoying your embarrassment from the stands. Mickey also once left a message in my locker with instructions to call a certain phone number and ask for Mr. Lion. I followed the instructions, only to learn I had been given the number of the Bronx Zoo.

Mickey could outrun anyone in the majors. A switch-hitter, he hit for power from both sides of the plate. Yet an opponent never knew when the feared slugger would decide to lay one down and beat out the bunt for a single. Excellent defensively with his speed and a strong, accurate throwing arm, Mickey drew the assignment of covering the cavernous center field of Yankee Stadium. Mickey could beat a pitcher and score a run with his power or with his baserunning, and then he could go out into the field and save his pitcher a run or two with a diving catch in one of the deep power alleys.

Even with his first-ballot Hall of Fame statistics, however, Mickey's career can't be discussed without the sad speculation of what might have been.

Like Roger Maris, Mickey played football in high school, received a football scholarship offer from the University of Oklahoma, and opted instead for baseball. In Mickey's case, however, football almost ended his athletic future—and his life. Kicked in the shin while playing during high school, he subsequently came down with a bone infection called osteomyelitis. Only a newly developed treatment with penicillin prevented Mickey from having his leg amputated, but chronic pain from the osteomyelitis would plague him throughout his career. He would have to wrap his legs with ACE bandages before games, yet he could still outrun everyone else.

To make matters worse, during the 1951 World Series, Mickey caught a spike on a drainage cover in the outfield and tore up his right knee. That injury would also cause him trouble for the rest of his playing life. Sports medicine back then was nowhere near what it is now, of course. I wouldn't be surprised if Mickey played essentially all his career with a torn anterior cruciate ligament that today could be repaired by surgery and rehabilitation.

Many people have speculated about how Mickey's career might have been negatively affected by his love of the nightlife. I think that if Mickey had taken better care of himself, his statistics might have been a little better, but not much.

For one thing, I don't think it would be possible for them to be *much* better. They were just too good. Second, tales of Mickey's partying have become exaggerated over time. His greatest excesses came after his retirement from baseball. (Like many others who spend their lives playing baseball, Mickey had a difficult time making the transition away from the game after retiring.) When Mickey was playing, he wasn't out getting drunk every night. He and Whitey were drinking partners, and Whitey not only curtailed his own drinking before games, but also kept Mickey—his center fielder and cleanup hitter—in with him. So I usually find speculation over how much better Mickey would have played without the drinking to be overstated.

Other than the constant battles with injuries, what I believe most limited Mickey's statistics—particularly his power numbers—was Yankee Stadium. When we played, straightaway center field measured 461 feet from home plate. (The monuments honoring Lou Gehrig, Babe Ruth, and former manager Miller Huggins, plus a flagpole, stood in deep center field. When Yankee Stadium was renovated in 1976, the center field fence was brought in to 417 feet, in front of the monuments.) I can't guess how many balls I saw Mickey hit at Yankee Stadium that would have been home runs in other ballparks.

I played one time—the 1962 All-Star Game—at the much more homer-friendly Wrigley Field in Chicago. The wind was blowing out from home plate during batting practice, and I hit a pitch just above my fists that stung my hands. I looked up from checking my hands to see the ball exit the park. As a power hitter, of course, I never came close to Mickey. So I can only assume that Mickey's playing his home games at Wrigley Field would have been downright frightening. On the days the wind blew out, with that powerful swing, all he'd have to do was get the ball up in the air, and it would have carried out.

I'm convinced that if Mickey had played his home games at

Wrigley Field instead of Yankee Stadium, he would have hit 800 home runs. Think about it. Mickey hit 536 homers over his eighteen seasons as a pro. To reach 800, he would have needed to average almost fifteen more home runs per season. I think he could have done that playing half of his games at Wrigley.

I once asked Mickey, "Do you ever go to bat trying to hit a home run?"

He answered, "Every time."

The hardest I ever saw Mickey hit a ball was in 1956, when he just missed becoming the only person to ever hit a fair ball out of Yankee Stadium. A home run off the bat makes a distinctive sound. Then there are the rare homers when that sound goes to a whole other level. I heard that sound that day and jumped off my seat on the bench to watch the ball. As it took off like a rocket toward the roof in right field, I just knew that would be a special home run. The ball hit up on the facade, about a foot and a half from leaving the Stadium.

Pedro Ramos of the Washington Senators threw the pitch, and he would later say, "I threw the ball fast; he hit it faster."

When Mickey returned to the dugout after circling the bases, he shrugged and said, "I didn't get it all."

Mickey was famous as a power hitter, of course. Less well known is that fact that he threw an almost uncatchable knuckleball. Position players like to think they could be pitchers. Mickey probably could have pitched in the majors if he'd had better control of that knuckleball. But he couldn't do that because it moved too much.

Mickey kept begging Casey Stengel to put him on the mound late in a blowout game, but Casey wouldn't let him pitch. Managers usually keep a position player from pitching for fear he might hurt his arm. In Mickey's case, considering how unpredictable his knuckler was, Casey might have been more concerned about the safety of his catcher, the batter, or perhaps even the umpire.

Mickey didn't throw one of those fluttering knuckleballs that meanders its way to the plate; he threw a hard knuckler that broke in all kinds of directions. I had a difficult enough time catching his knuckleball with a glove; I sure wouldn't have wanted to try to hit it with a bat.

We used to tell rookies we would give them one hundred dollars if they could catch three of Mickey's knuckleballs in a row. Jake Gibbs was a catcher who had been both an All-American third baseman and a quarterback at the University of Mississippi, and he is an inductee of the College Football Hall of Fame. Jake came up to the big leagues in 1962 and took us up on our hundred-dollar proposal. He caught Mickey's first knuckler, but the second danced right around his mitt and hit him in the nose. Jake's broken nose forced an end to our hundred-dollar offers to rookies.

Mickey kept me, Tony Kubek, and Clete Boyer supplied in gloves. He'd signed a contract with Rawlings and arranged for the three of us to receive two or three gloves per year. I had a contract too, with MacGregor, for a Bobby Richardson signature model. MacGregor paid me a nickel for every glove sold, up to a limit of three hundred dollars. I made the maximum, but MacGregor sold far more gloves than needed to reach my limit. Truthfully, though, I preferred Rawlings gloves. My whole career, I played with gloves Mickey gave me.

Leader and Encourager

Mickey was a quiet leader, not a rah-rah guy. He led by example, and if someone wasn't hustling, he'd make sure that player knew he needed to. He always did it in a tactful way, though, without making the other player feel put down.

His style was to pull someone aside and say something like, "Hey, you know what? You can run faster. You need to really put out 100 percent. We want to win this. Some of these guys need

that World Series bonus check. You need to give a good effort."
And the player would *want* to give 100 percent, not only because
Mickey told him he should, but because he knew Mickey was giv-
ing 100 percent himself—often despite being injured.

To me, Mickey was an encourager. If I was going through a
tough time at the plate, Mickey would be the first to come over to
me on the bench, give me a small pat on the back, and say something to pick me up. He wouldn't do that in a showy way, either,
to let the rest of the team know what he was doing. Mickey simply
motivated others in his quiet way, and everyone on the team recognized him as our leader.

Mickey had a way, without trying, of drawing people to him—
my kids included. Mickey was like an uncle to my sons. Like Roger,
he was separated from his own sons during the season, so Robby and
Ronnie served as stand-in sons for Mickey, too.

I remember one time when Mickey and I were signed up for a
golf tournament and I brought Robby and Ron with me. When
Mickey saw my boys, he motioned them over to his cart. "Come on.
You boys ride with me," he said. "You can see your dad anytime!"

When my sons visited the clubhouse, they wouldn't stay long
at my locker. My locker was to the left of the entrance, five spots
from the door. Mickey's was on the right, across the room from
mine. Robby and Ronnie would be with me at my locker for about
three minutes before they were crossing the floor to go see Mickey,
who always welcomed them with open arms and made them feel
special. He would joke around with them, tousle their hair, have
one-on-one talks with them, and wrestle around with them.

In fact, whenever my boys were involved in roughhousing in
the locker room, Mickey was likely in the middle of it. It wasn't
uncommon to see Mickey with Robby tucked under one arm
and Ronnie under the other, both trying to squirm free from
Mickey's grip.

One of our most prized photos appeared on the back cover of Mickey's book *The Quality of Courage*. Mickey and a preschool Ronnie are running side by side on the Yankee Stadium field, and both are wearing boyish smiles. That picture says so much. Mickey was a fun-loving kid from Oklahoma, and there was a sense that he never really grew up. That was part of his appeal—and also part of his problem.

As fun-loving as Mickey was, sadness also haunted his life. Mickey's father died at age thirty-nine, from Hodgkin's disease, during Mickey's second season in the majors. An uncle and grandfather also died young from Hodgkin's, and Mickey often stated that he, too, would die at an early age. He said it in a joking manner, but it was obvious that deep down he didn't expect to live long.

Mickey was insecure in his relationships, particularly with his family. He loved his four sons and missed them during the season, but he didn't seem to know how to properly relate to them as a father. When his sons were older, his relationship with them basically consisted of drinking together. That appeared to be the only way he knew how to connect with them. I believe they knew he loved them, though. Years later, in a *New York Times* article, I read these words from Mickey Jr. about his father: "I thought he was a great dad. He wasn't what you would call a regular dad. But then he didn't lead what you would call a regular life."

I had closer friends on the Yankees than Mickey, and there were others I spent more time with off the field. Yet my relationship with Mickey was very special. That special bond carried on well after our playing days. In fact, I believe it grew stronger after we both retired. I would see Mickey maybe two or three times per year or up to five or six times when we were playing in Old Timers' Games.

In the late 1970s a friend of mine wanted Mickey and me to help promote a resort, and he offered to give us a townhouse in exchange. Mickey liked that idea, so we shared a place at Adam's Apple near Grandfather Mountain in western North Carolina.

A friend of mine from Sumter, Betty Ann Klapthor, came in and picked out furniture for the place and had it decorated all nice and cozy. We enjoyed having that place available as a getaway and used it several times.

At one point, the resort arranged for us to be grand marshals of a huge ski festival. When we got there, they wanted to take a picture of us snow skiing, but neither of us knew how to ski. So the idea of getting us on snow skis was scrapped in favor of having us dress in ski clothing and pose on a ski lift. We couldn't ski, but we did know how to sit down!

We had shared the place about three or four years before the economy got in the way. Interest rates soared, there was a nationwide gasoline shortage, and the resort went bankrupt. When people asked Mickey what happened to the place that he and I shared, Mickey didn't want to say what really happened, so he came up with a better-sounding answer: "Bobby tithed that to the Lord."

Ready to Help

Retired baseball players are often invited to take part in or lend their names to fund-raisers for worthy causes. Mickey, being so famous, was asked to do that a *lot*. And because I was involved with so many charitable endeavors, there were times when I was the one asking. I was careful not to go overboard in requesting favors, but not once did he turn me down when I asked for one.

The time when Mickey and Tony Kubek came to Sumter to help me with the YMCA fund-raiser—when Tony's changeup wound up hurting Mickey's leg—Mickey must have signed two to three hundred bats for fans. He was pretty well known for not liking to sign bats, but on that occasion he volunteered. I know he offered to do it because he wanted my fund-raiser to be successful.

He would have signed more, too, but so many people were trying to get his autograph that a concrete wall the lined-up fans were leaning on gave way, and the signing had to be stopped.

After that event I put fifteen 100-dollar bills in Mickey's pants pocket to cover his plane fare and other expenses. About two months later when I saw him again, I started, "Mickey, I hope that fifteen hundred—"

"What fifteen hundred?" he asked.

"I put fifteen 100-dollar bills in your pocket."

"I keep 100-dollar bills in my pocket all the time. I didn't know they were yours."

Then it dawned on me: Mickey had thought nothing about paying his own way to come help me.

Later, when I ran for Congress, I didn't even need to ask Mickey to visit South Carolina on my behalf. He offered to come in and do anything I needed from him.

One of my favorite memories of Mickey involved an instructional video he helped me with when I was coaching at South Carolina. Mickey worked with a group of eight-year-olds on their swings, and he was great with those boys, just as he had been with my sons in the Yankee Stadium clubhouse. Mickey would ask a kid to swing a couple of times, find something to compliment, then say something like, "Maybe this is a suggestion for you. When I'm hitting, I do so-and-so." Then he'd have the boy take a few more swings and help him apply the tips he'd just received. He worked with all the kids that way, teaching them to hit the ball where it's pitched, to not try to pull every ball, and to get out in front of the ball and make solid contact there instead of trying to hit for power.

When we had completed filming and began picking up to leave at the end of a long day, one of the boys said, "Mr. Mantle, can we ask you something? Would you take one swing for us?"

Mickey looked at me. I nodded. Mickey took a couple of practice swings right-handed, because that was his natural side and he was a better hitter right-handed. Then, when the pitch was thrown, Mick crushed it. We had been filming on a youth field, so the ball sailed way over the short fence in left center. It flew across a football field and into a parking lot that, because we were on such a small field, seemed like it was five hundred yards away.

"Wait! Wait! Wait!" I ran screaming toward Mickey. "No more, Mickey! We've got to stop this—my car is parked over there!"

Mickey had already made a big impression on those young boys that day because of how special he'd made each one feel while the cameras were on. That long home run hit he'd made just for them, while the cameras were off, left them in awe.

Searching

The two of us were long considered a curious pairing—Mickey, the hard-living life of the party, and I, the clean-living homebody. I am frequently asked how our special bond grew out of such contrasting lifestyles. I believe that Mickey and I were drawn together spiritually, that God had a purpose for our friendship.

Christians tend to use the word *searching* to describe a nonbeliever who seems to feel a void in his life that he can't adequately describe. We Christians can identify that person as searching because we have been there and have experienced the joy of filling that void with the presence of Christ in us.

In that sense, for most of the years that I knew Mickey, I do believe he was searching.

I'd heard Mickey and his wife, Merlyn, say that they did not drink alcohol when they were young but that when Mickey got to New York, he was drawn into the fast life there. Truthfully, though, I don't think Mickey's going to New York was to blame. If he had played in a smaller city, such as Kansas City or St. Louis, I believe he still would have found the party scene. That was his personality, and he would have been drawn to that lifestyle no matter where he was. Mickey was searching, but he didn't know what he was searching for and went to the wrong places to try to replace the sadness in his life with something meaningful.

One spring in Fort Lauderdale, we had a team party at the home of a friend, Jack Matthews. Mickey had previously introduced Jack to me as "one of your kind," meaning a Christian. Jack didn't have alcohol at his party. Everyone had a fun night grilling hamburgers and playing pickup basketball games. "You're right," Mickey told Betsy and me as we were leaving. "You can have fun without drinking."

I believe what drew Mickey to me was that I had the relationship with Jesus Christ that he was searching for, even if he didn't realize it. I knew that I had the answer for Mickey's questions. My problem was that I did not know how to share that answer with him effectively.

And as I've mentioned, that problem was not limited to my friendship with Mickey.

I had no problem standing in front of an audience and sharing the gospel. I spoke in churches on road trips during the season and to church and civic groups during the off-season. After some early bouts with stage fright, I even found it relatively easy to get on the platform of a packed stadium during a Billy Graham Crusade and tell how I had come into a personal relationship with Christ.

I was even known throughout baseball as one of a handful of players who publicly shared his faith. When I signed an autograph for a fan, I liked to include the words *Romans 1:16* after my name.

One time I signed that for a fan at a hotel in Kansas City. The fan looked at my signature and asked, "You're in Room 116?"

"No, no," I said, "that's Romans 1:16—a Bible verse. Go look it up."

That verse begins, "I am not ashamed of the gospel of Christ: for it is the power of God unto salvation to every one that believeth." I was not ashamed of the gospel, and I felt a responsibility to accept almost every speaking invitation so I could tell others about the salvation that God offers. At the same time, I felt insecure and ill-equipped to share that same message in a one-on-one setting with a friend. It wasn't a natural part of my personality to open up about the details of my life.

In many ways we are influenced by the events of our childhood, and I grew up in an environment that was not very open or expressive. My dad never talked much, especially about personal things. I never doubted that he had great love for me and was extremely proud of my abilities and future as a baseball player. He made sure to spend time with me, coming home from work and throwing a ball in the yard with me every day. He was at every game of mine he could make. And yet our communication was mostly nonverbal.

Because of the way I grew up, I wasn't comfortable expressing deep feelings with others. Men of my generation tend to be fairly nonexpressive to begin with, and I'm probably even more that way than most. I wasn't—and still am not—much of a hugger, and personal, one-on-one witnessing is a challenge for me. Step behind a microphone in front of tens of thousands of people? Let's do it. Sit down with an individual and share my deepest feelings? That's a different story.

That prevented me from having conversations with Mickey, as well as other teammates, that perhaps I would have liked to have had. However, I tried to live a life in front of them that demonstrated my relationship with Christ and glorified God. And when I could, I did try to share my faith with them in a low-key manner.

I was glad to read that interview with Joe DiMaggio where he said I had shared my faith in simplicity as a friend. That's exactly what I always hoped to do. I didn't want to be too zealous and, despite my best intentions, turn someone off to the point that he would shut down my future attempts to share the gospel. I know this is a concern for people with a personality like mine who want to witness to others. It's a tricky balance to maintain and was especially challenging for me as a ballplayer. I was aware of the risk that thumping my teammates over the head with a Bible could lose me their trust, which was a key component of our success as a ball club.

There is a greater risk, of course, when we neglect the great commission of Matthew 28:18-20—an eternal risk. So in addition to living what I prayed would be an exemplary lifestyle in front of my teammates, I invited in speakers who were experienced and effective in sharing the gospel message in small-group settings. About five or six times on road trips during a season, I'd arrange for a room in our hotel and bring in a guest speaker. I would have sweet rolls and coffee ready for the guys because of the time-proven truth that free food always attracts people!

I liked to have the speaker come and visit me a day early so I could introduce him to my teammates and give them a chance to get to know him. I knew the guys would be more likely to come to our meeting the next morning if they first had a chance to connect individually with the speaker. And if the speaker happened to pick up the tab for dinner—as often happened—the guys were much more likely to give him a chance. Again, free food.

I didn't target Mickey specifically for those sessions, but I did invite speakers who I thought would relate well with him. I also made sure to invite him personally. He would usually try to give a type of nonanswer by kidding around, saying something like, "Oh, man, let me know tomorrow morning because I'll be out late tonight. I'm not sure I'll be up that time of day." But then, almost every time, Mickey would come walking in.

Mickey wasn't embarrassed to walk into one of our chapel services or into a church service, either. I think he actually liked being in church and looked forward to going if someone would ask him and make arrangements for him to get there.

Watson Spoelstra was a sportswriter for the *Detroit News*, and he'd told me, "If any of your guys want to go to church while you're playing in Detroit, I know where there's an early service." Tony Kubek and I liked to take up Watson on his offer, and we usually asked Mickey if he wanted to go to church with us. I remember several occasions when Mickey would say, "Yeah, I'd like to go." We would have coffee together, then Watson would pick us up at the hotel, take us to church, and get us back in time for the game.

Even though I kept my witnessing low-key, Mickey was well aware that his salvation was important to me. In fact, we often talked about "that decision"—referring to the prospect of his surrendering to Christ. As Mickey often did with serious topics, however, he would use the phrase in a half-joking manner.

Once we were together in a helicopter that lurched at takeoff. Mickey looked over to me and said above the noise of the helicopter, "Maybe this would be a good time to make that decision!"

Another time I showed up at a charity golf tournament that Mickey didn't know I'd be participating in. "I'm glad you're here," he told me. "This minister's getting on me about making that decision for Christ. I told him if he beat me in golf, then I'd make that decision."

Mickey and I talked enough about "that decision" that Phil Rizzuto, when he was broadcasting Yankees games, would holler out to Mickey, "Have you made that decision yet?"

Well after our playing days, in the late 1980s, Mickey opened a restaurant in New York City. On a couple of occasions I was asked to speak to groups that met there. I called Mickey's secretary ahead of time to let him know I'd be there. And both times he showed up, listened to me share my testimony, and joined in with the group asking questions about my story and faith.

My son Robby, who is in the ministry, also shared his faith once to a group in Mickey's restaurant. After the meeting started, Robby noticed Mickey slipping in and quietly taking a seat in the back of the room. Robby didn't mention Mickey so as not to draw attention to him. Afterward Mickey made eye contact with Robby and pointed toward a back office. Robby walked back to meet with Mickey, and Mickey told Robby how great it was to see him again. "You know," he told Robby, "you sound just like your dad—always talking about that decision I need to make."

It was about that same time that Mickey appeared in a televised interview with sportscaster Bob Costas. Roger Maris had passed away about three years earlier. Mickey, in his midfifties at the time of the interview, had joked for years that he wouldn't live past age thirty-nine. And his good friend Roger's death had affected him in a deep way. At Roger's funeral, Mickey had asked me to handle his own funeral when the time came. Three years later, during the interview, it was obvious Mickey was still thinking about his mortality.

Mickey told Costas that Roger's death had left "a void in my heart, an emptiness inside."

When the interview ended, my phone began ringing with calls from friends wanting to know if I had watched the interview.

"Did you see that?" one friend asked. "He's searching. God is working on his heart."

Chapter 20

THE DECISION

MICKEY WAS A courageous baseball player. He played through constant injury to earn a place among the game's best ever. I would watch in amazement as Mickey would have a leg bandaged from his ankle to the top of his thigh in the locker room, then drag his leg onto the field and clout one of his tape-measure home runs or track down a long fly ball in deepest center field that many fully healthy center fielders would not have been able to reach. And I could never forget that World Series game in '61, when he played with a hip so badly abscessed that he left the game with blood-stained pants.

Yet I don't think I ever saw Mickey more courageous than when he sat across from Bob Costas in another interview, in 1994. By then Mickey had recently completed rehab for alcohol abuse at the Betty Ford Center. And only two weeks earlier, one of his four sons, Billy—named for Billy Martin—had passed away at age thirty-six. Like so many in Mickey's family, Billy had contracted Hodgkin's disease and then, after receiving treatment, died of a heart attack. Another Mantle had died far too young.

In the interview, Mickey swept away a tear and admitted, "I was not a good father. . . . I wasn't ever there." He hadn't expected to live as long as he had. He certainly hadn't expected to bury a son. He added that he still had three sons, and "I need to tell 'em I love 'em."

Mickey talked about how he had looked up to ballplayers such as Stan Musial, Ted Williams, and Joe DiMaggio. "Those were role models," Mickey said, implying that he didn't think of himself that way. "I wouldn't want kids trying to be like I was at the end there."

Near the conclusion of that interview, with the camera zoomed tightly on his face, Mickey said, "I know there is something in there that's not fulfilled or something. I don't know what it is, Bob. I can't explain it." Then Mickey shook his head.

The year after that interview, Mickey was diagnosed with liver cancer and received a liver transplant. That summer, with the All-Star Game in Arlington, Texas, Betsy and I traveled to Dallas for a meeting with the Baseball Assistance Team. B.A.T., as it is called for short, provides financial assistance for players, umpires, and team personnel. I was on the B.A.T. board of directors with Whitey and Mickey, but Mickey was unable to attend the meetings because he was still recovering from the transplant.

The phone in our Dallas hotel room rang at six o'clock one morning while we were there. Betsy answered.

"Betsy, this is Mickey. I'm really hurting. I want Bobby to pray for me."

Betsy handed the phone to me, and Mickey and I prayed for his condition to improve. As I had with Dick Howser, I shared with Mickey the message of Philippians 4: Delight yourself in the Lord, tell Him your problems and anxieties, and He promises to give you a peace that passes all understanding.

I talked with Mickey two or three more times on that trip. "Now don't forget," he told me before I returned home, "you have my funeral."

We had been back in Sumter a few weeks when Mickey's wife, Merlyn, called. Mickey was back in the hospital, and his condition had taken a turn for the worse. We hastily arranged a flight back to Dallas. On the plane, as I realized this likely would be my final visit with Mickey, I prayed for my teammate's life. I prayed for my friend's soul. I prayed that I would be a bolder witness than I had ever been, in what would be our final times together. I wanted nothing more than for Mickey to spend eternity with me in heaven.

We arrived in Dallas that night. First thing the next morning, I headed to the hospital. I didn't know what to expect as I pushed open the door.

Mickey flashed his down-home, country-boy smile.

"I can't wait to tell you this," Mickey said right away. "I want you to know that I'm a Christian. I've accepted Christ as my Savior."

I was thrilled, of course, but I said, "Mickey, to make sure you understand, let me go over it with you again." Then I began to share again the story he had gone out of his way to hear me share when we were teammates.

"Mickey, God loves you, and He has a purpose for your life. He sent the Lord Jesus to shed His precious blood and promised in His Word that if you repent of your sin and receive Him as Savior, you may indeed have everlasting life. I did that very thing when I was a boy of about twelve. My pastor came to my home and opened up God's Word and talked about how Romans says, 'All have sinned, and come short of the glory of God.'

"Mickey, you and I are both sinners. We are in that same category. And the Bible says there's a penalty involved. 'The wages of sin is death'—eternal death. The good news is that Christ died for our sins. He was buried, and He rose again the third day, according to the Scriptures. That day as a young boy, I responded to ask God to forgive me for my sins, and I received Him as Lord and Savior of my life."

"That's just what I've done," Mickey told me. "I have received Jesus Christ as my Savior."

Tears filled my eyes. After a lifetime of decisions he regretted, Mickey had made "that decision"—the best decision any person could make. I didn't get the whole story about how Mickey accepted his salvation, but near his bed were audiotapes of Pete Maravich's testimony.

I couldn't wait to recount our conversation to Betsy when I arrived at the friend's home where we were staying.

"Let's go back to the hospital," Betsy said, "and let me talk to him." She and Mickey had become good friends over the years.

When Mickey saw Betsy, he said, "Let me get comfortable so we can talk." His sons helped him to a reclining chair. When his son David put his arms around Mickey to help move him, Mickey asked David, "Do you want to dance?" As sick as he was, he still couldn't resist a joke.

After we visited awhile, the boys left the room, leaving only Mickey, Merlyn, Betsy, and me. Betsy knelt beside Mickey, held his hand, and shared the story of how she had come to know Christ as her Savior. She told Mickey that even as a youngster, she'd needed her sins forgiven just as much as Mickey did. Finally Betsy paused, gave Mickey a serious look, and asked Mickey the same question she had been asked when she became a Christian: "If you were to stand before a holy God today, and He asked you the question, 'Why should I let you into My heaven?' what would you say?"

Mickey considered her question for a moment and looked to Merlyn before turning back to face Betsy. "Betsy, we're talking about God?"

"That's right."

Mickey thought a little longer before answering: "For God so loved the world, that he gave his only begotten Son, that whosoever believeth in him should not perish, but have everlasting life."

I suspect that verse had been planted in a young Mickey's heart long ago, perhaps in a church back in Commerce, Oklahoma. For all those years, that seed had been germinating. Now, in what a gospel tract would later call Mickey's final inning, in a hospital room in Dallas, the salvation message of John 3:16 had grown in and changed his heart.

Over the next couple of days, Mickey had to be heavily medicated for pain and began drifting in and out of sleep. His wife and sons were in the room with us. Whenever Mickey woke up, I would read to him from Psalms, and we would pray. Despite his condition, there was a genuine peace in that room—a peace I had never seen in Mickey before. At one point, a doctor checked in on Mickey, and Mickey told him, "I'm ready."

Mickey passed into the presence of his Savior early on Sunday morning, August 13, 1995. He was sixty-three. He was my teammate and friend, and I will spend eternity with him.

My Favorite Mickey Story

Securing a location for Mickey's funeral proved a greater challenge than expected. I had two friends who pastored large churches in Dallas, but both were on vacation and unable to be reached. Finally an assistant to Mickey's lawyer helped us connect with people at the Lovers Lane United Methodist Church in North Dallas. We could hold Mickey's service in that beautiful facility.

When I wasn't involved in the arrangements for the service, I isolated myself as much as possible at the home of our friends Sumner and Celeste Wemp. Robby and Ron, who both were pastoring churches in Sumter at the time, received a flood of phone calls from media outlets all across the country trying to contact me with interview requests. I like to help the media when I can, but that was a time when I chose to turn down all requests. I knew Merlyn and the family wanted to avoid publicity, and my mission was to be there for my friend Mickey and his family.

As I prepared my message, I thought of the friends and teammates of Mickey who would be at his funeral. What did they need to hear?

First and foremost, I wanted to let them know that the Lord had answered the prayers of so many—that Mickey had become a Christian. Because Mickey's final days had been kept private, few would know that Mickey had accepted Jesus as his Savior. I asked my family and close friends to pray for me, that I could present the gospel clearly and represent my friend in a way that would have pleased him and would comfort his family. This would be one more opportunity for me to share that message with my teammates. I knew Mickey would want them to know that he had finally made "that decision."

I felt a heavy sense of responsibility in communicating that message for Mickey—and that was when I was thinking only of speaking to his friends and teammates. I did not know the service would be broadcast live—not only by two Dallas TV stations, but also nationally on CNN and ESPN2.

Tony Kubek was at the funeral home for visitation the night before the funeral. I talked with Tony about what I was feeling as I prepared the message, and he was such an encouragement to me.

The next day more than two thousand family members and friends packed into that church. Folding chairs had to be set up in one of the aisles to make room for more people. A line began forming outside the church at five thirty that morning for a service that would begin at two in the afternoon, and many had to be turned away by security.

It's eerie how quiet that many people crammed into one place can become.

After being introduced as "a faith friend of Mickey's," I made some brief opening remarks. I chose to set a comforting tone for the service by reading from 1 Thessalonians 4:13-18:

> I would not have you to be ignorant, brethren, concerning them which are asleep, that ye sorrow not, even as others which have no hope. For if we believe that Jesus died and rose again, even so them also which sleep in Jesus will God bring with him. For this we say unto you by the word of the Lord, that we which are alive and remain unto the coming of the Lord shall not prevent them which are asleep. For the Lord himself shall descend from heaven with a shout, with the voice of the archangel, and with the trump of God: and the dead in Christ shall rise first: Then we which are alive and remain shall be caught up together with them in the clouds, to meet the Lord in the air: and so shall we ever be with the Lord. Wherefore comfort one another with these words.

Then I prayed, referencing the words of Moses in Psalm 90:9: "We spend our years as a tale that is told."

"We know that one day," I continued, "we will all stand before You as our Creator. We're just so thankful that You provided a way, the Lord Jesus Christ, who suffered and died for our sins on the cross so that we might have everlasting life with You. We ask Your blessing on this service and Your blessing on this family. Be a comfort to them, and meet each one here today at their point of need. We pray in Jesus' name, Amen."

Bob Costas, who had grown up admiring Mickey, was next at the pulpit. He hit a home run as he eloquently expressed the emotions Mickey had stirred up within so many baseball fans who became kids again at the sight of their baseball hero.

Bob drew a loud laugh from the congregation when he shared one of Mickey's favorite stories about being met by Saint Peter at the pearly gates of heaven. As Mickey envisioned it, the good saint shakes his head and says, "Mick, we checked the record. We know some of what went on. Sorry, we can't let you in. But before you go, God wants to know if you'd sign these six dozen baseballs."

I had heard that tale many times and had laughed because it's a funny story, but I'd felt a sense of sadness, too. This time, though, I just laughed. I knew that in just a few minutes I would be sharing a new Mickey Mantle story that would correct the part about him not stepping through heaven's pearly gates.

Before my message, singer Roy Clark delivered a haunting rendition of a song that was a hit for him in 1969: "Yesterday When I Was Young." Mickey had asked Roy to sing that song at his funeral. "A promise is a promise," Roy said as he stepped forward to the microphone with his guitar. "It just wasn't supposed to happen this soon."

The ballad, originally written by Herbert Kretzner and Charles Aznavour, tells the story of an aging man who reflects on his life and regrets the way he had wasted the years of his youth on meaningless pursuits. Mickey believed the song could have been the story of his life. And the final line Roy sang really is sobering: "The time has come for me to pay for yesterday, when I was young."

Those words seemed to hang heavily over the congregation as I took my place again at the pulpit. If Mickey had been next to speak, I knew he would have cracked a joke to lighten the mood.

"I want to make a transition now from crying and sadness to laughter," I began, "because if you knew Mickey, he was always laughing."

Then I began working my way down my page of notes, highlighting Mickey's favorite pranks and my favorite memories of him: the fake mongoose he scared us with in the Detroit clubhouse, the rubber snake he hid in Marshall Bridges' uniform pants in Kansas City, Yogi's high-interest loans, Phil Linz's harmonica, the basketball game at West Point. I pointed out his soft heart for others and for charity and his numerous good deeds, many of which went unpublicized—flying across the country during the 1965 season, for instance, to visit with former teammate Fritz Brickell, who was dying of cancer, or holding a missions benefit at the very church where we'd now gathered to remember him.

As I shared these memories of Mickey, I was building toward my last day in the major leagues: October 2, 1966. That was also the last day of the season, so Ralph Houk had asked me to lead a team devotion. I spoke briefly that day, and as I often did for our chapel services, I brought in a guest speaker: Billy Zeoli, my close friend from Gospel Films, whose messages in past chapels had touched Mickey's heart.

Billy's message to our team that day was that, according to the Bible, we all have a problem: sin. God's answer to that sin problem is Jesus Christ, but each of us must make a decision about that.

We can give one of three possible answers to the question of whether or not to accept Jesus Christ as Lord and Savior. We can say "yes." We can say "no." Or we can say "maybe," putting off the decision until a more convenient time. However, Billy warned, because of the X factor of death, "maybe" can automatically become "no."

I didn't fully comprehend what Billy meant until some years later, at a reunion of the 1961 team. We had a wonderful time remembering our great season together. But when I returned to my room that night, I reflected on the evening and the fact that three of our teammates from '61 had already passed away: Roger Maris, Elston Howard, and Duke Maas. I understood then why Billy had said "maybe" really meant "no."

In reality, I explained to the congregation, because we never know what tomorrow holds for us, there are really only two choices: yes or no.

Billy's message culminated with one question he wanted to leave in the minds of my teammates that day, the same question I wanted to present to those at Mickey's funeral: "What have you done with Jesus Christ?"

Then I began to walk the congregation through my last visit with Mickey in his hospital room, when he'd excitedly told me he had accepted Jesus Christ as his Savior and recited John 3:16 as evidence that he understood his choice to say "yes."

I knew that many in that church and in the television audience looked to Mickey as a hero, and I told them that if Mickey could talk to them from his new home, he would introduce them to *his* true hero: Jesus. The greatest tribute those listening to my words could give Mickey, I said, was to say "yes" just as he had.

In conclusion, I prayed, "Thank You, God, that You loved us so much that You gave Your only Son, and He willingly came and died for our sins, according to the Scriptures. And then He was buried and rose again on the third day, according to the Scriptures. May each of us today honestly answer the question, 'What have I done with Jesus?'"

Then I continued, "I'm so glad that someone shared with me years ago, and perhaps you'd like to pray now as I did then."

I then led those whose hearts might have been stirred by God's touch in a prayer:

"God, thank You for loving me and sending Your Son to shed His precious blood. And right now, I'm sorry for my sin. And I receive You as Lord and Savior. Thank You for coming into my heart. To God be the glory."

I know Mickey would be proud to read the mail I received from people who watched the funeral, saying the story of

Mickey's decision had influenced them to make that same decision. His testimony keeps making an impact too. The American Tract Society developed his story into a gospel tract titled "Mickey Mantle: His Final Inning." I include a copy in most of my answers to fan mail, and I have received replies from people letting me know they had checked the box that says, "I have just now prayed for Jesus Christ to save me." It's the same tract that Clete Boyer was reading in our living room when he prayed the prayer of salvation a year before he died.

And I know it would bring tears of joy to Mickey's eyes to hear that one of those most influenced by Mickey's final message was his oldest son, Mickey Mantle Jr.

Following Mickey's funeral, there was a private burial service for only his family, teammates, and closest friends. Fewer than fifty people were invited. I read the Twenty-third Psalm, and at the point where I was to pray, I felt led to have a young pastor there pray instead. I knew that the young pastor had spent a lot of time with Mickey's sons, sharing God's Word with them and helping them through their struggles.

I've been told that same pastor helped lead Mickey Jr. to the Lord before he passed away five years later, at the age of forty-seven, from cancer.

What a glorious reunion there must have been between Mickey and Mickey Jr.—in a place where there is no more sadness, no more insecurity—only joy.

Chapter 21

PROTECTING THE HOME FIELD

I DIDN'T REALIZE at the time of Mickey's funeral that his testimony and my testimony would become one. Following his funeral, my speaking invitations increased dramatically. I continue to tell Mickey's story for him, and I consider it a tremendous honor to have been placed in the position to do so.

Talking about Mickey has kept fresh in my mind the memories of him as a teammate and friend. Because I include his testimony in many of my speaking engagements and people ask me so many questions about him, I have spent a lot of time over the past decade and a half reflecting on our friendship and our time together. And from the perspective of hindsight, I've come to believe that Mickey was wrong about two things.

The first was thinking he had to change before he could become a Christian.

I am grateful that Mickey's life ended in such a way that he could see his death coming, and that by God's grace, his reasons for putting off a decision for God—saying "maybe," which actually means "no"—were removed as hurdles. I also believe Mickey realized he was a sinner and knew that the wages of sin is death, so he understood the penalty involved. But I think he wrongly believed that he had to completely clean up his life before he came to Christ.

We don't have to change our lives to become acceptable to Christ. In fact, we *can't* change our lives to become acceptable to Christ. There is nothing we can do to earn His salvation. It is a gift. The only "requirement" is that we acknowledge our sin and helplessness to change ourselves and then receive that gift. Paul writes in Ephesians 2:8-9, "It is by grace you have been saved, through faith—and this is not from yourselves, it is the gift of God—not by works, so that no one can boast" (NIV). John 3:16, which Mickey recited in his hospital room, says that God *gave* His only Son.

Grace, by definition, is unmerited favor. And also by definition, salvation—which comes through grace—cannot be earned.

Change comes not *before* salvation but *from* salvation. Salvation doesn't mean we change; it means we allow God to change us from the inside out. Change comes through the only way God has provided: our asking forgiveness for our sins and receiving His Son as Lord and Savior in our hearts and lives.

In 2 Corinthians 4:7 Paul wrote that the power of salvation comes "from God and not from us" (NIV). That is such a freeing thought—to know that I don't have to change myself. Because let's be honest: none of us has the power to make that change.

I think that Mickey's misunderstanding of that reality is one reason he delayed his decision for Christ. He had battled his insecurity in the areas of drinking and relationships for so many years that I don't think he believed he could make the changes he thought were necessary to become a Christian. He did not understand that when you give your heart to Christ and invite Him to be Lord of your life, He is the One who gives you the strength needed to overcome the temptations that come your way.

Another thing I believe Mickey was wrong about is more painful to admit. Mickey was wrong about me.

Mickey once told Betsy, "I can't live like Bobby." He knew I didn't cuss or drink, and he looked at me as living a good life—good in the sense that I didn't do any of the things that he would consider bad. But what Mickey didn't know was that I battled my own weaknesses too.

I always tried to live in a way that I hoped would cause my teammates to be drawn to my Savior. But I shudder at the possibility that in trying so hard to do that and not sharing my struggles with them, I might have given the wrong impression. Did they know and understand that the source of my strength was Jesus, not a religion or self-discipline?

When I speak, I like to emphasize two points. First, the way we Christians live our lives in front of others is important. Second, we need to guard against allowing our witness to break down at home. I failed at both many times, of course, and by grace I asked God to forgive me. But I have to wonder whether, if Mickey knew just how often I failed in that second area, maybe he would not have told Betsy he couldn't live like me.

The plain and simple truth is that all Christians have struggles. Ephesians 6:12 says, "Our struggle is not against flesh and blood, but against the rulers, against the authorities, against the powers of this dark world and against the spiritual forces of evil in the heavenly realms" (NIV). The implication in that passage is not that Christians *might* struggle but that we *do* struggle. And those struggles can come from places we do not expect.

For a professional baseball player, the obvious place to expect struggles is within the major league lifestyle. And there are plenty of temptations there.

I always recognized that my baseball ability was a gift from God, so I attempted to redirect praise from others to become praise to Him: "To God be the glory." I didn't put myself in positions where alcohol and drugs could become a problem for me. Because I made my faith known publicly, my teammates—even the ones who drank—became my helpers. My teammates knew I didn't want to drink, and they would not try to persuade me to go out with them. Often they would say something like, "We're going out to a bar, but we know you'll probably want to go to a restaurant with some of the others." It was as though they respected my decision to not drink and perhaps even encouraged me to be different. Even today it makes me feel good when Betsy says that when I was a player, she did not experience the same fears that some other players' wives felt when their husbands were on the road.

One of my biggest struggles, though, came in the place that probably would be the least expected: at home. While I was out sharing my faith in churches, at Billy Graham Crusades, in front of civic groups, and with my teammates, the enemy was diligently chipping away at my marriage. It happened so gradually that I wasn't even aware of it until more than thirty years after Betsy and I got married. By then, our marriage was in real danger.

Our marital problems were never a question of love. Betsy and I loved each other deeply. But we both had needs and issues from our past that affected the way we treated each other. Neither of us knew how to communicate effectively with the other. And our schedule, especially during my playing days, made things more difficult.

I've described how my father remained mostly silent and how my mother had the stronger personality in our household. So I went into my marriage not knowing how a husband and wife

should effectively communicate to work out their differences.
I also had anger issues, and the avenue through which my anger expressed itself was sarcasm. I could be quick with a sarcastic and biting remark. On top of that, I chose a profession that involved travel and a lot of time away from home. I take full responsibility, though, for my actions. I don't blame anyone else.

Betsy's father left his family when she was eight months old. She never met him. As would be expected, Betsy went into our marriage needing a husband who would affirm her, protect her, and be present for her. I'm not sure any professional baseball player would have fit the personality profile of Betsy's ideal mate. I know I didn't.

Remember, we didn't have a true honeymoon, and just about the first thing I did after we had completed the drive from Sumter to Denver after our wedding was take off on a two-week road trip with my team. *Here's our home—see you in a couple of weeks.* My baseball schedule immediately had an impact on our marriage.

Then while I was in the major leagues, Betsy had to take on more than her fair share of responsibilities at home. Her mother, Mary, and her friend and helper, Virginia Burgess, were a great support to her, but ultimately Betsy was the one responsible for packing up our family when school ended so she and the kids could join me for the summer. Then she was the one responsible for packing up our family again at the end of the summer to return to Sumter for the beginning of school.

Betsy also handled all the home and parenting duties when I was off on road trips. People saw our children play sports and assumed they benefited from having a major leaguer to work with them at home. They would be stunned to know how many times it actually was their mother throwing a ball with them in the yard or shooting baskets with them because their father was not home.

Even when our family was together at our in-season home in New Jersey and the Yankees were on home stands, my schedule still meant Betsy had to cover for things I should have been doing as the husband and father. For a day game, I had to leave the house at eight thirty in the morning to get to the ballpark, and I wouldn't return home until around seven or eight at night. For a night game, I would leave around noon and make it back home around midnight. That schedule did not leave much room for quality family time.

That was our schedule for eight months of the year. The off-season began in October and ran through February. But during the off-season I still traveled a good deal, sharing my testimony as much as I could because I had a difficult time saying no.

Even for the strongest marriages, that is a demanding schedule, and eventually it took its toll on our family. I wish I could go back in time armed with the knowledge of our differences I now possess. I certainly would have treated Betsy better.

As it was, when Betsy tried to express the areas in which she needed my help, I would take it the wrong way, think she was trying to run my life, become angry on the inside, and pop off a sarcastic remark. Betsy did not understand that the source of my anger and sarcasm was in my childhood. Because she grew up without a father, she would take my sarcasm as a rejection of her.

Betsy thought that if I really loved her—and I did, dearly— I would stop the sarcasm. Her solution, then, was to try harder to express her pain and need for affirmation. But because we were missing each other with our different levels of communication, I still wasn't providing the affirmation she needed from me. The more Betsy tried, and the more I didn't get it, the angrier I became, and the more my words made her feel like a failure. I'm telling this story in only a few paragraphs, but imagine that cycle slowly spinning within a marriage over the course of three decades.

I complicated matters by not recognizing my own deficiencies. I dealt with my anger and sarcasm like a ballplayer deals with losing a game: it happened, tomorrow's a new day, forget about it, move on. A baseball player has to be able to do that to make it in the majors. The obvious flaw in that approach to a relationship, though, is that it never deals with the problem. Perhaps worse, it does not even acknowledge that there is a problem.

That was me in our marriage. I understood Betsy's upbringing and wrongly believed that her father's absence was to blame—that the problem was Betsy's. I know now that it was *our* problem, and I was the one person who could bring the male affirmation that Betsy had missed and desperately needed. I am so thankful that she turned to her Savior and heavenly Father and not to another man to meet those deep needs in her loneliest times. Betsy has committed many Bible verses to memory, and her knowledge of God's Word is rooted in those times when she had to rely upon God's strength and wisdom every day.

Because I thought the problem was Betsy's, I had no interest in meeting with a counselor. If she wanted to talk to a counselor, that was fine with me, but I wasn't about to go anywhere near a counselor's office. She had issues; I was fine.

This wasn't funny then, but Betsy laughs while telling the story now, so I'll share it here. I did relent enough to Betsy's pleading to agree to attend a Christian marriage seminar with Betsy and two friends, Sam and Shirley Anderson. I didn't know then that Betsy had picked this seminar because of the way it was promoted. The speaker was going to tell husbands how to love their wives. That sounded great to Betsy.

One night of the seminar, the speaker focused on how wives are instructed in God's Word to be submissive to their husbands. The next morning he was to speak on how husbands are supposed to love their wives as Christ loved the church. But we didn't stick around for that part.

"That's it," I announced after the nighttime seminar. "I've had enough of this. We're going home." Hearing only the wives' role talk in the first part of the seminar, I left more convinced than ever that all our problems really were Betsy's fault. As we drove home—with our friends in the car—Betsy became so distraught over our leaving the seminar without meeting her expectations that she started crying. I looked over at her and said, "You didn't learn a thing, did you?"

I wasn't much help, was I?

In the late 1980s, while I was coaching baseball at Liberty University, our marriage reached the point that Betsy knew there was no hope for it apart from God. Only a handful of people were aware of the depths of our struggles—and that didn't include me! Betsy reached out for help to a counselor, who recommended strongly that she confront me with a "we must get help now or else" declaration. I finally agreed to seek outside help with her, and we were referred to an evangelist for spiritual counseling. Ron wasn't a marital counselor, but he was an expert in spiritual warfare who put his trust in the power of the Holy Spirit.

For two days Betsy and I put our lives on the table in front of the evangelist. As someone who had trouble getting below the surface and into a deep, personal level with others, I found it extremely difficult to open up my life like that to a person I did not know. But as we allowed not only each of our personal lives, but also our spiritual lives, to be evaluated in front of each other, I finally saw the depth of pain Betsy was going through and how I had contributed to it. For the first time, I understood that what we were going through was not Betsy's problem but our problem.

The evangelist helped us to see that our battle was not just with each other but also within ourselves. There were deep-seated issues in each of our lives that were being used to attack our marriage. Our battle was spiritual, as Paul had said in Ephesians.

I came out of that counseling knowing that my life had to change completely. And the changes that were needed were not ones I could make on my own; they could only be made by allowing the Holy Spirit to work within me to make me the kind of husband Betsy needed. They weren't changes I could make right there, on the spot, but I did have to make a commitment right then and there to work toward real change.

My sarcasm, for one, had to stop. That certainly wouldn't be easy. It remains a battle for me to this day. But at least I have come to understand the poison of sarcasm and why it needed to go. Sarcasm is sneaky. It has a habit of working its way out of our mouths before we suddenly realize, *Boy, that was the wrong thing to say at this time.* I still catch myself wanting to say something sarcastic or even making a sarcastic remark before I can stop it.

There were other changes I needed to make, of course, for Betsy's sake and for our marriage's sake. She had to do some adjusting as well. I won't say it was easy, but we kept at it.

That meeting with the evangelist occurred more than twenty years ago. I believe that God's mercy and grace kept our marriage together until those two days of counseling, His mercy and grace saved our marriage during those two days, and His mercy and grace have kept us married since. We recently celebrated with joy our fifty-sixth wedding anniversary.

I don't want to make it sound as though the battles within us have stopped—far from it. All Christians face battles. But the power of God that saved us is the same power that sustains us.

I also don't want to make it appear that one day, after more than thirty years of being married, I woke up to the realization that our marriage needed help. Just as the deterioration of our marriage was a slow process, so was the chipping away at my hardened heart that led me to consent to counseling.

Although I was saved when I was almost twelve and realized when I met Betsy that there was a deeper walk with Christ available, I understand now that I remained at that decision level for many years. I was a Christian, and I lived a Christian life that made an impact around me, but I didn't mature spiritually as I should have.

I definitely wasn't ashamed of the gospel; I can't guess the number of days I shared the gospel as a speaker. I was intentional in ministering, but I wasn't intentional enough about being ministered to. When I wasn't speaking in a church, I was attending church, but I was in a pulpit speaking much more than I was in a pew listening. The ratio of ministry going out compared with ministry coming in was way out of whack.

I also allowed my busy schedule—baseball and otherwise—to get in the way of my studying Scripture and having devotion time at home with my family. Betsy sometimes challenged me to be more consistent with my Bible study and prayer and to have devotions in our home, but it was easy for me to resent her efforts and say, "I have to meet someone for breakfast this morning, so I'll do it this afternoon." Then, of course, afternoon would come around, something else would come up, and I wouldn't have my quiet time.

As a result, I was unashamed but unequipped.

My inner urge to retire from baseball so I could spend more time with my family came at a time when I believe God was trying to get my attention, as He had in the earlier years of my marriage when there was a lot of spiritual growth in my life. Then after I did retire, I went to hear a friend, Bob Norris, who had just come to pastor a small church in our hometown. Bob's teaching made the Scriptures come alive in a way I had not heard in a long time. I told Betsy I wanted her to visit Bob's church with me the next Sunday. She felt the same way about how God's Word was being presented there.

We decided to begin attending that church, and my friend's messages caused me to see a deeper level within the gospel message—a level I had never reached. I came to the stinging realization that, while I was effectively sharing the gospel all across the country, I was not effectively living and sharing it at home. I had become so busy going to places where I wanted to make an impact that I had neglected the place where I most needed to make an impact.

Convicted by this realization, I began studying God's Word more and praying more, and I committed to having more devotion time at home. As a result, I began to grow more as a Christian. In a way, I think I began moving toward becoming the person some folks thought I already was.

That is why I still think often of that poignant interview Mickey Mantle had with Bob Costas. When Mickey said, "I was not a good father," I immediately understood what he was saying—because I wasn't a good father on numerous occasions either.

I also think of another interview during which Mickey said, "I'm no hero." Again, I understood. I was no hero either, despite all the people who considered me to be one. I failed my wife. I failed my children. I failed others. I failed my God.

My struggles and battles were very different from Mickey's. But what I want my testimony to include is that all of us, including Christians, battle sin—despite what others' perceptions of us might be. Some people's struggles, like Mickey's, are public, out there where everyone can see. Other people's, like mine, are more private. The struggles can even be within a person and known only to him or her.

I am so grateful that we have a loving God who came to save sinners—and that means me. It is only the daily influence in my life of that loving God that has enabled me to address some of my failures and grow as a husband, a father, a person, and a Christian. The power of His Son, Jesus Christ, and the presence of the Holy Spirit are made stronger in my life through Bible study, prayer, and fellowship with other believers.

So That Others Can Grow

My spiritual growth after I retired from baseball is one of the reasons I have invested myself and my resources in organizations such as Baseball Chapel and Fellowship of Christian Athletes.

Athletes enjoy an incredible platform from which they can make an impact, and athletes who are believers receive so many opportunities to minister. But they also need to be ministered to. I know that from experience. I often say that if Paul were to have his conversion on the road to Damascus today, the church would immediately put him on television and start him on a speaking tour instead of allowing him to go off to the desert to be prepared for ministry.

FCA began in 1954, the year before I made my Yankees debut, but it wasn't widely established in the majors while I played. I later served on FCA's board of directors and have maintained an association with the organization for probably fifty years because its acceptance within our public school systems has made it so effective. FCA enjoys an inroad among our youth that many other organizations and churches have not been able to establish.

Baseball chapels for the Yankees actually began out of that Sunday morning in Minnesota when Tony Kubek, Mickey Mantle, and I were unable to sneak out of the church service before our doubleheader. When Red Barber—the Yankees broadcaster and also lay minister—heard our comical story, he offered to lead private prayer meetings for the team when we were on the road. Red thought players should be able to have a time of Bible study and prayer without having to rush to the ballpark for games. Those team chapels were part of what led to the eventual formation of Baseball Chapel.

While some of us in baseball dreamed of every team holding chapel services, Detroit sportswriter Watson Spoelstra went to baseball commissioner Bowie Kuhn with the idea of a league-wide chapel program. The commissioner was sympathetic to our purpose and gave us a ten-thousand-dollar check from Major League Baseball to help start what would become known as Baseball Chapel. I had the privilege of serving as Baseball Chapel president for ten years, beginning in 1983, and I am so thankful for what it has become. Now it is organized systematically, so that when a player becomes a believer in the minor leagues and then progresses up the minor league ladder, a coordinator can ensure that proper spiritual care moves along with him. That continuity allows for more in-depth ministry to players and their families.

The presence of FCA, Baseball Chapel, Pro Athletes Outreach, and other similar ministries such as Idols Aside, UPI (Unlimited Potential, Inc.), and Global Baseball has greatly improved the environment for athletes of faith, though the organizations themselves had to go through some growing pains. In the early days, for instance, we had to watch out for outside speakers whose main interest was rubbing shoulders with the athletes or adding to their credentials: "I spoke to the New York Yankees." Also, some Christian athletes in the early days believed that if we shared what we were really battling with, God wouldn't be glorified. This misconception not only placed way too much pressure on the athletes, but it could actually hinder both their spiritual growth and their influence with others.

In time, though, the growing network of Christian athletes created a support system that made it okay for athletes to share their flaws honestly with others—to admit they face many of the same struggles as everyone else. Being a Christian doesn't mean that our struggles are necessarily different from those of non-Christians; it's just that our solution to the struggles is different. Because of Calvary and a personal relationship with Jesus Christ, we don't have to fight our battles alone. I believe that message is conveyed much more effectively today, and I'm glad of it.

Chapter 22
GOD'S HALL OF FAME

WHEN MY SON ROBBY was a boy, he liked to gather my fan mail from the Yankee Stadium clubhouse and open and read the letters on our way home after games. On one of those rides home, as we were crossing the George Washington Bridge, one particular letter grabbed his attention. "Hey, Dad," he said, "I've got to read this one to you."

It was from a man named Walt Huntley, who said he attended a church in Toronto, Canada. He had written a poem that he wanted to give to me because I was a Christian. The title was "God's Hall of Fame." Robby read Huntley's poem to me as I drove.

"Boy," I told Robby, "that is *good*."

When we arrived home, I went through the poem again, and as I read and absorbed the words, their meaning rang so true. I liked that poem so much that I knew it was something I wanted to use at my speaking engagements. I had no idea how many times and for how many years I would be requested to recite "God's Hall of Fame."

I have adapted the poem a little over time. It goes like this:

Your name may not appear down here
In this world's Hall of Fame.
In fact, you may be so unknown
That no one knows your name.

The trophies, the honors, and flash bulbs here may pass you by,
The neon lights of blue,
But if you know and love the Lord,
Then I have news for you.

This Hall of Fame is only good
As long as time shall be.
But keep in mind, God's Hall of Fame
Is for eternity.

This crowd on earth, they soon forget
The heroes of the past.
They cheer like mad until you fall,
And that's how long you last.
But in God's Hall of Fame,
By just believing in His Son,
Inscribed you'll find your name.

I tell you, friend, I wouldn't trade
My name, however small,
That's written there beyond the stars
In that celestial hall

For every famous name on earth
Or glory that it shares.
I'd rather be an unknown here
And have my name up there.

On three occasions I have recited that poem when giving the prayer at National Baseball Hall of Fame induction ceremonies in Cooperstown, New York. I've had Hall of Famers ask for a copy. I've heard Johnny Bench recite it on several occasions. The late Gary Carter said he used the poem a lot in public appearances. The late Coach John Wooden, one of the most revered college basketball coaches of all time and a faithful worker for God's Kingdom, included that poem in one of his books.

Mickey Mantle liked that poem a lot—especially the lines that say, "They cheer like mad until you fall, / and that's how long you last." He had planned to read the poem to the fans on the day he was honored in Yankee Stadium, although for a reason I can't recall, Mickey wasn't able to do so.

I reminded him of the poem when I visited him in the hospital. "You talked about using it that day," I said.

"Yeah, I should have."

"No, I'm not sure that was the right time," I told him. Mickey hadn't been a Christian when he wanted to read the poem at Yankee Stadium. He'd wanted to use the poem because he could relate to the part about the fans cheering like mad until he fell. But he hadn't truly understood the entire poem's meaning back then. He couldn't do that until he became a Christian.

I recited the poem at Mickey's funeral on national television as part of my message, and requests came from all over the country for a copy of the words.

The poem resonates strongly with athletes because it conveys how quickly athletic glory fades. Athletes can struggle when they cease playing a sport they've played most of their lives. They must adjust to an entirely new way of life where the earthly fame they've enjoyed often disappears.

When I see the lines, "This crowd on earth, they soon forget / the heroes of the past," I think back to Roger Maris in 1966. Only five years after the season when Roger hit more home runs than any player in baseball history, and despite his continuing to play through injuries that limited his power, New York fans booed Roger when he came to bat—so loudly and persistently that he wanted to retire.

Those two lines are so true! When you're doing well, the fans are for you. But when things go bad, they turn against you. The highs and successes of athletics are temporal—and temporary. But Christians have something else to look forward to—something time cannot diminish. As the poem states, "God's Hall of Fame / is for eternity."

To me, Walt Huntley's poem describes what a Christian athlete should portray. I pray that is what I have been able to portray with Christ's help.

I am seventy-six years old as I write this book. When I run through the lineups from the Yankees teams I played on from 1955 through 1966, I'm saddened at the reminder of how few of us are still living. And I'm acutely aware of my own mortality.

In September of 2011, I underwent a colonoscopy that revealed some polyps, and one of them was cancerous. Shortly afterward Betsy and I traveled to Yankee Stadium the last weekend of the regular season to be with Pat Maris and her children during ceremonies honoring the fiftieth anniversary of Roger's sixty-one home run season. The morning after we arrived home, surgeons removed a section of my colon.

The surgery was successful, and the doctors gave me a completely clean bill of health. I wouldn't need radiation or other cancer treatments. Still, having cancer found in my body caused me to consider more closely both the brevity of life and the scope of eternity. Psalm 90 came to mind, especially verse 12: "Teach us to number our days, that we may apply our hearts unto wisdom."

I don't know how many more innings of life I have yet to play. Perhaps I should be taking a peek over my shoulder to see if Casey Stengel is preparing to tell me to "hold that gun" and then send in a pinch hitter for me. But then again, Casey would pinch-hit in the first inning, so I'm not sure what that would indicate anyway.

What I do know, however, is that I have lived a blessed life. I played more than fourteen hundred games in the major leagues, all with the team I first fell in love with as a teenager watching a movie. I played in seven World Series, three times on the winning team. I received individual accolades and made lasting friendships.

The Lord has generously provided for our family, mostly through baseball. He allowed me to achieve my dream of playing for the Yankees, then turned my career with the Yankees into open doors for opportunities far greater than I could ever have dreamed. I was able to coach and show young baseball players in college the Yankee way of baseball and, I hope, God's way of living. I've been asked to share the story of my faith more times than I can estimate.

I have been able to retire in my hometown of Sumter, South Carolina. Betsy, my wife of fifty-six years, still loves me despite the storms we have encountered. I'll sign up for another fifty-six years with her if she'll agree to it. My three sons and two daughters either work full-time in ministry or are active in their churches. I have fifteen delightful grandchildren and four wonderful "grand-in-laws" who have married into the family, and all are excited about the Lord. That is God's mercy once again demonstrated.

I'm healthy enough to stay active in Sumter, to keep hunting quail and duck, and—even though I'm choosing now to cut back on my schedule—to travel around the country sharing the gospel message.

I have enjoyed a remarkably rewarding life. There have been struggles, no doubt, both because of the professional rat race and because of my own failure to walk by faith, trust God, and obey His Word as I should. But the Lord has given me wonderful opportunities, and He continues to do so.

If my life is a testament to anything, it is to God's mercy and grace. I have been blessed far beyond what I deserve.

My aim in both baseball and life has been simple: to make an impact by being used by God in the lives of others.

When accounts of my life are written, I hope two things will be said of me. First, that I played baseball in a way that made my team better. Second, and more important, that I lived my life in a way that drew others to my Savior.

To God be the glory.

ACKNOWLEDGMENTS

I WANT TO ACKNOWLEDGE my longtime friend Marty Appel, whose call started a process that eventually resulted in this book.

A big thank-you also to my sons, Rich, Robby, and Ron, whose encouragement and efforts helped make it possible. I'd also like to thank my daughters—Jeannie, who is my right-hand "secretary," and Christie, my cheerleader. The gracious love, encouragement, and prayers from you, your spouses (Karen, Darlene, Paul, and John), and our wonderful grandchildren have meant so much to your mom and me over the years. We love you.

Thank you, David Thomas and Carol Traver, for your patience and prayers, and for sharing your gifts and skills.

And most of all, I give my heartfelt praise to the One from whom all blessings flow! The song "My Tribute" says it all: "How can I say thanks for the things You've done for me?"

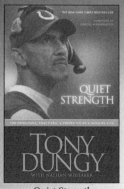
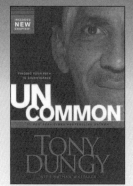
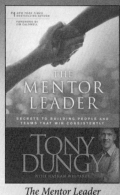
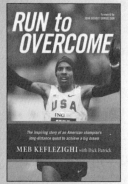
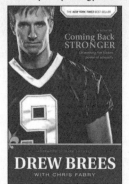

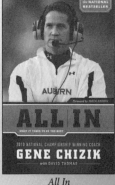